UNDERSTANDING THE FINANCE OF WELFARE

Other titles in the series

Understanding social security
Issues for policy and practice

Edited by **Jane Millar**, Department of Social and Policy Sciences, University of Bath

"This first-class text will fast become the definitive guide to the subject." **Jonathan Bradshaw, Department of Social Policy and Social Work, University of York**

PB £17.99 (US$26.95) **ISBN** 1 86134 419 8

HB £50.00 (US$59.95) **ISBN** 1 86134 420 1

240 x 172mm 352 pages tbc May 2003

Forthcoming

Understanding social citizenship
Themes and perspectives for policy and practice
Peter Dwyer
PB ISBN 1 86134 415 5
HB ISBN 1 86134 416 3
May 2004

Understanding work-life balance
Policies for a family-friendly Britain
Margaret May and Edward Brunsdon
PB ISBN 1 86134 413 9
HB ISBN 1 86134 414 7
May 2004

Understanding research for social policy and practice
Themes, methods and approaches
Edited by Saul Becker and Alan Bryman
PB ISBN 1 86134 403 1
HB ISBN 1 86134 404 X
June 2004

Understanding the policy process
Theory and practice of policy analysis
John Hudson and Stuart Lowe
PB ISBN 1 86134 540 2
HB ISBN 1 86134 539 9
May 2004 tbc

INSPECTION COPIES AND ORDERS AVAILABLE FROM:

Marston Book Services
PO Box 269
Abingdon
Oxon OX14 4YN
UK

INSPECTION COPIES
Tel: +44 (0) 1235 465538
Fax: +44 (0) 1235 465556
Email: inspections@marston.co.uk

ORDERS
Tel: +44 (0) 1235 465500
Fax: +44 (0) 1235 465556
Email: direct.orders@marston.co.uk

The **POLICY** **P~P** **PRESS**

SPA

UNDERSTANDING THE FINANCE OF WELFARE

What welfare costs and how to pay for it

Howard Glennerster

First published in Great Britain in May 2003 by

The Policy Press
University of Bristol
Fourth Floor, Beacon House
Queen's Road
Bristol BS8 1QU
UK

Tel +44 (0)117 331 4054
Fax +44 (0)117 331 4093
e-mail tpp-info@bristol.ac.uk
www.policypress.org.uk

British Library Cataloguing in Publication Data

A catalogue record for this book is available from the British Library

ISBN 1 86134 405 8 paperback

A hardcover version of this book is also available

Howard Glennerster is Professor Emeritus of Social Policy at the London School of
Economics and Political Science. He has been an advisor to HM Treasury and to the
Secretary of State for Health.

Cover design by Qube Design Associates, Bristol.
Printed and bound in Great Britain by Hobbs the Printers Ltd, Southampton.

Contents

Detailed contents		vi
List of tables, figures and boxes		xi
Foreword by Saul Becker		xiii
Acknowledgements		xvi
one	Meeting basic human needs	1
two	Market failure and government failure	15
three	How to pay for social programmes? The tax constraint	35
four	Financing healthcare	55
five	Financing social care	79
six	Financing education	103
seven	Financing income security	129
eight	Financing housing	159
nine	Rationing scarce resources: managing rising expectations	177
ten	Do public services have a future?	197
References		209
Index		225

Detailed contents

one   Meeting basic human needs   1

Summary   1
Basic human need   2
Someone has to pay   5
Need and the life cycle   6
The distinction between finance and provision   6
The social division of welfare   9
Choice and agency   11
Overview   14
Questions for discussion   14
Further reading   14

two   Market failure and government failure   15

Summary   15
Why markets work – sometimes   16
Market failure   18
    Public goods   18
    Externalities   19
    Income externalities and giving   20
    Information failure   22
Government failure   25
    You can't please everyone all of the time   25
    Self-interested voters   26
    Self-interested bureaucrats   27
    Budget maximisers?   27
    X-inefficiency   28
    Public servants as knaves?   29
    Exit, voice and loyalty   29
Privatisation and quasi-markets   30
The voluntary sector and mutuality   32
    Why a voluntary sector?   32
Overview   34
Questions for discussion   34
Further reading   34

three	**How to pay for social programmes?**	**35**
	The tax constraint	

Summary	35
Consent	36
Improving the popularity of taxes	40
Make employers pay	40
Stealth taxes	40
Hypothecation	40
Taxes on 'public bads'	41
Localise taxes	41
Convince taxpayers	43
Equity	43
Efficiency	46
The traditional view	46
A more complex picture	48
Taxing wealth	49
What alternatives are there to taxes?	50
Overview	52
Questions for discussion	52
Further reading	53

four	**Financing healthcare**	**55**

Summary	55
The cost of healthcare	56
Blair's promise and the Wanless Report	59
How the NHS funds are allocated	61
Measuring differential need	63
The 2003 English formula	65
The Scottish and Welsh equivalents	66
Raising the money	67
An insurance-based system	67
Private insurance	69
Local taxation	70
On balance	71
Improving choice and efficiency	71
Primary care trusts in England	74
Local healthcare cooperatives in Scotland	76
Taking the changes even further?	76
Overview	77
Questions for discussion	77
Further reading	77

five	**Financing social care**	**79**

Summary	79
The cost of social care	81
Informal care	81
Privately funded care	82
Not-for-profit providers	83
Local authority social services and social work departments' budgets	84
How social care funds are allocated	84
Changes to local government finance in 2003	85
The personal social services	86
Specific grants	88
Capital spending	89
Perverse funding	89
Fees and charges	91
Improving choice and efficiency	92
The spending on and organisation of social care in other countries	94
The funding and organisation of long-term care in the UK	97
Complex funding streams	97
Overview	101
Questions for discussion	102
Further reading	102

six	**Financing education**	**103**

Summary	103
The cost of education	105
How education funds are allocated	108
Schools	109
Colleges of further education	113
Higher education	113
The economists' case	115
'New' Labour's policy: phase one	116
The 2003 White Paper on Higher Education Funding	118
Improving choice and efficiency	120
Incentives in higher education	123
The finance of education in other countries	123
Schools	123
Higher education	124
Overview	127
Questions for discussion	127
Further reading	127

seven	**Financing income security**	**129**

Summary — 129
The state's role: income replacement or poverty relief? — 130
The case for insurance markets — 131
The cost of income maintenance — 132
    Public spending — 132
    Tax credits — 136
    Tax allowances — 137
    Spending in other countries — 138
How social security funds are allocated in the UK — 138
    The present structure of UK pensions — 140
    A way out of the maze? — 142
    Public assistance — 143
    Pensions in other countries — 145
Improving choice and efficiency — 149
    Work incentives — 149
    Saving incentives — 150
    To fund or not to fund? — 151
    To target or not to target? — 155
    Pensions for carers — 156
Overview — 156
Questions for discussion — 157
Further reading — 157

eight	**Financing housing**	**159**

Summary — 159
Housing policy evolves — 160
From producer subsidies to consumer subsidies — 162
Rent control and regulation — 162
A subsidy to the rich — 163
The costs of housing — 165
    Costs to the state — 165
The organisation of state finance — 168
    Supporting local authorities — 168
    Local authority capital spending — 169
    Housing associations — 170
    Housing Benefit — 170
Improving choice and efficiency — 171
    A gradual reform of Housing Benefit — 172
The finance of housing in other countries — 172

Overview	174
Questions for discussion	175
Further reading	175

**nine   Rationing scarce resources: managing rising   177
expectations**

Summary	177
Rationing	178
Containing public expenditure	182
Treasury control	183
Comprehensive plans	185
Self-imposed prudence	187
A more proactive role for the Treasury	188
Territorial rationing	189
The place of local authority spending	191
The Private Finance Initiative	193
The 2002 Comprehensive Spending Review	194
Overview	196
Questions for discussion	196
Further reading	196

ten   Do public services have a future?   197

Summary	197
Changing the tax structure	199
Stealth taxes and beneficial taxes	200
Charging	201
Selective universality	201
Squeezing more out of each pound spent	202
Whatever we do, it costs	203
Working longer	204
Vouchers and tax incentives	205
Tapping the willingness to pay	206
Overview: Dear Brutus	207
Questions for discussion	207
Further reading	207

List of tables, figures and boxes

Tables

1.1 Classification of countries by public–private mix of provision 10
and finance of healthcare

3.1 International comparisons of taxes including social security 38
contributions (1975-2000)

3.2 Public attitudes to taxation and social spending (1983-2001) 39

3.3 International comparisons of national and local tax 42
receipts (1998)

3.4 Taxes paid as a percentage of gross household income, 47
by income group, UK (2000-01)

4.1 Health expenditure per capita and as a % of GDP (1998) 57

5.1 The total cost of long-term care in the UK (1995-96) 83
(£ billion)

5.2 Central government grants to social services departments, 88
England (2002/03) (£ million)

5.3 Long-term care provision and spending in eight countries 96
(various years) (%)

6.1 Expenditure on educational institutions as a % of GDP 106
(1999)

6.2 UK education spending relative to GDP (1975-2003) (%) 107

6.3 Funding per pupil (1995/96-2003/04), real-terms index 108

6.4 Annual expenditure per student in different countries, 109
by level of education (1998) ($)

7.1 The UK National Insurance Fund (1999/2000) (£ billions) 135

7.2 Funding Income Support, UK (1999/2000) (£ billions) 139

7.3 Combination of public and private pensions, 140
international comparison (non-working males aged 65-69)

8.1 UK housing expenditure of households (2000) (£ billion) 165

8.2 Housing investment: (a) New housing completions in the 167
UK (1977-2000); (b) Value of housing construction (2000)

9.1 Identifiable expenditure by country (2000/01) 192

9.2 UK public spending: past and future (1984/85-2005/06) 195

10.1 Depth of support for additional taxation 199

10.2 The costs of 'going private' 205

Figures

1.1	A hierarchy of needs	3
1.2	A theory of human need	4
1.3	The finance–provision distinction	8
1.4	Classification of public and private welfare activity	12
1.5	Expenditure on welfare	13
2.1	Needs provision implied by economic theory	25
2.2	Types of public funding	31
3.1	The changing structure of taxation	45
4.1	Hospital and community health services' gross current expenditure per head, England (1999-2000) (£)	58
4.2	Where does the NHS budget go?	60
4.3	The flow of funds to the NHS (2003)	62
4.4	Allocating NHS resources	65
5.1	Social services departments' budgets, England (2000/01)	85
5.2	Residential care for older people, England (1980-2001) (total places)	93
6.1	Public expenditure on education: where it goes (2000/01)	107
7.1	Alternative principles of state pension schemes	130
7.2	State pension spending as a % of GDP (2000 and 2050)	146
8.1	Public expenditure on housing (1973-2001) (£ million, 1995/96 prices)	166
9.1	The economic concept of rationing	179
9.2	Types of rationing	180

Boxes

3.1	A glossary of tax terms	44
4.1	Market failures in health	56
5.1	Market failures in long-term social care	80
6.1	Market failures in education	105
6.2	The Scottish model	117
7.1	Market failures and Income Support	133-4
7.2	National insurance contributory benefits	134
7.3	Tax-funded benefits	136
7.4	Defined benefit and defined contribution schemes	152
7.5	The 'Ponzi Game' nature of unfunded social security	154-5
8.1	Market failures in housing	161
9.1	Department of Health objectives and performance targets	184

Foreword

As governments unleash their White Papers, social security reforms, new social programmes and initiatives (in education, housing, health, social care and other spheres of social policy), and as they implement their political and social objectives and priorities, we should not forget that someone, somewhere, at some time, has to pay for all of this.

Everything has a cost, from the introduction nationally of new pension provision or systems for community care, to the piloting of New Deals for specific groups of people, through to the implementation locally of homecare for frail or vulnerable people, or local services for family carers, lone parents, children and other groups. What is spent on any one of these means that there may be less to spend on something else. *Understanding the finance of welfare* addresses *what welfare costs and how to pay for it*, and asks questions such as:

- What does it cost to provide a modern welfare system, including healthcare 'from cradle to grave', education 'for all', a social security 'safety net', and means-tested benefits for the poorest in society?
- Who pays for these social programmes and what is the best way to finance them?
- Are there limits to what can be paid for out of general taxation?
- What is the role for the market, or for private insurance?
- What is a fair or equitable system of finance?
- Do we need to ration social welfare services in order to control expectations, demand and supply?
- Do public services have a future, and what are the options that need to be considered?
- How do social welfare programmes in the UK compare with those in other countries?

Howard Glennerster has long been recognised as the pre-eminent thinker and writer on the finance of welfare. He is also well known for his research and publications on other themes and issues central to social policy. One of his books (in its many editions), *Paying for welfare*, has been an essential read for all students of Social Policy and Administration, and for the many others who have needed to know about the choices and costs of providing and paying for welfare services and income security. His work in this field has informed countless students and academics, and he has brought his knowledge and expertise to bear on UK government policy making through his various advisory roles.

Understanding the finance of welfare has all the hallmarks of what is certain to become the definitive text on the subject. It deals with a broad range of complex and highly contested policy areas, including the finance of health and social care, education, housing and income security. Howard Glennerster cuts through the policy rhetoric to set out the details, debates and options in an engaging style. His analysis is always authoritative yet accessible. The book contains a wealth of information and data that are rarely found in one volume.

Howard Glennerster's book will be read eagerly by students and teachers of Social and Public Policy, Sociology, Social Work, Economics and Politics; and it will inform the thinking, and hopefully the choices, of politicians, policy makers, managers and practitioners who work in, or are concerned with, social welfare programmes in health and social care, housing, education and social security.

Understanding welfare series

This emphasis on policy making and delivery is a key feature of all the books in the *Understanding welfare: Social issues, policy and practice* series. The series was commissioned by the Social Policy Association (SPA) and is published in partnership with The Policy Press. It is the first book series that the SPA has initiated and it has clear aims and objectives, not least of which is to provide over time a library of key texts that are central to understanding major social issues, such as income security, the finance of welfare, and the policy process, to name but a few.

The subject matter and orientation of the books have also been informed by the requirements of various subject benchmark statements produced for the Quality Assurance Agency for Higher Education (2000). These benchmark statements provide a means for the academic community (and others) to describe the nature and characteristics of programmes in particular subject areas, including Social Policy and Administration, Social Work, Sociology, and so on. Books in the *Understanding welfare* series have been especially mindful of the Social Policy and Administration and Social Work subject benchmark statements produced in 2000 by a group chaired by Professor Pete Alcock. *Understanding the finance of welfare*, and the other books commissioned for the series, are the first which could be termed 'benchmark compliant'; that is, their content (and the knowledge and skills which they hope to foster) are central to the subject areas of Social Policy, Social Work and other applied social sciences.

Useful website resources

The Social Policy and Administration and Social Work subject benchmark statement can be found at: www.qaa.ac.uk/crntwork/benchmark/socialwork.pdf

The SPA website can be found at: www.social-policy.com

Saul Becker, Series Editor

Acknowledgements

I would like to express my thanks for permission to publish the following extracts, tables and figures from other publications:

The Controller of Her Majesty's Stationery Office for the following items which are Crown copyright:

Table 4.1 from HM Treasury (2001) *Wanless interim report*.

Figures 4.1, 4.2 and 5.2 from the *Department of Health annual report 2002*.

Box 9.1 from HM Treasury (2002) *Public service agreements 2003-6*.

Figure 8.2 from L. Doyal and I. Gough, *A theory of human need* (1991), Macmillan Press Ltd, reproduced with permission of Palgrave Macmillan as Figure 1.2. Permission from Guilford Press in the US has also been sought.

Figures 7, 13 and Table 10 from T. Burchardt, J. Hills and C. Propper from *Private welfare and public policy* (1999), with permission of the Joseph Rowntree Foundation (now Figure 1.4, 1.5 and Table 1.1 respectively).

Figure 3.1 and Box 3.1 are reproduced from *Paying for progress: A new politics of tax for public spending* (2000) by the Commission on Taxation and Citizenship published by the Fabian Society, with their permission.

Table 5.3 is reproduced from *Health Affairs*, vol 19, no 3, published by Project Hope, with their permission.

Box 7.4 is reproduced from *A new contract for retirement* (2002, p 32) published by the Institute for Public Policy Research.

Box 7.5 is reproduced in part from R. Disney's article 'Crises in public pension programmes in OECD: what are the reform options?', *The Economic Journal*, vol 110, pp F12-13, February 2000, published by Blackwell Publishers.

I am indebted to an ex-London School of Economics and Political Science PhD student, Phil Agulnik, for Figure 7.1.

I am grateful for the support the Economic and Social Research Council (ESRC) has given the Centre for Analysis of Social Exclusion (CASE). Colleagues at the London School of Economics and Political Science (LSE) in the ESRC CASE and in LSE Health and Social Care have been remarkably generous with their help. Without drawing on their expertise this volume would have been impossible. At various points they have allowed me to reproduce or revise tables and figures they have produced. They are acknowledged at appropriate places, I hope, but my particular thanks are due to Tania Burchardt, John Hills, Martin Knapp, Jules Forder, Jeremy Kendall, Julian Le Grand, Phil Agulnik and Tony Travers. Many other colleagues at the LSE have been unstinting in their help and expertise. Such collaboration is one marvellous feature of the place. I also have to thank my past students. The book is an expanded version of a lecture course I gave for 20 years to an enthusiastic and critical group who seemed to get better and better each year. I miss them.

Finally there is the secretarial, administrative and computing staff of CASE/ STICERD. I have never worked with nicer or more helpful colleagues.

The whole idea of the book and encouragement to do it have come from the Social Policy Association, especially Saul Becker who persuaded me to do it. Dawn Rushen has been a most efficient editor and support.

My more personal thanks have to be to Ann. We celebrated our 40th wedding anniversary just as I completed the first draft of this book. We met writing a Fabian pamphlet together. The proof copies were to arrive the day of our wedding. Somehow she has coped with similar deadlines and demands ever since. This time, because my eyes do not take kindly to long hours at the computer, she has typed much of this book and been as critical as ever of what I am writing. It would not have been completed without her.

Howard Glennerster
London School of Economics and Political Science
January 2003

Meeting basic human needs

Summary

- Social policy is concerned with the way societies meet the basic needs of their populations over an individual's life cycle.

- Some of these needs are met by the market, with the state supplementing the incomes of the poor. Other needs are met by families.

- There are a wide variety of modes of financing these basic human needs, but all have to be paid for in one way or another.

- It is important to distinguish who pays – the finance of a service – from who provides it.

- Governments may affect welfare through direct provision, varying taxation or by requiring employers to provide.

> All collectively provided services are deliberately designed to meet certain socially recognised 'needs'; they are manifestations, first, of society's will to survive as an organic whole and, secondly, of the expressed will of all the people to assist the survival of some people. 'Needs' may therefore be thought of as 'social' and 'individual'; as interdependent, mutually related essentials for the continued existence of the whole. (Titmuss, 1958; and Alcock et al, 2001, p 62)

The starting point for the study of social policy is: how have societies evolved ways of meeting the basic needs of their populations? How are their populations fed, housed, supplied with clean water, and trained with sufficient skills to survive? The answer in many parts of the world is imperfectly, or barely at all. Where people are starving this may be because of temporary climatic disasters or agricultural failure but, as the Nobel prize-winning economist Amartya Sen (1981) has shown, it is often that *individuals, or families and communities, do not have the purchasing power to buy the food that they need to survive.* This not only occurs in times of general poverty or economic decline; it can also happen in times of general prosperity, when some sections of the community lack the capacity to *buy* enough food when food prices are high and rising. This was the case in the Bengal famine of 1943, about which Sen originally wrote. The long-term answer may lie in a system of income security that gives families enough money to buy food that the market then produces. (Those interested in the basic issues of supplying people with enough food could read the collection of essays edited by Jean Dreze, Amartya Sen and Athar Hussain, 1995, notably the paper by Sen.)

Sen himself argued that the reason Western Europe had not suffered large famines, despite serious economic recessions, was precisely because it had developed forms of community-financed income support that enabled poor people to buy a minimum food entitlement even in times of economic or personal disaster. Other basic requirements of life, such as healthcare, have come to be supplied and financed collectively by society as a whole. Yet others, such as love and companionship, remain beyond the reach of either governments or markets to provide.

Basic human need

Just what constitutes a basic human need is the subject of much academic debate. Maslow (1954) listed human requirements in an ascending order of importance. Each higher order need presupposed the meeting of a more basic need (see **Figure 1.1**).

Some needs are more tangible, such as food and shelter – what Maslow calls *physiological needs*. *Safety* is less easy to ensure. It is partly the responsibility of

Figure 1.1: A hierarchy of needs

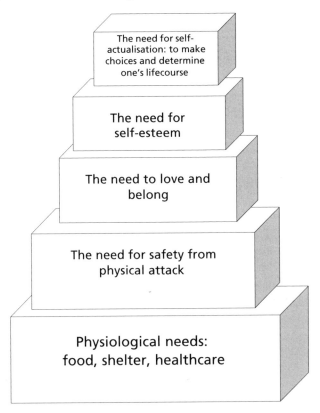

The need for self-actualisation: to make choices and determine one's lifecourse

The need for self-esteem

The need to love and belong

The need for safety from physical attack

Physiological needs: food, shelter, healthcare

Source: Adapted from Maslow (1954)

parents when children are small, later it is the responsibility of many agencies – the police, traffic engineers, employers and, at its most serious, the armed forces and the security services. It also depends on good government and a society that is perceived to be just. Other needs are more intangible but crucial, such as *love, companionship,* and *self-esteem.* Self-esteem may depend critically on having a job and enough income to buy trainers or a decent sweater. Rawls (1972) talked of 'primary goods', and also included self-respect. T.H. Marshall (1950) talked of 'rights of citizenship'. Without them no human being can be a full individual or will survive. The chain of reasoning differs in all these accounts and in what is seen as basic, but the outcomes are not that different. Doyal and Gough (1991) have come closest to elaborating a full theory of human need (see **Figure 1.2**).

They argue that all, or virtually all, political and moral theories start from the presumption that individuals ought to be able to survive and live healthy autonomous lives. Some more Left-leaning theories may argue that everyone would be better off if they agreed to exercise some of that autonomy collectively.

Figure 1.2: **A theory of human need**

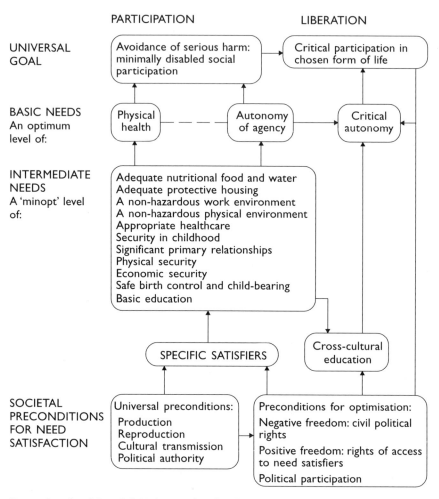

Source: Doyal and Gough (1991), reproduced with permission of Palgrave Macmillan and permission sought from Guilford Press, US

Others will want to minimise that collective activity. But if people are too weak from hunger or too ill or too cold to care or to choose, neither Karl Marx's world nor Mrs Thatcher's will have any meaning. Democracy cannot function well if voters are ignorant or incapable of reasoning and discussion. Even Malthus (1798), who believed that the state should not help the poor because to do so would lead to overpopulation and hence starvation for the many, had a social policy. We may think it misguided, but its ultimate objective concerned a basic human need – the need for food.

People not only have needs as individuals. Conservatives, liberals and socialists all agree that there is more to life than individual ambition and satisfaction. The group identity we all seem to need may be at the level of the family, or the local group, mosque, synagogue or church. It may be at the larger collective level of a trades union or voluntary society. It may be at the level of the nation state – even if it is limited to support for the national football team! It may increasingly be global in its membership. Doyal and Gough recognise this in distinguishing individual human needs from social participatory ones. They interconnect. Starving people cannot be very effective members of any group. They argue that it is not enough to have adequate food and shelter but that we also need 'critical autonomy' – the capacity to choose and to participate in political action. They restrict this attribute to the wider political system. Conservatives and liberals argue that this is the basic case for giving people choice of school, doctor and form of housing. Very few would now accept that the government should decide what poor people should eat each day, as they used to in the Poor House or the soup kitchen. Instead, public assistance is usually given in the form of cash. Refugees in the UK were, for a while, given food vouchers, which many felt was a denial of their human dignity, although food stamps are an accepted form of support for the poor in the US. Autonomy and agency matter in the way we meet human need. They are linked to self-respect.

Someone has to pay

What concerns us in this book is *how to ensure that all citizens do indeed have access to these basic needs or entitlements*. Someone has to pay. Even in the simplest society food production will involve many hours of backbreaking work in the fields, planting, weeding and harvesting. Those hours could be spent doing other things. And it is women who often carry this burden more than the men. They pay. In more complex societies this labour power is used to generate wages that are then used to buy the food. The family pays for its own food and a sophisticated system of world food suppliers produces it.

Much education takes place in the family, even in modern economies. Perhaps the most important building blocks are set in place before a child is five, and much of that takes place in the family. And so does the largest element of caring for children, disabled people and older people. Family care and child-rearing are not without their costs. Women do more of this caring than men, and their lifetime earnings, if they have such caring responsibilities, are markedly lower than those of men. On average the lifetime incomes of women are, or were in the 1980s, half that of men (Falkingham and Hills, 1995). Even basic legal and political rights of voting and a fair trial have to be paid for. Parliament and the courts take money to run. So *meeting basic human needs costs money*. Who pays, who should pay and how we make these decisions as a society is the subject of this book. For the rest of this chapter we make some basic distinctions between the kinds of ways in which we finance our basic needs in all modern advanced economies.

Need and the life cycle

One of the main difficulties that families face is that basic and costly needs arise at precisely the time in our lives when we are least able to pay for them. When we are sick and medical bills are high we are unable to work and earn. When we are old we may not only be unable to work but may need looking after in ways that can be very expensive. It can cost more than £25,000 a year to look after a very old person – more than many people earn in a year. Most old people are unable to pay for that care out of current income or savings. Some families are able to pay for their own children's education. Most cannot. The average cost of private education for a family of two would again take more than the whole of many families' incomes. Rowntree (1902) drew attention to the mismatch between the life cycle of need and the life cycle of the typical family's earnings pattern. Families are under most pressure when they are bringing up children and in old age. Young childless people at work and couples after they have ceased to have children in the household have large 'surpluses'. For a detailed discussion of these issues see Falkingham and Hills (1995).

Nowadays, some of the mismatch between earnings and need over the life cycle can be bridged by private insurance. Financial markets have grown up to provide products that enable people to invest savings to pay a pension, to pay for long-term care as an old person, even to pay for a child's education. But, as we shall see, all these markets have drawbacks as well as some advantages. They do not tend to work well for the most sick or for those with poor or uncertain incomes. Women are especially disadvantaged as a result. For some they give more choice and freedom. Nevertheless, much of social policy is concerned with spreading families' incomes from their working lives to their non-working lives, and from periods of high earnings to periods of limited earnings and greater family responsibilities. Indeed the Falkingham and Hills study concluded that in the UK in the 1980s roughly three quarters of all the redistribution welfare spending achieved was of this kind – *horizontal redistribution*. Only a quarter was concerned with redistributing incomes to the lifetime poor – *vertical redistribution*. Most people gain from this better lifetime matching of need and income, not just the poor.

The distinction between finance and provision

Our basic needs are financed in a variety of ways, and it is wrong to think of the state as the *main provider* for each of those needs. Food is one of our most basic requirements; for that reason it formed the basis of early attempts to measure a poverty line and still does in the US today. Food takes about a quarter of the budget of the poorest fifth of families but only a seventh of the budget of the richest fifth. However, the state does not provide us with food outside disasters such as floods or earthquakes. Most families pay for food out of their regular income from paid work. The same is true of that other critical need – housing. Families usually need the help of some private financial service agency – a building society or bank or insurance company – to spread the financial burden of buying a house over time, and market agencies are only too happy to oblige. This is the case unless you are poor or have an uncertain income. In the case of both food and housing the state steps in to help poor families to buy the basic necessities. In the UK, **Income Support** is available to those with no other income and no significant savings. **Working** and **Child Tax Credits** boost the incomes of those in work and with children. Public pensions help poorer people who are also elderly. **Housing Benefit** is available for those who could not otherwise afford minimum standards of housing. Similar schemes exist in other advanced economies. But here the state helps by giving cash. In the case of both housing and food the consumer, even a poor consumer, is deemed well able to make the choices involved in buying what they need. The market works reasonably well in responding to the very different preferences families and individuals have for the different kinds of food they like. It does less well in the case of housing for poor people for reasons we shall discuss in Chapter Eight. The big debates are over whether the market is as good a provider of education or healthcare. We know much less about the kind of medical care we need and it is much more difficult to get a private company to provide insurance for a person who has a long history of poor health. A child is not in the best position to decide on his or her educational needs. There are systematic reasons why markets for health and education and the long-term care of older people work less well than markets for food. We shall discuss these arguments in the next chapter.

In most countries these services are largely paid for out of some public budget, whether for rich or poor people. These may be social insurance funds not general taxation but the sources of funds are mostly social and not private fees. However, there is a lot of divergence in the kind of agencies that actually *supply* the services. In Germany most of the funds raised to pay for healthcare come from social insurance contributions. But the sick funds, which receive this money, frequently buy healthcare for their patients from private hospitals and clinics; often these are not-for-profit private hospitals run, for example, by a religious foundation. Throughout the book we shall therefore be drawing a sharp distinction between *who pays for a service* and *who provides it*. See **Figure 1.3** for an illustration of why public finance does not necessarily entail public or state provision. Here we draw only on the UK examples to show how the pattern of funding varies even within one nation state. If we had included German or French or Dutch and Belgian examples the picture would be more varied still.

Across the top of the figure we distinguish between different kinds of formal organisations that have different legal bases. The first column includes

Figure 1.3: The finance–provision distinction

				Provision		
Public sector bodies				**Private organisations**		**Private – informal**
	Central government	Public trusts	Local government	Profit	Non-profit	
Types of Institution	eg HM Prisons	eg NHS hospital trusts	eg LEA schools, old people's homes, council houses	eg language schools, nursing homes	eg church schools, universities, housing associations, Barnado homes	
Finance — Public	Home Office payments	Purchases of services by health authorities	Grants from central government, Council Tax	LEA purchase of nursing home places	Government grants to housing associations, universities, church schools, and places bought for children by LEAs	Social security payments to carers of disabled people, payment by local authorities to foster parents
Finance — Private	Sale of products made by prisoners' charitable gifts	Fees paid by private patients	Charges by old people's homes, fundraising by parents	Fees paid by households	Rents to housing associations	Income lost in giving up work to care for a family member

organisations directly run by central government such as Her Majesty's Prisons. In the next column we have arm's length organisations such as health trusts or foundation hospitals. They are semi-independent with their own governing bodies. Then there are bodies run by, or coming under the ultimate control of, a local authority. These include local schools and housing estates. Even here schools have been given a large degree of independence with their own governing bodies and budgets devolved to them by local education authorities (LEAs), as we shall see. All these bodies are, however, statutory agencies – they are governed by acts of parliament and accountable to elected members of local or national government and to bodies such as the National Audit Office and the Audit Commission. Private organisations are different in their legal oversight. If they are private for-profit organisations they will be subject to the companies' acts; if they are not-for-profit they may be a charity or a friendly society and covered by different charities' acts and Friendly Society rules. They will also have to be regulated and inspected by statutory bodies. Examples include private nursing homes looking after old people, and earning profits for their owners. Housing associations, church schools and universities are not-for-profit organisations. Then there are private families and neighbours – the informal sector – who are an important provider of care (Park and Roberts, 2002).

Down the left-hand side of **Figure 1.3** we distinguish the types of funding that these bodies receive. Her Majesty's Prisons are one of the last examples of something provided *and* almost exclusively funded by central government, although there may be charitable gifts from private individuals, books for the prison library or time given to help with basic skills training. Essentially, however, Her Majesty's Prisons are an unusual case, wholly run and financed by central government. They therefore occupy the top left-hand box. A *private* prison would be in the profit-making organisation column but funded exclusively by public funds.

NHS hospital trusts have to rely for their income on agreements or contracts made with them by local health authorities or primary care trusts to treat patients from their areas. They may also take private patients into their private pay beds. These individuals pay for their own treatment. Hospitals receive a lot of voluntary help from people coming in to help out on the information desk or selling tea to visitors or raising money for the hospital. Thus even an ordinary NHS hospital has a small stream of income that is not from central government and the taxpayer. Foundation hospitals will have power to borrow money on the open market to set limits. In 2002 the Blair government made it clear that it would be prepared to sanction the use of private hospitals where NHS ones were failing to provide services in good time. In some other healthcare systems private hospitals deliver most of the care even though the funding is public. The wide variety of mix of health funding and provision in other countries is illustrated in Table 1.1. We discuss the arguments for and against in Chapter Four.

Local schools are financed by an allocation from their LEA, which receives money from central government and from local taxes. A school may also call on parents to cover the cost of school trips and parents may raise more themselves through, for example, car boot sales, and give the proceeds to the school to fund extra computers. Universities, as not-for-profit organisations, receive grants from central government but also get fee income from local authorities and from students. They earn money from the research they do for government and private firms. They have one of the most complex income streams of any of the agencies in the table. We discuss this further in Chapter Six.

Housing associations, as not-for-profit agencies, are now responsible for nearly all the newly built social housing. They receive capital grants from the government and borrow from private lenders to cover the building costs. They also receive rents from tenants, some of which are essentially paid for by the government in the form of Housing Benefit. We cover more of that in Chapter Seven. Here it is only important to grasp that the social policy world is more complex than a simple dichotomy between publicly funded state organisations and private profit-making ones. Almost every combination of funding streams and public and private providers of services can be found in the UK and in other countries.

The social division of welfare

The government can help individuals directly with specially targeted *cash support* for particular needs. It can provide services in kind such as education; it can also reduce the costs of, for example, childcare for low-income families

Table 1.1: Classification of countries by public–private mix of provision and finance of healthcare

Public–private mix	Country	
Mainly public provision, public finance	Denmark Finland Greece Iceland Ireland Italy	Norway Portugal Spain Sweden UK
Mixed provision, public finance	Australia Austria Belgium France	Germany Japan Luxembourg New Zealand
Mainly private provision, public finance	Canada	
Mixed provision, mixed finance	Turkey	
Mainly private provision, mixed finance	Netherlands	
Mainly private provision, private finance	Switzerland US	

Source: Burchardt et al (1999), reproduced with kind permission of the Joseph Rowntree Foundation

by reducing their tax bill. This can be given as a capped sum per child – a tax credit – or it could be a sum taken off the taxable income of a family – a tax allowance (see later in Chapter Three). The name given by Titmuss (1958; Alcock et al, 2001) in his classic lecture on the 'Social division of welfare' to assistance through the tax system was *fiscal welfare*. Economists later came to call this *tax expenditure*. The current Labour government has come to rely on some kinds of fiscal welfare more than ever before. They have used it to target poor families, whereas the kinds of fiscal advantages Titmuss talked of largely favoured rich families. Hence the tax system we shall discuss in Chapter Three is not just a way of taking money from individuals; rather it can also be used to give money to certain needy groups.

Employers may also help their employees by paying contributions to their pension schemes, or by meeting their housing or healthcare costs. Titmuss called this *occupational welfare*.

The task of the rest of the book is to explore the different ways in which our basic needs are financed. It is important to grasp now, however, that there are many different ways to do it and each have their advantages and disadvantages.

Choice and agency

One important element in designing a social policy is that of *agency*, or the sense of control a user of a service has. Indeed, a sense of being in control of one's own destiny is in itself a human need. In most of our transactions and relationships we have and make choices. We generally choose our own partners. We have what seems an endless choice of different kinds of bread and cookers and bathroom designs. Of course, we need money to realise those choices, but even poorer people, as we touched on earlier, are not told what to eat in our society. Where there is a high degree of consumer choice, limited though it is by the nature of the market, consumers of public services expect some option when it comes to consumption of education and healthcare. Students do not expect to be told what university to go to. Their choice may be constrained by the A-levels they have gained but they are not assigned to an institution or to a subject to study by the state, as they were in some former Communist countries. Parents resent being told "That is the school to which you must send your child" or "That is the general practitioner you must use". In the US, where the practice was traditionally to assign children to schools by strict zoning limits – your zip-code determined your school – parents did not buckle down and accept it; they simply moved to the suburb of their choice. School districts are relatively small in the US, so moving house became a means of school choice. Formal choice of school in any local authority area has become part of the English school system since the 1980s. Many good schools are over-subscribed, just as many private ones are, but some element of choice has grown and seems likely to grow in the state system. Without it parents will simply leave the state system of education if they are able. It is in response to pressures of this kind that funding systems in the UK and elsewhere have given users of services more choice. They are able to choose their university, school or doctor, and government funding then goes to the university, school or doctor the user has chosen. However, there are drawbacks as well as positive gains in such moves, as we shall discuss in later chapters. Here it is important to take such moves into account conceptually. Burchardt et al (1999) extended the analysis presented earlier to distinguish between public decisions and private decisions about the way money is allocated between producers of services. **Figure 1.4** illustrates the distinctions they make.

The quartered circle distinguishes between *public* provision and *public* finance – an NHS hospital – from *private* provision and *public* finance – a private hospital funded by NHS funds. It shows *public* provision and *private* finance –

a private pay bed in an NHS hospital. It also shows *private* provision and *private* finance – a private hospital where patients pay for their own care. These are the distinctions we have already made. But Burchardt et al go on to distinguish between the extent of agency or choice involved. The top right-hand segment of public provision and finance might include a school to which all parents in the area *have* to send their children. That would be an inner-circle situation. But it goes on to distinguish an outer circle where individuals have greater power of decision over the service they choose. The comparative example here would be where parents can choose their children's state school. In England today the choice of a school by a parent triggers a sum of money for that school. (Later chapters describe these mechanisms in more detail.)

Similar distinctions apply to the other inner and outer circles. In the bottom left-hand segment of the outer circle is a purely private purchase unaided by the government. An example would be the purchase of a course in computer keyboard skills from a private firm. The inner circle represents the purchase of a contracted-out service, say, for example, private schooling for disabled children in a school usually used by a local authority, but in this case the parent is paying the full cost themselves.

The top left-hand inner circle quadrant represents public services that are financed in part by charges on their use. Courses in further education are a prime case. So are the charges made for a local authority old people's home or home helps by local social services departments. Prescription charges are another example. In European systems of healthcare, charges for hospital stays

Figure 1.4: **Classification of public and private welfare activity**

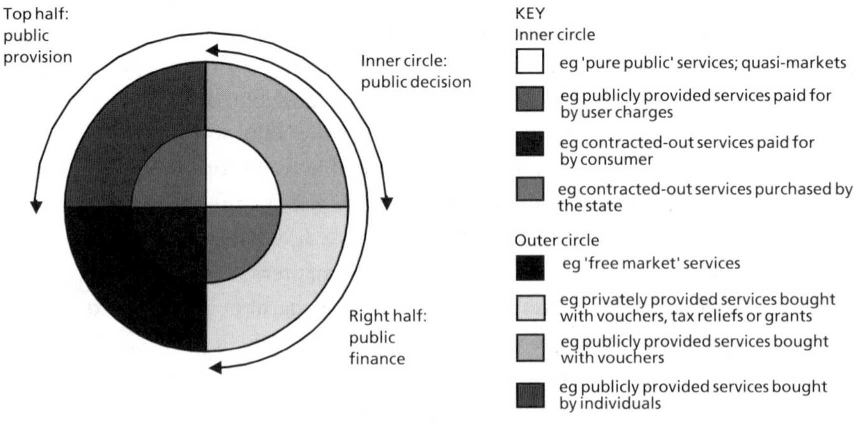

Top half:
public
provision

Inner circle:
public decision

Right half:
public
finance

KEY

Inner circle

☐ eg 'pure public' services; quasi-markets

■ eg publicly provided services paid for by user charges

■ eg contracted-out services paid for by consumer

■ eg contracted-out services purchased by the state

Outer circle

■ eg 'free market' services

☐ eg privately provided services bought with vouchers, tax reliefs or grants

■ eg publicly provided services bought with vouchers

■ eg publicly provided services bought by individuals

Source: Burchardt et al (1999), reproduced with kind permission of the Joseph Rowntree Foundation

and visits to the doctor are significant sources of funds. The outer circle includes the example we gave earlier of a private bed with the consultant acting as a private agent but operating within an NHS hospital.

In the bottom right-hand quadrant we have in the inner circle services that the private sector provides under contract to the state. Nursing homes for older people are a good example. The homes are inspected and deemed the kind of facility a social services department should use. A fee is set and the local authority decides who shall have the place. There is not much agency or choice on the part of the client here despite the fact that the service is privately provided. In the outer circle the privately purchased service has been bought with *some* government help, for example, tax relief on the cost of the school place.

Burchardt et al (1999) calculated how much spending on meeting social need fell in each quadrant – inner and outer cells (see **Figure 1.5**).

They found that only half of all spending fell in the top right-hand quadrant – 49%. That is, services that are both funded *and* provided by the state. In 1979, at the beginning of Mrs Thatcher's period in office, the comparable figure was 52%. This apparently small shift towards 'privatisation' overall hides big changes in each service. Essentially, big shifts towards the *public* finance of *private* provision in the personal social services and housing were masked by a big increase in the share of public social security spending in the total welfare budget. We shall explore each service later. What is important here is to note how small the 'state monopoly welfare state' is in reality.

Figure 1.5: **Expenditure on welfare**

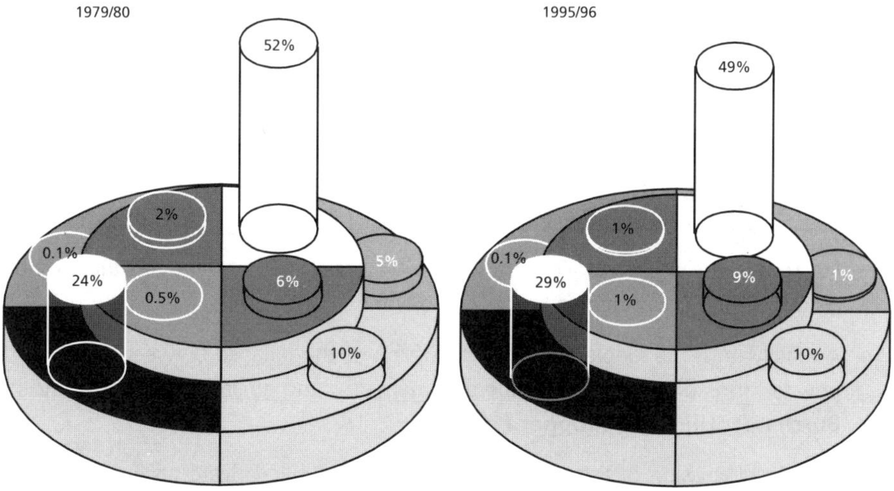

Note: For key please refer to Figure 1.4.

Source: Burchardt et al (1999), reproduced with kind permission of the Joseph Rowntree Foundation

In the last decade of the 20th century the role played by the voluntary sector organisations grew substantially. They did not raise more money relatively speaking. Indeed, charitable giving declined somewhat. But they were used more by the state as the means of delivering social welfare services. Thus the share of state funding for this sector grew. In both the cases of housing and the care of older people this was especially true. Kendall et al (2003) estimate that income from government received by charities grew by 40% between 1991 and 2001 while their total income grew by about a third.

In the following chapter we consider what economists have said in more theoretical terms about the reasons why some basic needs are best left to the market, and why others are perhaps better left to various collective forms of provision and funding. Economic theory has advanced a very long way since the 1980s in helping our understanding of these issues.

Overview

- Human needs are met in a wide variety of ways by different human agencies.
- Government plays a large role in redistributing incomes from periods of work to periods of dependency and from the lifetime rich to the lifetime poor.
- The market and families also play a large role but meeting human need is a costly and growing task.

Questions for discussion

1. What constitutes basic human needs?
2. What kinds of agency provide for them, if at all, in any society that you know or have read about?
3. Roughly how much does it cost to meet these needs in the UK and how, in broad terms, is the cost met?
4. In what variety of ways is government involved in ensuring that basic needs are met?

Further reading

For those who wish to follow up on the discussion of human need the **Doyal/Gough (1991)** treatment is a classic beginning.

A readily understandable and brief discussion of the balance between public and private forms of financing and the arguments for and against are to be found in **Burchardt, Hills and Propper (1999)**.

A wider discussion of the case for, and limits to, public–private partnerships is to be found in the **IPPR (2001)**.

Falkingham and Hills (1995) use a dynamic computer simulation model to trace the impact of the state on incomes through the life cycle.

Market failure and government failure

Summary

- Markets, according to classical economic theory, are an efficient way of meeting needs and wants. They have proved effective in many respects.

- Markets, however, fail in particular circumstances, many of which concern social policy. Individual actions affect others in ways that are not reflected in market signals – the public health dangers of untreated sewage are a classic case.

- Markets require good information equally shared by purchaser and provider. In health, education and long-term care especially this does not hold true.

- If markets fail, so too do governments and for systematic reasons. It is difficult to reach agreement on what people want government to do. In the absence of a market test, those who work for the government may prefer to work for their own interests, not their clients.

Why markets work – sometimes

Who is best placed to meet human needs and why? Standard classical economic theory, certainly since Adam Smith (1776), has been founded on the claim that the most efficient form of economic organisation rests on self-interested exchanges made between many individuals:

> Give me that which I want, and you shall have this that you want ... it is in this manner that we obtain from one another the far greater part of those good offices which we stand in need of. It is not from the benevolence of the butcher, the brewer, or the baker that we expect our dinner, but from their regard to their own interest. We address ourselves, not to their humanity but to their self-love, and never talk to them of our own necessities but of their advantages. Nobody but a beggar chooses to depend chiefly upon the benevolence of his fellow-citizens. Even a beggar does not depend on it entirely. The charity of well-disposed people, indeed, supplies him with the whole fund of his subsistence. But though this principle ultimately provides him with all the necessaries of life which he has occasion for, it neither does nor can provide him with them as he has occasion for them. The greater part of his occasional wants are supplied in the same manner as those of other people, by treaty, by barter and by purchase.... With the money which one man gives him he purchases food. The old clothes which another bestows on him he exchanges for other old clothes which suit him better, or for lodging, or for food, or for money, with which he can buy either food, clothes, or lodging, as he has occasion. (Adam Smith [Penguin edn, 1974], 1776, pp 118-19)

There are several basic economic assumptions and theories embedded in this famous extract.

- *Self-interest is more consistent and reliable than good will.* Are we so sure that self-interest is the only human driving force we can rely on? May not the love and care a mother has for her child be far more sustainable than a paid professional's willingness to care for the child for money? Just because it is a cash exchange relationship the carer has the undoubted right, written into their contract of employment if they have one, to give up and move on to another job. The mother has no such 'right' in accepted social practice. Yet, as we move away from such intense personal ties, Smith's proposition gains force. Even internal family decisions, who works, should we marry, have children, are susceptible to economic analysis using the self-interest presumption (Becker, 1976). Philip Abrams (Bulmer, 1986) long ago showed that even caring neighbours' willingness to shoulder burdens gives out after a relatively short period. Henry Aaron (1999) and Julian Le Grand (2003) delve into the psychological and experimental literature to question the self-interest assumption that lies at the heart of modern economics. We shall return to the issue later in this chapter.

- *Dynamic efficiency and the profit motive.* The promise of profit encourages new entrants to the marketplace to keep thinking of new ways to meet consumers' needs and wants. Is there a market niche they could fill? Arguably, it also encourages firms to create consumer desires that make life very difficult for poor families. But the lure of profit does encourage innovation by companies who want to prevent new entrants capturing their market. The recent history of computer technology and dot.com companies are classic examples of both the force of this competitive drive and the penalty paid if you get it wrong. As a result, economists argue, a market economy will show *dynamic efficiency*. The failure of centralised socialist monopoly economies in Eastern Europe to foster such a climate of innovation arguably led to the demise of the whole system. But the modern capitalist system is not fully efficient in this sense either.
- *Consumer sovereignty.* In theory, where individuals have cash in their pockets they can encourage firms to respond to their preferences – what they want and need. If *enough* consumers want organic foods the supermarkets and the farmers will, in the end, respond. New producers will threaten or replace old non-organic farms. If enough people want free-range eggs and are prepared to pay more for them supermarkets will stock them. If consumer preferences are met the economy will exhibit *allocative efficiency*. Resources will be allocated in a way that is required to produce what consumers need and want.
- *Productive efficiency.* Free markets also ensure that firms produce what consumers want at the lowest price consistent with their survival. The market will minimise *X-inefficiency* or unnecessarily high cost output.

This leads economists to argue that in most cases, where there are multiple providers and many customers, and where both consumers and producers have perfect information, free markets will be the *most efficient* form of organisation in every sense of the term discussed above.

Such an outcome will not necessarily be fair or *equitable*. That is especially true in a free market for labour. There is no reason why employers should pay their employees what society may think is a 'living wage'. There is no reason why they should pay an employee more if they have children. A rival employer will always be able to out-compete the more generous one by pushing wages down to a level nearer that which single or childless couples will accept. (Remember that there are relatively few families with dependent children at any one time compared to the population as a whole.) If the community does not like the outcome of such competition in the labour market it can impose a minimum wage – a social policy. However, every time it interferes in this way, economists argue, there will be an efficiency cost (Okun, 1975; for an extract see Barr, 2001a).

Despite caveats you may have about the force of these arguments, it is widely accepted, at least by economists, that, in relation to much economic activity, markets work rather well. At least no one has invented a wholly superior system. Economists have also long recognised that, in practice, their ideal world of free markets rarely if ever exists. One, or a few firms, may come to dominate a market – *monopolies* or *oligopolies* as economists call them – and this leads to 'imperfect competition'. It may be very difficult for new firms to enter the marketplace. Here the case is not that the theory is wrong but that there are systematic reasons why a free market may be difficult to achieve. That leads to a policy recommendation that governments do all they can to prevent monopolies occurring, to enable markets to operate as near the ideal as possible. Hence, there is powerful legislation in a country such as the US or the UK to prevent price-fixing between a small number of firms.

A particular kind of monopoly affects social services – a *geographical monopoly*. Often there may be a population big enough for only one effective school to operate in a small village or town. Travel times may be too great or costly for most parents to contemplate using an alternative. No new school could have any hope of gaining ground. The existing school may have no real competition.

All these limits to markets have been well recognised by economists for many years. Recently, economists have gone further and have come to develop a body of theory which suggests that markets do not work well, or at all, in a wide range of circumstances that are of particular importance for social policy. Much of this theory has been formalised since the 1970s. Some has its origins in the work of Adam Smith himself.

Market failure

Public goods

Adam Smith (1776, see page 16) first elaborated one kind of limit to market exchange. Public works were necessary where "the profit could never repay the expense of any individual or small number of individuals" – roads, bridges and harbours were his examples (1776, 1974 edn, p 78). The state had to step in and provide them. In the 1950s this theory came to be elaborated more fully.

- For a market to exist, a product or a service has to benefit only the person who buys it. It cannot also be available to everyone else free of charge. Clean air is costly to achieve but no one individual could buy it and stop others enjoying the benefits. Economists call this the property of *non-excludability*. Policing is another example – someone could pay for a security firm to police a neighbourhood, and everyone else would gain as well. The cost would be vast, however, and no one is likely to do it. Such a person may then try to live in a gated community and turn safety into a private good.

- If some people club together to pay for the whole neighbourhood to be policed the cost could be reduced. But even here there is a problem. Others in the neighbourhood will benefit and do not have to pay – they can *free ride* on the rest of the community. This may lead to a collapse in the whole agreement. The solution, which may not satisfy everyone, is to levy a *tax* – a compulsory levy – to pay for the police and courts of law. On an even larger scale, if we want to make sure we are safe from invasion as a country we may be willing to be taxed to pay for an army and navy. Individual armies, owned by competing warlords, do not have a good history of promoting safety. But we cannot avoid the benefits of our country being defended. For centuries public safety, in its different forms, has been paid for out of taxation.
- Another characteristic of a public good is *non-rivalry*. If someone drives along an uncrowded road they are not preventing others from doing so. Therefore driving along the road should be free. If the road becomes congested then they are slowing others down by their presence. As rivals they now impose a cost on others and should pay.

Goods that conform entirely to these conditions are called *pure* public goods. Given that they exist, they require some kind of non–market action to sustain their supply. Something other than the self-interest of the butcher and the baker is required. That leaves open what kind of collective action to adopt. Some public goods require public provision, some public finance, some state regulation. They do not necessarily require state provision. For example, the state could ask private prison operators to compete to provide a prison. Those who produce smoke pollution may be fined if they persist in breaking smoke control regulations. The purer the public good and the larger the community it applies to the more appropriate is public provision. It is unlikely that the British Navy will ever be put up for tender.

Externalities

Important though they are, pure public goods are not that common. But there is a class of products or services that are more common and share some of the same characteristics.

It may be perfectly practical to produce something that is bought by an individual – a car, for example – but the process of production may harm others. It may pollute the air or water. It may damage the health of those who use it or others who inhale the exhaust fumes. Economists call this a *negative externality*. If making steel causes smoke to reduce the life expectancy of those who live near the steelworks, then the firm should be forced to reduce its emissions or to pay a fine that covers the cost of the emissions. Forcing the firm to pay for the costs imposed on others would make the market work more efficiently. The full social costs would be imposed on those who were causing them. The market price for their product would reflect those costs and hence the demand for the product would probably fall.

At the other extreme a product may confer benefits on others beyond the cost of producing it. If, for example, I choose to educate my daughter and to pay her school fees I am benefiting others by doing so – those she can talk to, her future children, her husband, her employer. A society that only relied on parents to pay for schooling could end up with too little education because the benefits do not accrue directly to the family. Families, even if they had the money to do so, might not invest the socially optimum level of resources in their children.

Many forms of social policy derive from the existence of some kind of externality as we shall see. The following are but a few examples:

- Pure market exchange tends to impose costs on future generations in the form of environmental damage. The cars we use today and the fumes they emit are causing damage to the world our grandchildren will inhabit. It is difficult to quantify but in theory we should be paying now for the costs of that damage. That is one justification for the *high taxes* on fuel.
- Emissions from factories that endanger health can be *regulated* or *taxed*.
- Danger of infectious disease leads to governments having power to *detain* and *isolate* those suffering from such illness.
- Access to the family doctor or clinics for sexually transmitted diseases are free in order not to deter those who need help early and could be a danger to others.
- Schools are free because the whole of society gains from a better educated population.
- Public transport carries subsidies where the costs of congestion would be higher without it.
- Motorists in London and other big cities are charged if they drive into the city centre and cause congestion costs to fall on others.

Income externalities and giving

If we all acted as if we were islands, unaffected by those around us, the simple model of the market might work. In fact, however, we are social animals. If the free market in labour produces large numbers of poor people unable to feed their children, that may affect not just these poorer families but those who are greatly disturbed by seeing starving children on the streets or on their televisions. We may go and live in the suburbs and try to forget or ignore such people in our inner cities, which has been the American response, but even that has its costs. In short, our happiness or utility may depend not just on our income but on others' income. The classic formulation of this problem was by Hochman and Rodgers (1969). In a two-person world the problem of seeing a poor person in the street can be met by one person sharing their income until such a point that they are no longer disturbed by the poor person's plight. Even then there are problems. Money received as charity may not be as acceptable as money earned or gained as a right. My utility as a poor person may not be enhanced; it could be worsened by the shame. One way to avoid or reduce that difficulty would be to give money to some impersonal agency that specialised in treating poor people in a sensitive way.

The problem becomes more complex in a world with more than two people. Others may also dislike seeing poor people on the street. But they can free ride on the generosity of other people. That will mean that poor people are less well treated than everyone wants ideally. So poverty relief becomes something we agree to do together on a community-wide basis and tax people to pay for social security and Income Support. This has the disadvantage that some taxpayers who dislike the poor will feel imposed upon. They may feel as if, in the view of an American philosopher, Robert Nosick (1974), they are being put in a labour camp and forced to work to keep such work-shy characters alive.

There is another problem with private giving which concerned the Victorians. Charity may make beggars of people. Some may learn to rely on charity and lose the desire to work. The wider community loses their value as a worker and has to support them permanently. This is, of course, not just a problem of private charity but is seen to apply to state benefits as well. However, some argue that it is easier for the state to regulate such perverse incentives – pauperisation – than it is for private uncoordinated giving. Others argue that the stigma and uncertainty that is attached to private giving is a good thing and discourages 'scrounging'. By and large societies worldwide have chosen the first option and see it as the state's job to relieve poverty supplemented by private charity for special cases.

So far we have discussed some classic market failures. Since the 1970s another class of market failures has been identified. They are usefully grouped under the heading of 'information failure'. (For a collection of the seminal papers see Barr, 2001a.)

Information failure

For a market to work effectively, as we have seen, there has to be perfect knowledge, or at least good enough knowledge, about the product by both the producer and the consumer. If there are a lot of people buying a particular model of a new car they may not be car mechanics but they may know someone who is. Other users will have experience of such a model. *Which?* magazine will have done a survey. The level of knowledge of the consumer may not be perfect but it is generally good enough to be able to make a reasonable judgement. In some markets that may not be the case, and a series of information problems arise.

Consumer information weaknesses

- Individuals going to a doctor do not usually know what is wrong. They want to know what is causing the pain. Is it serious? The patient is not demanding a service; they are asking the doctor to act as their proxy demander, to refer them to hospital if necessary. The capacity to judge the quality of eventual treatment is also small. You may go to your garage frequently for the same car service. You may go to several garages to get second and third opinions. In any medical system this is more difficult; you are only likely to have one appendix out. This is not to say that patients cannot form judgements about the quality of their treatment, particularly the speed of care or the cleanliness of the hospital. But the more specialist the care, the more unequal the knowledge between the doctor and patient and the more vulnerable the consumer.
- Choosing a good quality school is difficult because so much depends on the children in the school. The users of the service themselves are part of the production process. How well the school is doing in a league table depends, above all, on the social background of the children. It may be doing very well given those children but the overall score the school gets looks poor. Yet your child, given their background, is likely to do well there. How are you to know that? Now it is not impossible to think of a statistical procedure that could disentangle such an information problem – it is called a *value-added measure* – but such information is costly to produce. Much the same problem is found throughout human services.

In short, professionally provided services, where the quality of the value added by the producer is difficult to measure, pose problems for traditional markets.

Seller and buyer imbalances in information

The lack of information may not be confined to the consumer. The reverse situation can also pose a difficulty for market exchange. Sellers of health insurance and long-term care may find that their clients know a lot more about their potential to use such services than the insurer. This was a problem discussed over 30 years ago by an American economist, George Akerlof (1970).

- If you are selling your car second hand you may know it was part of a bad batch off the production line. You have driven it for two years. The car has all kinds of bad traits. You are a particularly bad driver and have damaged the car in ways that the buyer is unlikely to find out about on a test run. The car is a bad buy – a 'lemon' in American slang. Equal knowledge about the product between seller and buyer does not exist. There is an incentive for owners of 'lemons' to sell them. If it becomes general knowledge that second-hand cars are a bad deal, the price will be low. That makes it difficult for the owners of good cars to get a fair price. They hold onto them. There is a less than optimal market in second-hand cars because the seller knows more than the buyer about the product.
- Akerlof pointed out that this phenomenon was not confined to second-hand cars. It was particularly found in healthcare and long-term care. Older people have a lifetime of knowledge about their bodies and what factors are likely to make them costly to care for in the future. Few older people were able to get health insurance cover in the US, at the time when Akerlof was writing. The private insurance company will, of course, be very wary of taking on an older person and will assume that they are a 'lemon'. Only the most sick are likely to apply, and insurance companies will expect the worst and therefore charge high premiums. They may exclude older people altogether. Gay men may find health insurance very hard if not impossible because of fear of AIDS. Such a person will be seen as a 'bad risk'. The price rises and the average medical condition of insurance buyers worsens as the price rises. It may be that this cycle goes on until no medical insurance is sold to this group.
- The phenomenon of the user knowing much more about the likely risks than the seller of insurance is an example of unequal knowledge that leads to the market not working properly. This is called *adverse selection*.
- The insurance company's response, to exclude the bad risks, is called *cream-skimming*. Human services are personal and intimate and the risks and costs of care are closely linked to information the individual or their family will know best. Hence human services are particularly prone to adverse selection and cream-skimming in free markets. Those in most need will be systematically likely to receive less. Vulnerable groups may find the private market is unavailable.

- The formal economic literature is largely concerned with insurance markets and healthcare in particular. But the same issues arise in other human services. Old people's homes paid a flat sum for every person they take will tend to select the healthiest and reject those who seem to need the most care. Schools who get a common fee for educating every child will aim to take the most able or the least troublesome. This will ensure apparently good results for the school and hence attract high-income parents.
- *Moral hazard.* Economists point to the fact that if someone takes out insurance against theft they may be less careful about locking their door. If your car is insured you may be less careful when driving. Insurers do not know whether you will respond like this or whether you are ultra-cautious; they cannot predict your behaviour. Hence they will assume the worst, and they will charge a high premium. This produces a below optimal sale of car insurance. They may take measures to be more selective, such as giving big discounts for no claims and other incentives. These are essentially to counter the moral hazard problem. (For a classic treatment of this issue see Pauly, 1974.) The phenomenon is not confined to private insurance, of course. A high level of state sickness benefit may make me less worried about being sick and more prepared to take time off work.

Uncertainty

- Markets do not like uncertainty. Uncertainty means you cannot predict from past human behaviour what is likely to be the future pattern of events or risks. We have good information on people's life expectancy, so pension companies know the probability of their policy holders living to the age of 70 or 80, or dying before they reach pension age. A whole profession of actuaries exists to advise on such probabilities. What they cannot cope with is uncertainty – unpredictable events about which there is no way of assigning a probability to the event occurring. Inflation is one such example.
- An additional problem is that many uncertainties may be linked. If the event happens to one person it is probably happening to many more. Unemployment is an example of this. If the economy is facing difficulties, many people will be affected. My chance of being unemployed is not just random and unconnected to your chance of being unemployed. This is a disastrous combination for private insurers, and they will not insure against unemployment except to a very limited degree.
- There are other examples of uncertain and linked futures. What level of inflation will occur in the next 40 years? What will be the nature of care for older people that far ahead? How many older people will need long-term care and what will it cost? Private markets for insurance work very poorly in all these cases. Private insurance companies do not give fully inflation-proofed pensions. They cannot forecast future inflation, and they are very

careful to offer limited promises to those who take out long-term care policies and to price them highly. For a discussion of the economics of long-term care see the Royal Commission on Long-Term Care report (1999, Chapter 5). (For an extended discussion of unemployment and pensions uncertainties see Barr, 1998.) We return to these topics later in Chapters Five and Seven.

This whole catalogue of market failures helps to explain why there is a powerful *economic efficiency* case for public funding and provision if people's needs for security, health and education are to be met (see **Figure 2.1**). On the other hand, economists also have grave doubts about the efficiency of public sector organisations. These doubts have been formalised in a set of arguments we may call 'the theory of government failure' (Le Grand, 1991).

Government failure

You can't please everyone all of the time

The trouble with public goods, particularly ones that can only be consumed at a national level, is that different people want different amounts of them. Take national defence, for example. Some people are pacifists, some are militarists and want national conquest of neighbouring countries to ensure their safety. Others want a small, but mobile, army capable of peacekeeping operations. There is no way they can agree on the one defence policy that the country can have at any one time. This is a rather simplified account of the kind of problem with which economists have struggled (Arrow, 1951). Coalitions may emerge which swing from one compromise to another, but

Figure 2.1: Needs provision implied by economic theory

Basic human needs	Market	Public finance and provision	Informal sector
Self-actualisation Self-esteem	Choice in a free market may contribute to these	State finance needed to ensure universal access to basic education finance and loans to enable access to higher and lifelong learning	Family
Love and belonging	Not marketable		Main source family, partners
Safety Personal National	Only marketable to a limited extent	State provision of police and courts	Close communities help
Physiological Public health	Not marketable	State provision and regulation	Public education helps families and individual healthy living
Healthcare	Major market failures	State finance at least on a significant scale	
Education	Market failures, tendency to under-provide	State finance on a significant scale	Parents as partners
Care of dependant – elderly, children, disabled	Significant market failures	State finance for major care	Large element of family care
Shelter	Market mostly provides	State pays rent/housing costs of the poor	
Food	Market mostly provides	State provides income for the poorest	

no single solution dominates all others. We may be right in saying that national defence has to be carried out by government but that is only the beginning of the problem. What kind of defence? How much should we spend? In practice we tend to accept that there is no perfect solution and that it is better to accept some compromise. But the more fundamental the disagreement the less acceptable compromise is. To the pure pacifist any compromise to agree on moderate defence spending will be unacceptable. The political market for public goods can never, in theory, produce a 'perfect' solution.

Where the public good is a *local* one there is a partial solution. If a voter wants lots of local road space, or very good schools, they can move to an area where most other voters seem to want that too and are prepared to vote for higher taxes. The theory was first advanced by Charles Tiebout (1956). It assumes that people can move freely. To the extent that they cannot, some people will be getting levels of service they do not want. The rich are able to move more readily than the poor. They will be able to choose the mix of taxes and services they prefer more easily than the poor. Where people do have a choice and a chance to move, voters can exert some pressure on the local council.

Self-interested voters

A naive view about the way politics works might assume that once a case has been made for redistributing income to the poor, altruistic voters will tax themselves to ensure this happens. If we want our schools to be well run we provide them with a decent budget and let the teachers get on and provide the best level of education they can. Drop that naive assumption and we have got problems. That is essentially what public choice economists began to do in a systematic way from the late 1950s on. (For a discussion of the intellectual origins and development of this branch of economics see Mueller, 1997; for an extract see Barr, 2001a.)

Let us assume, they said, that voters simply see elections as opportunities to maximise their *own* self-interest (Tulloch, 1976). Voters want to minimise their tax burden if they are moderately well-off. Car owners want more roads and low petrol duties. Parents want more schools, pensioners higher pensions. Only a minority of people are poor so there are few votes in higher benefits for lower income groups.

Reality is far more complicated. Voters do seem prepared to pay taxes to help the poor, particularly some groups such as older people, but less so groups like the unemployed (Hills and Lelkes, 1999; Hills, 2001a; Taylor-Gooby and Hastie, 2002). But it is also true that self-interest drives many public attitudes to social policy. Given that the middle class is large, influential in the media and critical in key marginal seats, we might expect them to be the main beneficiaries of social policy. Where a social service, such as state pensions, ceases to be of much benefit to the middle class, political support erodes. A tipping point may come where the middle or median voter no longer has an interest in preserving that service. People leave for the private sector and a service for poor people becomes a poor service. Willingness to pay taxes erodes. The service lacks the politically effective sharp elbows of the middle class, as Frank Field puts it. That may be exactly what has happened to pensions policy in the UK since 1945 (Glennerster, 2000). Thinking of the voter as a self-interested player is very important for designing and thinking about social policy but it is not the whole story. (For an extended discussion see Goodin and Le Grand, 1987.)

Self-interested bureaucrats

It is not just voters who seek to maximise their own interests:

> Bureaucrats are like other men. This proposition sounds very simple and straight-forward, but the consequences are a radical departure from orthodox economic theory. If bureaucrats are ordinary men, they will make most of (not all) their decisions in terms of what benefits them, not society as a whole. Like other men, they may occasionally sacrifice their own well-being for the wider good, but we should expect this to be exceptional behaviour. (Tullock, 1976, in Hill, 1993, p 110)

This assumption came to dominate Conservative views about public servants in the 1980s and 1990s. It remains today in many New Labour attitudes. Two strands in this literature are evident. One saw all claims for improved spending on public services as a reflection of public servants' and professionals' desire to earn more and run larger organisations – to be budget maximisers. The other strand concentrated on the fact that public services were usually monopolies and hence exploited their users just as private monopolies did.

Budget maximisers?

The classic book that began this whole debate was written by an economist who had been employed in the American equivalent of the UK Treasury, the Bureau of the Budget, later the Office of Management and Budget (Niskanen, 1971). Congress decided on big spending programmes in collusion with the big agencies like the Social Security Administration and the Department of Defence, Niskanen argued. From this searing experience Niskanen developed a whole theory of government spending. He argued that bureaucrats benefited in direct proportion to the size of the budget they held. Hence they were always seeking to increase their budgets regardless of the public good. They had particular power because they knew more about their field, social security for example, than anyone else. They could thus 'hoodwink' legislators into believing that there was a need to expand public spending. They controlled the research budgets of their agency. They could ask social policy departments in universities to undertake research knowing that they would be likely to make the case for more money to be spent on long-term care or schools. Doctors employed in the NHS regularly complain that it is about to collapse, and that their patients are dying needlessly. 'Shroud waving', Treasury officials call it. Worried voters believe it and the NHS ends up with more money.

This line of reasoning is not to be dismissed. One of the reasons we have very large hospitals and schools may well be that those who run these institutions get paid more the larger the institution they run. Doctors *are* actually very effective at shroud waving. You might like to read recent debates on public service spending in the UK and see how well the theory fits. But there are difficulties too:

- It is a one-sided account. There are powerful pressures working against spending departments. Unlike the US the UK has a powerful Treasury (see pages 82-9). Powerful economic interests resist higher taxes and spending. Politicians have to worry about imposing higher taxes if they want votes. Since 1976 it is these pressures that have held public spending in check.
- It also gives a narrow and inaccurate description of what motivates public servants. Large budgets do not regularly bring those involved larger salaries and even if they do they also bring more headaches for those who run them. Dunleavy (1991) presents a detailed critique of this theory. He does not dismiss the idea of civil servants and social services providers using their power for their own ends, but argues that this may often take other forms than budget maximising. They may, for example, seek to 'shape the bureau' in which they work for their own ends. They may structure the NHS or local schools for their own ends rather than the clients'. Why, for example, do schools end long before parents have finished work?

X-inefficiency

Another American economist, Leibenstein (1966), coined the term **X-inefficiency**. By this he meant the tendency of firms in a non-competitive situation to be less than wholly efficient in the way they produced their product. Working practices may be slack, responses to consumers slow or rude. The 'monopoly profit' may not be reaped by the shareholders but by the workers and managers not being as responsive and effective as they could be. That is the kind of inefficiency many critics argue besets public services.

Public servants as knaves?

It is not necessary to see public servants as wicked to see the force of this argument. Let us assume that someone in a social services agency is doing a boring or stressful job. They want to get home to their family. They go for a night's drinking and do not turn up the next day. They call in sick, and are unlikely to 'get the sack'. If they do a bad job their hospital or school is not going to go out of business. The users cannot transfer their custom to another hospital. Managers have weaker sanctions over their employees as a result. There is no self-interested reason why workers should not try to get by doing the minimum. It is difficult for any manager to see what is going on in a classroom or social work client's home. Such social services professionals may spend their time 'getting through the day', minimising stress, not going 'all out' to help their clients (Lipsky, 1980).

It may be worse than that. The incentives may be perverse. If I am a consultant, the slower I work the longer my waiting list. The longer my list, the more of my patients will ask to transfer to become a private patient. The more that happens the higher my income. May this not affect the eagerness with which I seek to clear my waiting list (Propper and Green, 2001)?

It is quite wrong to see all public servants, teachers and doctors as driven only by self-interest. In Julian Le Grand's phrase (1997, 2003) some may be 'knaves' but others may be 'knights' or angels. Many, probably most, will be a mixture of both. The more intrinsic satisfaction that a professional gains from their work, saving lives in a hospital, for example, the more like an angel they may behave. If their work is boring and repetitive the less incentive they have to work extra hours or go the extra mile. If we seek to run organisations assuming everyone in them is a pure altruist and needs no monitoring, we shall encourage sloppy practice. If we assume no one can be trusted we lose the goodwill of the altruists. A balance that can bring sanctions on the poor performers and retain the goodwill of the altruists is difficult to strike. This is at the heart of current debates about introducing market incentives and better accountability into public services.

Exit, voice and loyalty

One of the most influential and convincing accounts is that by A.O. Hirschman (1970) in his book *Exit, voice and loyalty*. He argues that there are two kinds of sanction or power that consumers or populations have over organisations to make them respond:

• One is by taking their custom elsewhere, as we have described. He calls this *exit*. In fact, there are often reasons why it is difficult for users to exit. One may be purely physical. Another choice of shop or school may be a long way away. It may be that a patient has been with that doctor for many years and has a sense of loyalty to the doctor. It may be that a child would be upset if moved from their school.

- Another way to influence a service is through *voice*, belonging to the school parents' association and having your say. That may not be effective. If you have no chance to move your custom, to exit, why should anyone listen? It is also costly in time and effort, and few parents go to school meetings.
- Where neither voice nor exit operate, and where loyalty to the institution has been eroded, high standards may steadily decline. Is the NHS a case in point?

The failings of *both* the market and traditional state monopolies gave rise, in the late 20th century, to two kinds of response. One was to introduce a degree of competition into the supply of public services, and the other was to draw more on the not-for-profit or voluntary sector. We explore the theoretical underpinnings of both strategies below. Another approach was to increase the scale of central regulation (see pages 181-5).

Privatisation and quasi-markets

Perhaps, some reformers thought, it was possible to gain the benefits from public finance and to avoid the efficiency losses that came from relying on state monopolies. The basic idea was simple. Finance services through taxation or social security contributions. Keep them free at the point of use. But let diverse agencies compete regularly to provide those services – schools, hospitals, old people's homes or community care companies. This was called Compulsory Competitive Tendering (CCT). Those who seemed to offer the most efficiently run services would get the contracts. Regular tendering for new contracts would ensure that if a company or public agency were not performing well, it would lose its contract. X-inefficiency would be squeezed from the service.

Examples from the US were quoted to suggest that where local authorities had sought tenders to operate, local refuse collection and other services efficiency had improved (Savas, 1977, 1982). Thatcher's government required local authorities in the UK to put services out to tender. Under the 1991 NHS and Community Care Act, social services departments were required to spend the majority of the special community care money they received buying services from private agencies. The NHS was required to put services such as hospital cleaning out to tender to private agencies.

A different approach was adopted for mainstream health services. Here NHS hospital trusts and community services were required to compete with one another for the tax funds that were held by the new district health authorities. These latter bodies purchased services from the hospitals of their choice on behalf of their whole populations.

Another model enabled *users* to choose the agency that did the contracting on their behalf. Some doctors were given a sum of money by central government that enabled them to buy treatment from a hospital chosen by their doctor. This was called *GP fundholding* (see pages 72-3). In Germany and the Netherlands in the 1990s competition between sick clubs (see page 69) was introduced. Each was free to make different arrangements for the care of its members. When someone joined the sick club the social security scheme paid that sick club a sum of money. On average that sum should cover the health costs of the members. It was very like the GP fundholding principle in the UK.

A more radical version left the choice of the provider to individuals. In many European healthcare systems the patient chooses which hospital to go to and the sick club or social health insurance society pays the bill. In Belgium and the Netherlands the system of schooling works in very much the same way. Parents choose the school and the state pays. This is a 'quasi-voucher' – it has the same effect as if the state were to issue a piece of paper that could be cashed for schooling. In Britain a combination of school choice and funding schools on the basis of the number of pupils they attracted had similar effects (see pages 110-13). **Figure 2.2** summarises these distinct types of quasi-market.

As we saw, the Conservative government required social services departments to buy from private providers for a period of time in the 1990s. More recently there is meant to be a 'level playing field' so that all types of provider have a fair chance of winning a contract, including 'in house' public sector service providers. This is the present situation with local authority contracting in the UK under the Labour government's 'Best Value' regime. Local users are meant to have a say in how those contracts are let. The contracts are meant to be less competitively bargained, with more informal negotiations and continuous

Figure 2.2: Types of public funding

	No competition between providers of services	Competition between providers of services for public money
No choice of purchase or provider	Pre-1991 NHS	Post-1991 district health authorities
Choice of purchaser		Gp fundholders; Netherlands and German sick clubs
Individual choice of provider		Post-1988 school choice plus formula funding of state schools. Netherlands and Belgian public and private school funding

contact between the local authority and its suppliers (Bovaird and Halachmi, 2001). But the basic change remains. There has been a move away from the 1940s model of state monopolies to a more diverse kind of provision. There is no one version of privatisation or quasi-markets. In subsequent chapters we discuss how well this experiment has worked.

The voluntary sector and mutuality

Why a voluntary sector?

The voluntary, or not-for-profit sector, as Americans call it, presents a problem for economists. There is a clear theoretical case for either the market or for the state as a provider of services. But why do *not-for-profit* organisations exist? The standard argument that economists have advanced is not that dissimilar to the quasi-market logic (Weisbrod, 1986). Where both governments and markets fail, not-for-profit organisations come in to fill the gap. But what gap? Weisbrod couches his argument in terms of the collective choice problem we discussed earlier. If people are voting to decide how much of a public good they want government to provide, many will be disappointed. Some may object to any form of support to AIDS victims, for example. They may find that government is providing too much, and there is not much they can do about this except campaign for less provision at the next election. Many, although not a majority, may want much higher levels of provision. It is open to them to give money to an organisation that collects money from similarly dissatisfied voters. There is no profit in helping AIDS sufferers, so it will be a non-profit group that receives the donations. Weisbrod couches his case entirely in terms of pure public goods. Yet, as Hansmann (1980, 1987) has pointed out, most voluntary organisations are not providing pure public goods. Our example of support to an AIDS sufferer is not a pure public good, but the essential point remains valid. The function may be one that the market is unlikely to undertake. Hansmann adds other explanations. If we are *giving* time and money to an organisation, we are unlikely to give to a profit-making one, fearing that the owner may simply take our gifts to line their own pockets. We are more likely to go to organisations we feel we can trust to allocate our gifts fairly and with due care and sensitivity. Such organisations compete to be more trustworthy than others.

This does not mean that such organisations are perfect. Far from it. They may not have profit maximising owners but they may give their staff too lavish offices and salaries. They may spend far too much on administration and fund-raising. Salamon (1987) calls such behaviour 'voluntary failure', analogous to market and government failure.

Billis and Glennerster (1998) have argued that these theories are only partially convincing. Previous authors had concentrated on the demand side – why other organisations fail – not on the supply side – what was unique about voluntary organisations. Billis and Glennerster develop an argument that while the state may be good at providing services which the average voter cares about, and has regular experience of – schools and healthcare – it is much less good at providing services for smaller and more stigmatised groups. This may be true of some ethnic groups, lesbians and gay men, and mentally ill people. Here the average voter is either ignorant or positively hostile. Funding may be too small or non-existent. Where this is so, public spending may be misapplied because there is little pressure and knowledge to push for the right priorities. Here voluntary organisations, perhaps set up by parents or partners of sufferers, come into play. They operate in more informal ways, perhaps having sufferers or victims on the governing committee. They use volunteers often related to victims and sufferers or past victims. They are able to keep the organisation in tune with the needs of those they serve. Their comparative advantage comes from their smaller size, less formal rigid structures, the involvement of close kin and past sufferers, and the use of volunteers. Here voluntary organisations may have a comparative advantage.

A rather different set of arguments leads to somewhat similar but distinct conclusions. Here the emphasis is not on economic efficiency or responsiveness to need but on the value of civil society – a complexity of non-state non-market institutions. State monopolies may, in addition to being inefficient, be driving out local self-help and community activity. A healthy society depends on such mutual giving and active involvement. Populations have come to leave human service provision to distant bureaucrats and professionals. They resent paying taxes to some authority to which they cannot relate. Hence both public services and the whole notion of what it means to belong to a social group decline. Voluntary, or not-for-profit, agencies can fill that gap, but many of these are as large and distant as a local authority or primary care trust. Perhaps some new forms of local community providers are needed to fill the gap (Mayo and Moore, 2001). These could be both more efficient and help revive local democracy. To some extent they already exist. Housing cooperatives owned and run by tenants are a growing part of the social housing sector. The school governing bodies created after the 1998 Education Reform Act have wide responsibilities and have parents and teachers and representatives of the local community as members. But there are many other more radical experiments quite free of the state that are inheritors of the old mutual aid societies that flourished centuries ago (Christie and Leadbeater, 1998). They include community shops, time banks, social care cooperatives, self-help self-build schemes. Here much of the exchange is not in the formal market. It relies on and builds trust. Yet it is difficult to see such small informal organisations ever being able to deliver sophisticated medical *cure* provision; they may well be able to provide better intimate personal *care*.

Overview

- Markets have their advantages. They hold producers to account. At their best they respond to consumer preferences.

- Modern economic theory has elaborated a range of market failures but also ways in which large-scale government monopolies fail.

- Social policy has to balance these effects. The balance may be different in relation to different services.

Questions for discussion

1. Why do economists think markets are a good way to allocate resources?

2. What are the most important market failures that affect social welfare?

3. What is meant by 'government failure'?

4. What are some ways of mitigating the effects of government failure?

Further reading

For those who want to follow up the economic theories of market failure as they apply to social policy the best source is **N. Barr (1998)** *The economics of the welfare state* (3rd edn, 4th awaited), Oxford: Oxford University Press. Barr has also edited a three-volume collection of seminal papers on the economics of social policy **(2001a)**. Volume 1 is the most helpful for this chapter.

Le Grand (1991) is the most succinct account of the theory of government failure.

The origins of quasi-markets are discussed in **Glennerster and Le Grand (1995)**.

The question of whether there is an economic explanation for the existence of a not-for-profit sector is discussed in **Billis and Glennerster (1998)**. For a discussion of the voluntary sector's role and the taxpayers' contribution to it, see **HM Treasury (2002f)**.

For a brief introduction to the idea of mutualism, see **Mayo and Moore (2001)**.

three

How to pay for social programmes? The tax constraint

Summary

- Most collectively provided welfare services are paid for out of taxation.

- Taxation is a compulsory levy on citizens and history tells us that it can only be collected when there is widespread consent.

- Currently the electorate seem willing to pay a little more to finance improved services but not a lot more.

- This chapter examines the scale and nature of taxation in the UK and how it differs from other countries. It is relatively low and most is collected nationally, not at a local level.

- Taxes and the way they are raised have important equity and redistributive consequences.

- Ways of improving the readiness of citizens to finance the services that they expect are discussed, as well as other forms of revenue raising such as charges.

We saw in Chapter One that roughly half of UK citizens' expenditure on basic needs is funded not through personal purchases but through some kind of collective action. We saw in the last chapter that there are some good economic reasons why this should be the case. So how do societies pay for collective actions they wish to undertake?

Here we come to what is perhaps the central dilemma in social policy. How do we persuade a population that has willed the ends – a generous or humane social policy – to will the means – a significant level of taxation? What are the limits to the levels of tax that can be imposed on a citizen? Does it matter how we raise taxes? Economics, or more accurately, *political economy*, can help us with these questions. The form taxes take matters both in terms of their acceptability and the impact that they have. It is no help to the poor if the benefits they receive are more than taxed away in a harsh tax system. No one, least of all the poor, gains if an economy is crippled by an inefficient tax system, which promotes unemployment. The tax system can be and is extensively used to act as a benefit-giving system. The study of taxation is as important a part of social policy as the study of the benefit system.

Consent

In very simple or small closely-knit communities it may be enough to rely on a sense of duty or religious obligation to contribute to the poor. The 'tithe' is an interesting example. This was originally part of one's income given spontaneously by the faithful – part of their crops each year – to pay the local priest or the monastery. It is still possible to see tithe barns in some villages in England where the crops were stored. Then, as the population grew and obligation weakened, 'free riding' began. People began to evade these religious duties, and gifts fell away. The church had to enforce the tithe and it became a tax. The duty to pay your tithe became part of canon or church law and failure to pay was punishable by the church courts. When they ceased to operate tithes became a tax paid as a rent enforceable in the Crown's courts. Since it was paid to the established Church of England it aroused the fury of the non-conformists and in the end had to go. (Tithes actually lasted until 1936!)

The King or Queen required tax revenue to maintain a navy to defend the nation: a 'public good' as we saw in the previous chapter. Ship money was first levied to raise a navy to fight the Danes in 1007. Charles I imposed it without the permission of Parliament in 1634; it was fought in the courts by John Hampden and the Parliament of 1641 repealed it. 'No taxation without representation' was a principle established in revolutionary England and passed on to form the basis of the American Revolution in 1776. In short, a collective will to achieve some common purpose requires some form of *compulsory* levy – a tax – to finance its purpose. Yet compulsion in tax matters actually requires a large degree of consent. Overstep that consent and kings, colonial regimes and governments fall. The long Conservative administration of 1979-97 fell in large part because it promised not to raise taxes and did so. In autumn 2000 a protest against high petrol duties threatened to bring Britain to a standstill. The Chancellor made concessions.

As rates of tax rise so it becomes increasingly advantageous to employ a good accountant to find ways to either legally *avoid* taxes by using loopholes in the law or to risk unlawful *evasion*. Working for cash in the black economy, not returning income fully on a tax return are examples. In some countries (Argentina is a recent example), it is claimed that *half* of all potential tax revenue is not collected. Beyond a certain point in all countries high tax rates actually produce less revenue because it becomes so financially advantageous to avoid or evade tax. An additional problem countries have faced more recently is that both capital and labour are able to move between countries more easily. Big corporations can move their manufacturing base to another country with lower wages and low taxes. Some people are able to move to places where taxes are lower. Governments certainly believe that this poses a real limit to the taxes that they can impose on corporations and the rich. This phenomenon is called 'tax competition'. Most advanced industrial countries have lowered their corporation tax rates and ceased to raise taxes on labour to avoid losing capital and highly productive workers.

The oil-induced economic crisis of the 1970s checked a long post-war trend to higher levels of taxation throughout the advanced economies. The UK was not alone but its experience was instructive. The UK economy ceased to grow for a few years in the mid-1970s. Taxes rose while incomes stagnated. People's take home pay, after tax, fell in real terms. This produced a sea change in political attitudes (Glennerster, 2000). Much the same happened in the US, Denmark and the Scandinavian countries. People were prepared to see taxes take a rising share of their *rising* incomes. They were not prepared to see it *reduce* their living standards. Tax restraint became a major political goal. After rising steadily from the Second World War, taxes levelled off as a share of the national cake in most advanced economies (see **Table 3.1**).

Sweden remained a relatively highly taxed country but it moderated its tax take. In 1970 its government took 46% of all Swedish incomes in taxes. This had risen to 54% in 1990. By 2000 it was still 54%. The US and Japan (since 1980) remain persistently low tax countries. France and Germany are moderate tax levying countries. They stabilised their tax rates from the mid-1980s on. Italy was the one country on a strongly rising trend until recently.

UK citizens used to be taxed at rather more than 40% of their total income. After the impact of the economic crisis that we referred to and Mrs Thatcher's period in office the tax share fell to around 35%. In the early 1990s the John Major government increased public spending but not taxation. The resulting high level of borrowing required first Kenneth Clarke and then Gordon Brown

Table 3.1: International comparisons of taxes including social security contributions (1975-2000)

	Taxes and social security contributions as % of GDP (total incomes in a society)[a]				
	1975	**1985**	**1990**	**1995**	**2000**
Sweden	42	49	54	48	54
Denmark	40	47	47	49	49
Finland	37	40	45	45	47
Norway	40	43	42	42	40
Netherlands	42	43	43	42	41
Belgium	40	46	43	45	46
France	36	44	43	44	45
Germany	35	37	36	38	38
Italy	26	34	39	41	42
UK	**35**	**38**	**37**	**35**	**37**
Spain	19	28	33	33	35
Canada	32	33	36	36	36
US	27	26	27	28	30
Japan	21	27	30	28	27
Korea	15	17	19	21	26

Note: [a] National accounts basis figures rounded to nearest percentage.

Source: Data from OECD (2002a)

to raise taxes again. Brown aimed to stabilise the tax ratio at about 37% of the GDP. That was the target set in the Comprehensive Spending Review of July (HM Treasury, 2000). The next Review (HM Treasury, 2002c) raised the target to just over 38%. If the GDP fails to grow as fast as predicted it may have to be raised again. Taken over the long period it is the *stability* of these rates that is surprising.

Economists lump all these limiting factors together and call them a country's *taxable capacity*. The problem with this concept is that we do not really know how to measure it. How much would a society be prepared to be taxed if a charismatic politician was able to sell high taxes to an electorate in the way that Mrs Thatcher was able to sell low taxation? Yet, as Table 3.1 indicates, a country's history does seem to present a substantial constraint on citizens' notions of a reasonable tax level. The Swedes have grown accustomed to 50% and the UK to less than 40%. The relative positions of the high and low tax countries have changed little in the past 30 years. The UK stubbornly remains a low taxed country.

But would voters be prepared to pay more? Recent surveys suggest that they might, but not much more. The repeated British Social Attitude Surveys do suggest that there has been a marked shift towards support for higher taxes since the beginning of Mrs Thatcher's term of office (see Table 3.2).

However, Hills and Lelkes (1999) and Taylor-Gooby and Hastie (2002) show that enthusiasm for higher spending is largely confined to health and education and, to some extent, to older people, and that 'higher taxation' means only a little more taxation. When a 3p in the pound sum is discussed most people disagree (see Chapter Ten, this volume). This view is supported by the research done for the Fabian Society Commission on Taxation (Commission on Taxation and Citizenship, 2000). It sponsored in-depth focus group discussions on people's attitudes to taxation, and the results were rather depressing. People simply did not trust politicians to spend their money effectively. There was no majority support for a general increase in taxation, and there was overwhelming support for earmarked extra taxation for the NHS but only for one or two pence in the pound, quite insufficient to do what people said they wanted done. The *Wall Street Journal* correspondent reporting on the 2001 General Election said "The trouble with the British Electorate is that they want European standards of public services but American levels of tax". You might like to consider whether this is a fair comment.

The whole debate about how far the general public is prepared to support higher taxes to pay for the services it seems to want was rekindled in 2002. The Budget proposed an across-the-board increase of 1% in national insurance contributions for employers, employees and the self-employed. This is the first significant rise in basic direct taxation since the Conservative Chancellor, Geoffrey Howe, reduced income tax rates in 1979.

Table 3.2: Public attitudes to taxation and social spending (1983-2001)

Question	% of respondents replying positively				
	1983	**1986**	**1990**	**1998**	**2001**
If the government had to choose, should it:					
Reduce taxes and spend less on health, education and social benefits?	9	5	3	3	3
Keep taxes and spending at the same level as now?	54	44	37	32	34
Increase taxes and spend more?	32	46	54	63	59

Source: Data from Taylor-Gooby (1995); Hills and Lelkes (1999); Taylor-Gooby and Hastie (2002)

Improving the popularity of taxes

How might it be possible to link people's evident desire for improved standards of public services and their willingness to pay? We consider some strategies that have been used or advocated.

Make employers pay

One strategy Chancellors may use is to increase those taxes they think voters will not notice. This is one reason why social security contributions paid by employers have been increased faster than those by employees at various times in the UK. Some governments in Europe raise much more of their revenue from employer contributions than the UK does. The French government raises a quarter of their total revenue from social security contributions levied on employers. The figure is just under a quarter in Italy and is a fifth in Germany (ONS, 1999). This looks politically convenient. Let the bosses pay. They do not have many votes. Yet in practice there are penalties in such an approach. Economic theory and empirical studies tell us that one of two things happen (Brittain, 1972; Nickell and Quintini, 2002). In a competitive labour market, employers can either respond to the higher cost of labour by reducing wages or by employing fewer workers. They use more capital equipment instead. Usually some of both responses occur. Either way workers end up paying.

Stealth taxes

Another approach is to impose taxes in ways that many people do not understand. In Gordon Brown's first Budget in 1997 some of the tax privileges enjoyed by private pension funds were abolished – the advanced corporation tax. Few understood the significance. Only later when individuals' pensions came to be threatened did the political costs begin to be paid. Altogether stealth is neither a good nor a lasting strategy for raising revenue.

Hypothecation

More justifiable, but still controversial, is a policy of matching a particular tax to a particular purpose. Social security taxes are one example. A specific health tax is sometimes advocated. The Fabian Tax Commission case for doing so was that instead of thinking of taxes disappearing into a black hole the electorate will associate the taxes with the purpose – improved healthcare – for which they are raised (Commission on Taxation and Citizenship, 2000). The whole argument is more complex and evenly balanced than that.

- Some classical economists arguing for *hypothecation* believe that forcing governments to relate particular taxes to particular purposes would mean that the whole tax voting procedure was better informed (Buchanan, 1975). Parties would campaign on competing platforms: 'Vote for 10p not 12p in the pound for health' and 'Vote 12p not 10p for education'. Improved information would enable voters to get a result nearer their preferences. There are, however, a series of theoretical and practical problems with hypothecation.

- There is no reason in principle why the outcome of such a competition for votes should produce more money for social policy overall. Indeed, the very fact that the Right advances the idea may give us some pause for reflection. Those who advocate it on the Left usually do so in the case of health or other services of which they think voters approve. A hypothecated tax to benefit unemployed people or lone parents could reduce the amounts those less favoured groups obtain. Advocates tend to assume that people, prepared to vote for a higher health tax, would keep their support for other taxation unchanged. That may not be right. Support for other taxes could fall, and evidence from existing hypothecated taxes is not encouraging. Social security is now the only tax dedicated to a specific fund to pay for that spending (see page 135). Social security has done much less well than health in attracting spending in recent years. Pensions have done especially badly. In the US schools are funded by a special education tax levied on property and voted on by local communities. It has not produced big revenues, and indeed, reactions against high property taxes to pay for schooling provoked the famous Proposition 13 tax revolt in California in the 1970s.

- The widespread application of the principle would result in a highly complex tax system and be administratively costly. The selective application of hypothecation to one or two purposes is difficult to justify on theoretical grounds.

- The strict application of the rule would mean that if the revenue derived from a particular tax fell in a particular year spending would too.

Taxes on 'public bads'

It may be possible to win public approval by taxing activities that are generally disapproved of or produce social or economic harm. This was the Labour government's strategy used in its first term of office from 1997-2000. Smoking tobacco, alcohol consumption, the emission of carbon gases or driving cars into congested city centres are all examples. There is a strong efficiency case for such taxes, which we discuss below. However, they are not necessarily popular. The environmental case for high petrol taxes may be sound but that did not prevent a powerful backlash against them in autumn 2000 throughout much of Europe.

Localise taxes

There is an efficiency case to be made for local people to make their own tax preferences clear by localising decisions. Voters will have richer information about the direct link between the taxes that they pay and the quality of services they get. If local councils do not provide effective services they will not get additional revenue. Those who want more and better services can move to areas that provide them. Such a threat will also force local politicians and providers to improve services, some economists argue (Tiebout, 1956). Overall, a greater degree of local control over revenue and spending may increase voters' sense of control and trust and hence their willingness to part with their money. The UK relies more on central taxation than almost any other advanced economy. Only 4% of its revenue is raised from local taxation. In Germany the figure is 30% if state (Länder) revenue is included. Sweden raises 30% of its revenue locally, for example, to pay for healthcare (see Table 3.3). No wonder there is a sense of 'disconnection' between local voters and local services in the UK. (For a discussion of the case for raising taxes locally see Commission

Table 3.3: International comparisons of national and local tax receipts (1998)

| | % of a total tax revenue from: | | | |
	Federal/central taxation	State/Länder taxes	Local taxes	Social security contributions
Federal states				
Australia	78.4	18.0	3.5	–
Belgium	36.7	23.3	4.9	35.1
Canada	41.0	36.3	8.9	13.7
Germany	29.4	22.0	8.0	40.6
US	45.1	19.2	12.0	23.7
Unitary states				
France	43.6	–	10.6	45.8
Italy	58.8	–	11.7	29.5
Japan	36.2	–	25.4	38.4
Korea	71.4	–	17.6	11.1
Netherlands	56.5	–	3.0	40.5
New Zealand	94.2	–	5.8	–
Norway	59.4	–	18.3	22.2
Spain	40.0	–	17.0	35.0
Sweden	58.1	–	30.8	11.1
UK	78.2	–	3.9	17.9

Source: Adapted from OECD (2002a)

on Taxation and Citizenship, 2000, Chapter 9.) Pure localisation is difficult though. Poor areas produce low revenues and high need. If we were to go down this route central government would have to retain a significant capacity to allocate more national revenue to areas of high need (Glennerster et al, 2000).

The Labour government has reduced controls on local authority spending and taxing but some still remain. Devolution has given Scotland some revenue-raising freedom. The 1998 Scotland Act enables the Scottish Parliament to vary the basic rate of income tax in Scotland by 3p in the pound, up or down. This power has not yet been used (as of 2003) but, at the first Scottish elections, the Scottish Nationalists argued that taxpayers in Scotland should pay 1p more than in England. (It did not win them many votes.) Neither Welsh nor Northern Irish Assemblies have tax varying powers. The Greater London Authority exercised its power to impose a congestion charge on motorists entering certain crowded areas early in 2003. More local freedom is practical but it will not necessarily increase revenue overall.

Convince taxpayers

There seems to be no easy short cut to the hard political task of convincing voters that higher taxes for social purposes are necessary and will be effectively spent.

Equity

Electorates are unlikely to support taxes they feel are unfair. Britain recently demonstrated this in a notable way. A poll tax is a tax regime that requires the same sum from each citizen. It was simple to work out what everyone paid and was used by the ancient Greeks. But it meant that the Duke in his castle paid the same as the poor man at his gate. Such unfairness led to Wat Tyler's rebellion in 1380 and Mrs Thatcher's brief attempt to impose it again in the 1980s helped to bring about her downfall. For a detailed and fascinating account of how a modern government could ever have landed itself in such a mess read Butler et al (1994). Despite the fact that many middle-class people stood to gain, the Poll Tax was widely unpopular, even among those who gained. Adam Smith (1776) argued that if government were to tax it should do so as nearly as possible according to people's ability to pay. (He actually advocated a flat percentage of a person's income should go in tax, a position advocated by some in the US today.) That is why early taxes were levied on the value of people's property, a way to roughly measure someone's wealth. The modern equivalent is a *progressive* income or wealth tax – one that takes a greater share of your income or wealth the more you have of either. (See **Box 3.1** for a set of tax definitions.) Smith also argued that taxes should be 'certain'

Box 3.1: A glossary of tax terms

- **Direct taxes** are levied on individual and corporate income. They can take various forms, including income tax, employees' national insurance contributions, corporation and capital gains taxes. **Indirect taxes** are taxes levied on expenditure. These include VAT, excise duties on vehicle fuel, tobacco, alcohol and other taxes on expenditure such as air passenger duty.
- A tax is **progressive** if the proportion it takes out of income is lower for the poor than for the rich. A tax is **regressive** when the reverse applies. If the share is the same for all income groups it is **proportional** or **neutral**.
- **Vertical redistribution** occurs when a tax and spending system takes money in net terms from higher income groups and gives it to the poor. **Horizontal redistribution** occurs when a tax and spending system gives money or services in net terms to a particular group in the population (irrespective of income) – such as households with children or older people.
- The **incidence** of a tax describes where its cost ultimately falls – that is, who pays it. A tax may be levied on one economic agent (a business, say), but its effective incidence may lie elsewhere. For example, the business may decide for competitive reasons not to 'pass on' the full amount of a sales tax but to absorb part of it. The net affect on the customer will be smaller than the full tax. So the incidence will be shared.
- Response to a tax is **price-elastic** if demand for the taxed product changes by more proportionally than the change in tax. The concept of elasticity can also be applied to behaviour in relation to income.
- The **average tax rate** is the percentage of total income or expenditure taken in tax. The **marginal tax** is the percentage taken on the last pound of income.
- A tax **allowance** is an amount of income (or expenditure) exempted from tax. A tax **threshold** is the level of income at which a certain tax rate starts. A tax **relief** is an expenditure (such as contributions to a private pension) that can be deducted from gross income before tax is charged. **Taxable income** is the range of income on which tax is charged, after reliefs and allowances.
- A **tax credit** is a deduction from an individual's or household's tax liability. A **'non-refundable' tax credit** can only be claimed up to the limit of tax liability. By contrast a **'refundable' tax credit** can be claimed in full even where it exceeds tax liability. The Working Families' Tax Credit (WFTC) was an example. Often taxpayers are left with more than their pre-tax earnings.
- Non-refundable tax credits and allowances are treated in the public accounts as **tax expenditures**. Whereas cash benefits count as public spending, these do not. They are taxes forgone.

Source: Commission on Taxation and Citizenship (2000)

and not arbitrary. Favourites of the King or the party in power should not be exempted and laws changed rapidly and for no good reason. People make decisions about whether to own a house or to take a certain job. They should be able to rely on those decisions not being upset by constant tax changes. Taken too far this would prevent any change in tax policy but it remains a sound principle modern Chancellors would do well to remember. Taxes should also be convenient to pay, Adam Smith argued, and not be costly to collect.

Although many people associate taxation with income tax and assume that the higher your income the more taxes you pay, this is not true. Income tax only provides about a quarter of all tax receipts and this share has fallen in recent years (see **Figure 3.1**).

Much of our national revenue is raised from *indirect taxes*. One is the Value Added Tax (VAT) which adds 17.5% to the price of most products that we buy, excluding food. There are separate taxes levied on spirits, wine and tobacco.

Figure 3.1: The changing structure of taxation

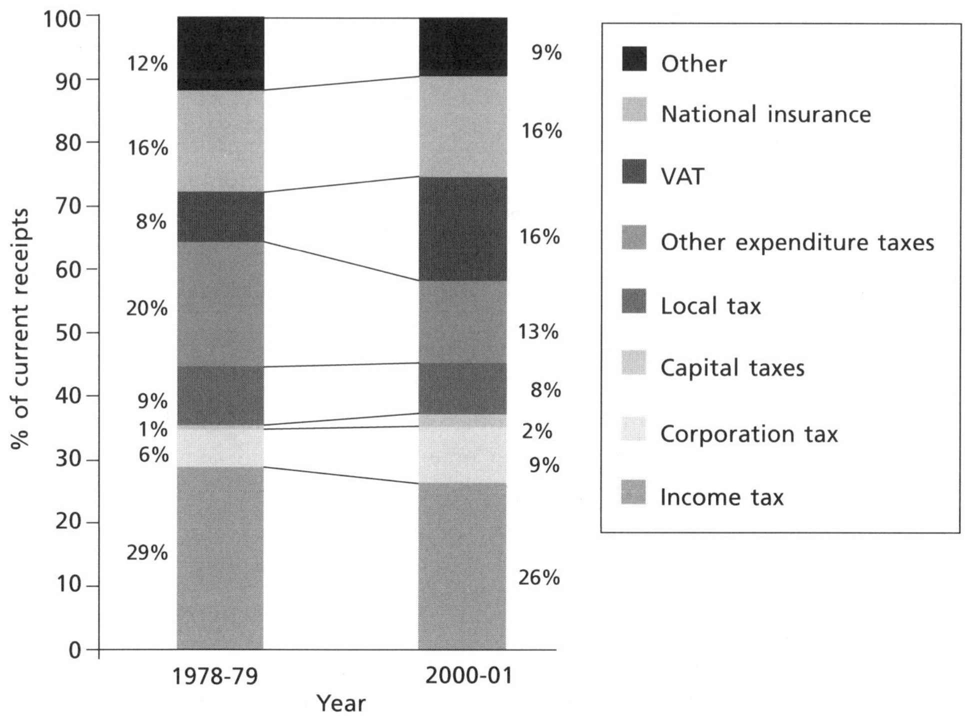

Note: Local tax is comprised of local authority rates, both domestic and business, for 1978-79 and Council Tax plus (national) business rates for 2000-01.

Source: Commission on Taxation and Citizenship (2000), reproduced by kind permission of the Fabian Society

Companies pay tax on their profits. We pay Council Tax on the value of our houses, which is to some degree related to our wealth.

National insurance is a contribution levied on both employers and individuals (see page 134) While low-income employees escape payment or pay at a lower rate, higher-income employees' contributions are capped. The justification is that since benefits do not rise with income beyond a certain level, neither should contributions. However, if we think of national insurance contributions as a tax it ceases to be progressive for the top range of incomes.

Economists debate just how we should calculate who pays taxes, such as the employers' national insurance contributions. One reasonable assumption is that employers pass them on in higher prices. These bear heavily on the poor. The Office for National Statistics (ONS) regularly work out what taxes are paid by each income group. The most recent results are shown in Table 3.4. From this we can see that the levels of indirect taxes – VAT, taxes on drink and tobacco paid by the poor – are very high. As a result the very poor contribute a higher share of their income to finance public services than do the richest 10%.

Efficiency

The traditional view

Economists argue that taxes should minimise the impact they have on the efficient running of the economy and where possible promote it. They further argue that taxes drive a 'wedge' between the preferences of consumers, workers and producers. The bigger taxes are the bigger the wedge and the less efficiently the market works. According to one theory, if a woman wishing to work faces a high marginal tax rate on her working hours she will be less likely to enter the labour market at all. Or if she does, the fewer hours she will work. That person values the time she spends with her children. Only if the wages she can bring home outweigh that valuation will she consider taking a job. She may consider the higher income will enable her to buy better clothes or accommodation for her child. At £20 an hour the judgement tips in favour of finding and paying for childcare and taking a job. If tax is introduced and take-home pay is not £20 an hour but £15 then the judgement is reversed.

She might decide to become trained as a social worker. That would take an investment of time and money, and it would take her away from her child. What she knows of social work salaries just makes that investment in her future worthwhile. Then the Chancellor raises income tax sharply. Her training now looks much less worthwhile. Work or looking after a child is not the only trade-off that individuals make. Another is between work and leisure. The more that work is taxed the more it tilts the scales in favour of leisure. This is the 'substitution effect' of tax.

Table 3.4: Taxes paid as a percentage of gross household income, by income group, UK (2000-01)

Taxes	% of total income paid in tax				
	Bottom decile	3rd	5th	8th	Top decile
Direct					
Income tax	2.5	5.4	10.1	14.0	18.1
National insurance	0.8	1.8	3.7	4.9	3.5
Council Tax[a] and water charges	10.0	5.5	4.0	2.8	1.0
Total direct taxes	**13.3**	**12.7**	**17.8**	**21.7**	**22.6**
Indirect					
VAT	12.2	8.4	8.1	6.9	5.2
Tobacco and alcohol	4.5	3.6	3.0	1.8	1.1
Car tax and petrol	2.9	2.5	2.6	2.4	1.4
Taxes on employers[b]	8.4	5.4	4.9	4.1	3.0
Other (TV license, betting tax and lottery)	9.4	2.4	1.7	1.3	0.8
Total indirect taxes	**31.4**	**22.3**	**20.3**	**16.5**	**11.5**
Total taxes	**44.7**	**35.03**	**38.1**	**38.2**	**34.1**
Average gross income, including cash benefits (£ pa)	(5,078)	(11,028)	(18,540)	(34,970)	(78,999)

Notes: [a] Council Tax Benefit meets housing costs for poor families who apply. This is a net figure *after* subtracting Council Tax Benefit.
[b] Taxes on employers are deemed to be passed on in prices.

Source: ONS (2002a, Table 24)

In practice things are not that simple. Many workers are not able to balance small adjustments in hours worked with changes in marginal tax rates. Many workers value their work over and above what they get in wages. Once in the labour market and in a good job they may be relatively little affected by monetary rewards. They may be more driven by ambition, power or the pure satisfaction of helping others. In contrast, however, many more may not find work that enjoyable and be much closer to the model worker that economists have in mind.

Another view is that individuals have some target income in mind. They may have a house in a particular area and a car in mind. They will work as long as it takes to earn such an income. If the Chancellor takes some of their income away they may work even longer. This is called the *income effect*. We should not think that longer hours worked for this reason are a good thing, that they are economically efficient. Here again a wedge has been driven between what the individual wants to do and what they do because of taxation.

While economists have written much about such disincentive effects of taxation they have devoted less attention to the effect of means testing. If social benefit is withdrawn at the rate of 50p for every pound earned it has an effect identical to imposing a tax on individuals of 50p (see Field and Piachaud, 1971, for the first statement of this case). As governments have increased the scale of means testing so they have increased the rates of effective taxation that poor families face. These rates are much higher – as high as 80% – than those faced by richer families (Evans, 1998).

Taxes and means testing can both have an effect on the amount people save. Taxing interest on savings may reduce the attractiveness of savings compared with spending. Reducing a person's state pension as their private pension income rises may well discourage others from saving (Boadway and Wildasin, 1996).

A more complex picture

The limitation of these older economic theories about taxation is that they tend to ignore the purposes for which it is levied. Taxes are treated as a black hole into which people's money disappears. In fact taxes are voted because they contribute to purposes people desire, helping the poor, reducing pollution or improving the efficiency of the economy by investing in public goods. The more people's desire is for collective action or income redistribution the less true it is that public taxes will be viewed as a reduction in an individual's welfare. Leading economists such as James Mirlees, Nic Stern and Tony Atkinson have produced some rather technical discussions of this issue and how far it affects what might be an 'optimal tax structure'. Those who want to explore this work could begin with Heady (1996). The essential point is that if we make assumptions about how much people want the incomes of the poor improved, we can see that their overall satisfaction may be raised with higher rates of tax.

Taxation is but one of a range of distortions that state intervention brings to the marketplace, as we saw in the last chapter. There will be benefits as well as costs in such interventions. Many economists tend to assume that the costs will always outweigh the benefits. Others have tried to test whether countries with high social spending have performed less well or not. Atkinson (1999) reviewed a large number of studies pointing out some significant problems with many on both sides of the case. In those that simply compare the size of the GDP with total welfare spending, the direction of the causal link is difficult to discern. High-income prosperous countries can afford high welfare spending and taxes to match. Their prosperity cannot be said to result from their high taxes! However, analysing growth rates, overall and in labour and capital productivity, may be more valid. Here Atkinson found no consistent results. Countries with high social transfer spending could not be shown to have suffered worse economic performance. The structure of benefits may have an effect, however. High poverty and unemployment traps, with poor incentives to return to work, can damage prosperity. A careful economic study of Swedish social policy (Freeman et al, 1997) shows that compressing wage differentials, and sustaining high benefits, can go a long way to eliminate poverty if it goes along with high incentives to work. But strong intervention and high taxes do entail some economic losses.

Taxing wealth

So far the discussion has largely centred around taxing people's earnings, the interest on their savings or on things that they buy. Why not tax their wealth? The US is in the process of abolishing its Estate Tax, which is what people pay at death on the wealth they then own. We do impose a tax on inheritances in the UK, and some other countries tax wealth owned during a person's lifetime.

The arguments for a wealth tax are:

- wealth inherited is not merited and may discourage further work – you are able to live on your parents' efforts;
- extremes of wealth are unfair; they prevent equal opportunity and give rise to unequal power;
- taxing wealth may have little effect on incentives to work.

Arguments against taxing wealth are:

- it is unfair on those who have saved and worked hard to hand on an inheritance to their children;
- it will be a disincentive to saving;
- it is extremely difficult to collect – people find ways to move capital to other countries and find loopholes in the system.

For a more detailed discussion see the Commission on Taxation and Citizenship (2000, chapter 12).

What alternatives are there to taxes?

If politicians find raising taxes difficult what else could they do to raise funds for social policy?

Charging

A frequent candidate for raising public money is to charge for the service. This has been one of the main ways in which continental European healthcare systems have contained their tax burdens in recent years.

The case for charging:

- it reduces the tax wedge and moves nearer to a market;
- it reduces unnecessary or frivolous use of a service or doctor's time;
- it makes people value the service they receive.

The case against:

- in political reality it is difficult to charge groups such as older people, children, disabled people or frequent users. This severely reduces the revenue collected; 85% of all prescriptions in the UK are dispensed free for this reason;
- charges act as a deterrent to those who need early access to healthcare and it can be more costly to the health or social work service in the end;
- charges destroy the point of having a free service in the first place and are often paid at the point when incomes are lowest and need is greatest, for example, when someone is sick, old or disabled.

For an extended discussion of charging see Parker (1976) and Judge and Matthews (1980).

Charity

It might be possible to encourage individuals to give more money or time to organisations that provide care. For reasons of free riding we discussed earlier, the scale of monetary giving is very small compared with taxation. The sum total of all charitable gifts for all purposes in the UK amounts to about 1% of the GDP. That includes giving for the arts, the environment and dogs' homes as well as social services. Even in the US, which has large tax advantages for giving, the total is only 2%. There is an important role for giving in any society and for agents other than the state to provide services (Titmuss, 1970; Deakin, 2001). However, taxation is likely to remain the main means for funding a social policy. For an extended discussion of the scale of the 'voluntary sector' and the small scale of funding, which actually comes from giving, see

Kendall and Knapp (1996). For an introduction to the economics of charity see Collard (1978) and Jones and Posnett (1993).

Fiscal welfare

So far we have discussed taxation as if it were merely a revenue-raising machine. In fact the tax machinery can be used to distribute cash benefits or their equivalent, and it is increasingly being used in this way. Richard Titmuss (1958) was the first to point out how tax allowances formed a kind of parallel welfare state (Alcock et al, 2001). A *tax allowance* is a band of income on which you do not pay tax. Tax law in Titmuss' day had many examples of allowances which enabled individuals or households to reduce their tax liabilities because they had children or were paying contributions to a private pension. It was possible, for example, to reduce the income on which you paid tax to the full extent of the interest you paid on your mortgage.

Taking a band of income out of taxation did not benefit everyone in the same way. Clearly if you were too poor to pay income tax at all the allowances had no value. If you paid tax at 20p in the pound the allowance was worth 20p for each pound. If you were paying tax at 50p the effect was the same as if the government paid half your mortgage interest for you. The government lost revenue. At one time this was more than equivalent to the government's spending on housing subsidies for those in council houses and Housing Benefit combined (see pages 164, 166). That is why economists call the practice *tax expenditure*.

By their nature tax allowances favoured the rich. Their scale was considerable in relation to actual public expenditure. Criticism by Titmuss and colleagues became more widely accepted and the range of tax allowances has been narrowed. Child tax allowances were replaced by the cash Child Benefit. This goes to everyone with children. Mortgage tax allowances were ended in 2000. We discuss these changes in later chapters.

On the other hand, there are disadvantages in having two separate administrative systems both assessing individual and household incomes and paying benefits. Many critics argued that the two systems should be merged. Benefits could be given out by the tax system to the poor and then taxed away as the household's income rose. This was the basis of what was called *negative income tax*. (For a succinct assessment of the idea see Barr, 1998, pp 255-67.) There were inherent practical problems with this approach as well as its disincentive effects. Incomes for tax purposes are calculated on an individual basis and the employer is responsible for deducting tax at source depending on an individual income. Income relevant to giving benefits is usually calculated on a household basis. It matters what your partner is earning and how many dependants you have.

Benefits also need to be claimed in an emergency, and household incomes and circumstances can change markedly and quite rapidly. Income tax liability is calculated annually, and there are therefore some practical limits to the merging of benefit and tax systems. But considerable progress has been made in recent years:

- The rules and definitions of the two systems have gone some way to being moved together.
- The Inland Revenue has been persuaded that their organisation can be adapted to hand out cash to people who qualify. The WFTC was a good example. It has now been replaced by the Working Tax Credit and the Child Tax Credit (see pages 136-7). In practice the parts of the organisation determining benefits and taxes are still rather distinct.
- The pro-rich elements of the tax allowances have been replaced in several instances by tax credits. These are absolute sums of money that can be deducted from your tax bill or paid to you if you are not eligible for tax. They do not rise in value as your income rises, and they can even be phased out as your income rises. (For definitions of different kinds of tax credits see Box 3.1.)
- Occupational and personal private pensions still attract pro-rich tax allowances. Exchequer support for pension saving could be better targeted on the poor by switching it from a tax allowance to a tax credit basis (Le Grand and Agulnik, 1998). This would set a ceiling to the amount of support the government gave to any individual.

Overview

- There is no easy way to raise more taxes. Taxing employers and taxing by stealth have economic drawbacks.

- Hypothecation may improve some services' chance of funding but at the expense of less popular services.

- Taxing environmental polluters has strong economic reasoning behind it but has not proved popular electorally.

- Consent has to be won and improved service performance is a necessary if not sufficient condition. So too is the perceived equity of the tax system.

Questions for discussion

1. What are the most important taxes in the UK, and how does its tax structure differ from that in other countries?

2. Outline the ways in which more revenue could be levied and the limits to each of these proposals.

3. What are the limits to charity and giving as an alternative source of resources for social purposes?

4. How far can the tax structure be used as a benefit-giving system and what are the advantages and disadvantages of recent moves to do this?

Further reading

Even if you do not agree with its conclusions or its political starting point the **Commission on Taxation and Citizenship** report, *Paying for progress* **(2000)** is an excellent discussion of the issues covered in this chapter. It contains background statistics and summaries of the tax laws as they stand and ways of raising more taxes to fund public services.

For an introduction to the economics of taxation, see the collection put together by the Institute of Fiscal Studies, *The economics of tax policy* **(Devereux, 1996)**. This combines a treatment of economic theory with a discussion of recent tax policy in the UK. Chapters from it have been referenced throughout this chapter.

The Chancellor's *Pre-budget report* each autumn sets out the fiscal position and possible tax changes. The actual budget report with firm proposals for legislation comes each March. Consult the Treasury's website (see www.hm-treasury.gov.uk).

The **Institute of Fiscal Studies Green Budget** always contains a good independent critique of the government's tax policies and basic statistics in an accessible form (www.ifs.org.uk). Also consult the journal *Fiscal Studies*.

Financing healthcare

Summary

- Healthcare markets suffer from significant failures of the kind that we examined in Chapter Two (see **Box 4.1**).

- Less of the UK's healthcare is financed through private payments than elsewhere.

- We have spent less on healthcare than most other advanced countries.

- The way we finance that spending and allocate it is relatively pro-poor and targeted on those in most need.

- Yet in many cases the NHS does not promote speedy treatment or consumer-friendly efficiency.

- We could get more out of what we spend.

Box 4.1: Market failures in health

- Individuals have *poor information* about their medical situation – they cannot diagnose their own condition or prescribe their own treatment. Information is expensive to gather and the opportunity for extensive research is not available in an emergency. Markets require good consumer information.
- *Power and information in the marketplace are very unequally spread*, both between individuals, the sick, the very old and the active healthy, and between doctor and patient.
- *Uncertainty about future needs is high*, both about potential illnesses and the medical knowledge that will be available to treat you. Medical science is changing all the time. So how much you should put aside for medical care is unclear.
- If you have a high probability of needing care over a long period, are chronically sick, disabled, mentally ill or aged, *private insurance will not cover you*. The risk of needing care is a virtual certainty.
- *People know more about their own bodies*, social habits and medical experience than insurance companies ('adverse selection', see page 23). Insurance companies respond by excluding potential bad risks and hence exclude those who need care most.
- There is a *separation* of the individual who is claiming medical care, their doctor and the eventual provider. At each stage 'moral hazard' (see page 24) problems arise. The doctor has little reason not to refer unnecessarily or the hospital to treat. The patient has less reason to be careful about their health. To counter this, insurance companies will take measures to restrict or ration access but not on the basis of need. (For a full discussion see Barr, 1998, Chapter 12.)

The cost of healthcare

The UK has traditionally spent much less on healthcare than most other advanced economies (see **Table 4.1**). This is for a mixture of some good and some bad reasons.

The first 'good' reason dates back to long before the National Health Service was founded in 1948, and it is called the 'gatekeeper' principle. Except in cases of emergency you will only be seen by a specialist doctor in a hospital if you have a referral letter from your General Practitioner (GP). They undertake a preliminary diagnosis and decide whether you need to be seen by a specialist. Ninety per cent of all contacts with the NHS get no further than the GP despite the fact that GPs take only 10% of the NHS budget. Other relatively low spending healthcare countries have a similar arrangement.

Table 4.1: Health expenditure per capita and as a % of GDP (1998)

Country	Per capita[a] Total	% of GDP Total	Public	Private
Australia	2,085	8.6	6.0	2.6
Canada	2,360	9.3	6.5	2.8
France	2,034	9.3	7.1	2.2
Germany	2,361	10.3	7.8	2.5
Netherlands	2,150	8.7	6.0	2.7
New Zealand	1,440	8.1	6.3	1.9
Sweden	1,732	7.9	6.6	1.3
UK	**1,510**	**6.8**	**5.7**	**1.1**
EU-15 average:				
Unweighted	1,764	7.9	5.9	2.0
Weighted[b]	1,824	8.4	6.4	2.1
Other countries				
US	4,165	12.9	5.8	7.1
Japan	1,795	7.4	5.8	1.6

Notes: OECD health data 2001. Public and private may not sum to total due to rounding.
[a] Expressed in US$ economy-wide purchasing power parities.
[b] Health spending per capita is population weighted. Health spending as a percentage of GDP is income weighted.

Source: HM Treasury (2001)

Another partly good reason for the low cost of the NHS is that it is tax financed. Other tax-financed systems, notably those in Scandinavia, Denmark and New Zealand, are also relatively low cost. The reason is that their central ministries of finance are better able to control spending than in countries where numerous agencies reimburse medical fees charged by diverse providers like Germany. After the UK Treasury took over the funding of healthcare in 1948, the share of the GDP spent on health fell sharply. It was about 4% before the Second World War, in the mixed private, local and national health insurance schemes. That figure fell to 3.75% in 1948, the first year of the NHS, and to only 3.2% by 1953/54. Capital expenditure on NHS hospitals dropped to one fifth of the level it had been when local authorities and charities had raised the money in the 1930s (Guillebaud Committee, 1956). This powerful role played by HM Treasury has its drawbacks too and may have been overplayed.

In some other countries patients have been able to go to their GP or chosen specialist hospital and merely send the bill to their private or social insurance fund. Such 'demand-led' systems were very expensive. Since the 1980s no country has been able to sustain this open-ended arrangement. Charges or 'co-payments' have been introduced in both public and private insurance schemes in Europe and America. It is this private spending, either in the form of charges for treatment or private insurance, that explains why health expenditure is higher in many other countries. This has led some to argue that the UK should move in the same direction.

In short, international research suggests that four institutional factors are associated with countries' lower spending, holding other factors like income and demography constant (Propper, 2001, quoting Gerdtham and Jonsson, 2000). They are:

- the existence of primary care gatekeepers;
- the use of payments for care such as hospital charges for accommodation or prescription charges or payments to visit the GP;
- the use of capitation payments: a GP gets paid for the number of patients on their list not how many times they see patients or how many drugs they dispense;
- the scale of public provision and finance.

The UK NHS has all these characteristics, but relatively low charges at the point of use. Scandinavian tax-based and especially European insurance-based systems charge patients directly at the point of use far more widely than the UK. The bottom line is that the NHS is both more efficient in some ways *and* less well supplied with doctors, nurses and equipment than most other European or North American arrangements (European Observatory on Health Care Systems, 1999; HM Treasury, 2001, 2002b; Propper, 2001).

The bulk of health spending goes on the very young or the very old (see Figure 4.1).

Figure 4.1: Hospital and community health services' gross current expenditure per head, England (1999-2000) (£)

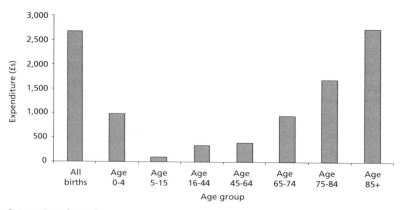

Source: DoH (2002c)

These figures need interpreting. It is sometimes argued that because the costs of those over 80 are so high, ageing will put huge burdens on the NHS. In fact, most of this extra expenditure on the very old is connected with the costs of dying and most people now die from old age. The good news for the Exchequer is that we only die once. As we age that high cost of dying moves up the age scale with us. Over the period 1998-2008 the ageing of the population will require the NHS to expand by 0.4% per year merely to stand still. This is rather less than in the previous 10 years. The most important pressure comes from the rising expectations we have of any healthcare system. Patients expect prompt treatment in modern facilities whereas 40 years ago they were grateful for free treatment. Modern consumers seem less tolerant of illness. Replies to the National General Household Survey over the past 25 years certainly suggest this. The percentage of respondents saying that they were 'not in very good health' has increased from 14% to 27% in that period (ONS, annual). It is difficult to believe that illness has really doubled in that time. We are simply less prepared to accept it. The range of costly treatments available to us has grown, and for all these reasons demands on the NHS will continue to grow.

Every healthcare system in the world is having to ration its resources more fiercely. In the US private insurance companies decide whether they will accept your physician's judgement that you need treatment. Some European countries have sought to define core services that their insurance schemes will fund and those for which patients must pay extra. In the UK the new National Institute for Clinical Excellence (NICE) (see page 74) has begun to advise health providers on what are the most cost-effective forms of treatment. It also advises ministers on what treatments or drugs are so ineffective (or costly compared with existing treatments) that they should not be provided on the NHS. We discuss rationing further in Chapter Nine.

Blair's promise and the Wanless Report

Following the influenza crisis in the winter of 1999 Prime Minister Blair promised that the UK government would increase spending on the NHS substantially. It would move to the average level of health spending in Europe. Whether this was a simple average of countries' spending or one weighted by their size was never made clear (see **Table 4.1**). Since then the rate of increase in real NHS spending has risen sharply. (By 'real' we mean excluding the general rate of inflation in the economy as a whole.) From a standstill in 1996/97 the NHS since 1999 has been receiving about 6% more each year. Within a total budget of £40 billion in England in 1999/2000 two thirds went on hospital and community services and half of that on acute hospital care (see **Figure 4.2**).

Figure 4.2: **Where does the NHS budget go?**

Hospital and community health services, gross current expenditure by sector, England (1999-2000)

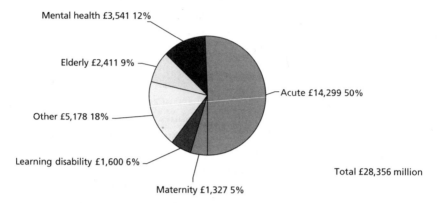

Mental health £3,541 12%

Elderly £2,411 9%

Other £5,178 18%

Learning disability £1,600 6%

Acute £14,299 50%

Maternity £1,327 5%

Total £28,356 million

Family health, personal medical and dental services, England (1999-2000)

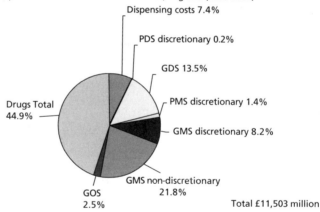

Dispensing costs 7.4%

PDS discretionary 0.2%

GDS 13.5%

Drugs Total 44.9%

PMS discretionary 1.4%

GMS discretionary 8.2%

GMS non-discretionary 21.8%

GOS 2.5%

Total £11,503 million

Note: PDS = personal dental services; PMS = personal medical services; GDS = general dental services; GOS = general optician services, free sight tests and other services; GMS = general medical (ie, GP) services.

Source: DoH (2002c)

The Wanless Report

Gordon Brown asked for an independent review of the scale of spending that would be required to deliver a first class health service taking a long view over the two decades up to 2022/23. The enquiry's final report (HM Treasury, 2002b) took account of underlying factors such as ageing and changing patterns of disease. Most important of all it costed commitments to shorten waiting times so that maximum hospital waits should fall to two weeks by 2022. It costed the consequences of introducing the new *National Service Frameworks*, which recommend best practice. They then existed for coronary heart disease, renal disease, mental health, diabetes and cancer. They will be steadily extended. The review team considered a range of scenarios making different assumptions about disease patterns and individuals' own capacity to undertake health-improving lifestyles. The report should be read in full by those wishing to understand the cost pressures on the NHS.

The conclusion was that UK spending should rise from 7.7% of the GDP in 2002/03 to between 10.6 and 12.5% in 2022/23. The assumption was made that the private component would remain at 1.2% of the GDP, which may well be an underestimate. The review team also commissioned a study of health and cost trends in eight countries, including their systems of finance. It was prepared by colleagues at the London School of Economics and Political Science (Dixon and Mossialos, 2002) and it is an extremely useful source of comparative material.

In the April 2002 Budget (HM Treasury, 2002a), Chancellor Gordon Brown committed the Labour government to spending 7.4% per annum more per year in real resources from 2002/03 to 2007/08. This would increase the share of the GDP going to health from 7.7 to 9.4%. The Wanless Report also made recommendations on social care spending, as we shall discuss in Chapter Five.

How the NHS funds are allocated

The NHS is usually described as being entirely financed out of general taxation. This is not strictly accurate. In total, about 80% of NHS spending is funded in this way. Another 12% has been transferred from the national insurance contributions that are deducted from employees and employers. Beveridge recommended this small link with the insurance system and it has remained ever since. In his April 2002 Budget the Chancellor raised national insurance contributions as from April 2003, adding 1% to all employees' contributions above the starting point (from 10% to 11%). He raised the employers' contributions from 11.8 to 12.8%. This applied to the whole of earnings above the lower earnings limit. The promise was that the extra revenue would be spent on the NHS. Charges bring about 2% of total revenue; charges made for prescriptions and for dentistry. They do not in levied by hospital trusts for private treatment.

Government makes no distinction between these forms of allocates money to various purposes and areas as if it were a money. Despite its title 'national', the NHS is, in fact, administer four distinct services: those in England, Wales, Scotland and Nor each with their separate budgets which are allocated somewh

Distinct formulas are used in each country to decide how much each local area needs. There is one system of allocation that funds hospitals and community services and another which funds family healthcare – GPs, dentists and opticians (see **Figure 4.3**).

Figure 4.3: The flow of funds to the NHS (2003)

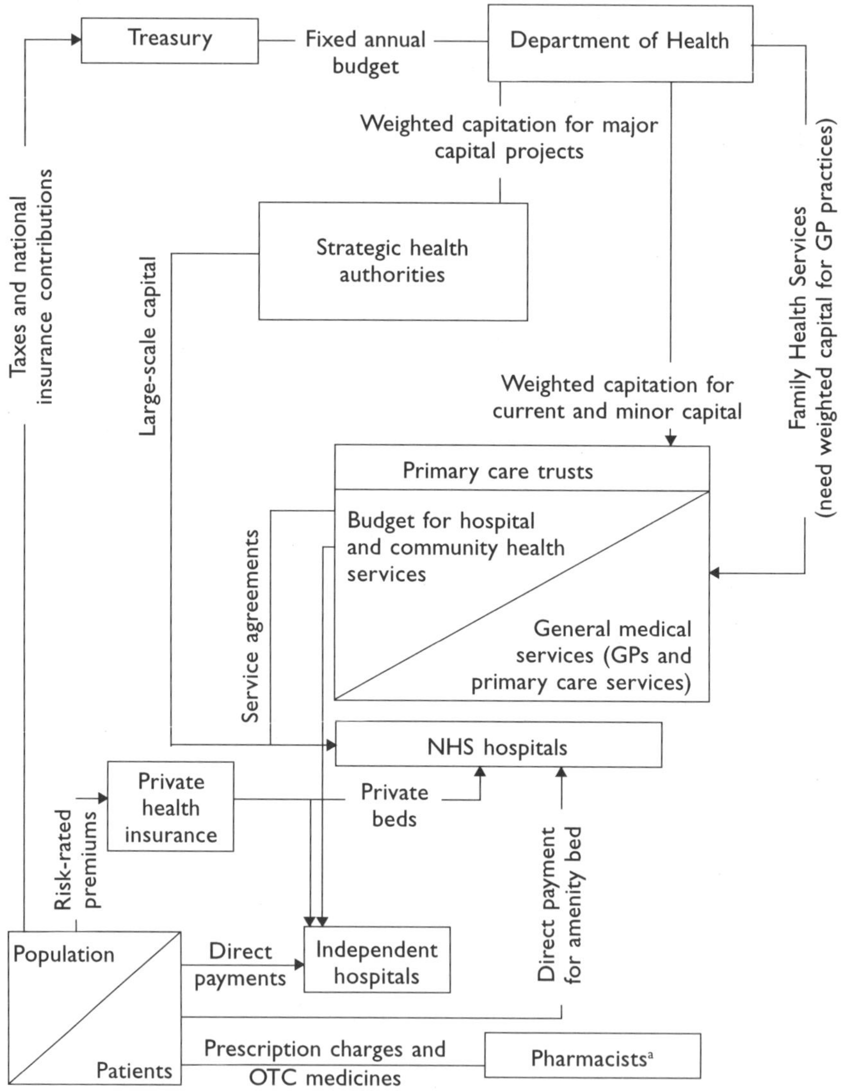

Notes: [a] Pharmacists are reimbursed by the Prescription Pricing Authority, a special health authority of the Department of Health.
OTC = over the counter.

Source: Adapted from the European Observatory on Health Care Systems (1999)

Dentists and opticians have been paid for each item of service that they provide ever since 1948, although the amounts and the regulations have changed. Part of a GP's income has also come from payments received for undertaking particular duties such as looking after pregnant mothers or running baby clinics. But most has come from two other kinds of payment. One was to keep the practice open and operating in line with the standards laid down in the GP's national contract. The second and larger element has been a capitation payment. This is a sum paid to the GP practice for each patient who 'signs on' to be treated at that practice. You cannot sign on at more than one practice or go to a GP practice unless you are registered with them. The capitation sum has varied with the age of the patient and GPs have received more money if their patient lives in a poor area. The 'Jarman' index, named after its inventor, was meant to compensate GPs for the additional demands put on the practice by poorer patients living in poor social conditions. From 2003 the intention is to use a more comprehensive measure of need to fund practices in a way that will compensate them for the additional workloads which deprivation and other social conditions impose. Instead of payments going to individual GPs the 'contract' will be made with the whole practice. The 55-year-old *Red Book*, setting out the fearsome 250,000-word payment system for GPs, will go. All GPs will have to provide essential core services. They will be able to opt out of out-of-hours care if alternative arrangements are made. Doctors wishing to provide extra services will be paid more. (At the time of writing, March 2003, their new contract had still to be agreed by the BMA's members.) The incentive to manage large lists and provide limited services will be removed under this new arrangement.

Measuring differential need

This proposal follows the relatively successful application of need formulae to the allocation of hospital and community health expenditure ever since 1976, and the Report of the Resource Allocation Working Party (RAWP) (DHSS, 1976). Before that date money was allocated to regions and then to individual hospitals on the basis of last year's budget plus some extra. If a new facility was built, more money was given to the region to keep it running and then the same procedure of incremental budgeting took over. The main beneficiaries were the richer areas, that had been able to open most hospitals in the era before the NHS was formed, and areas of population growth. RAWP proposed using population size weighted by a measure of the relative health needs of each region. These weights partly took account of the age of the population and partly its relative health as measured by the region's standardised mortality ratio (SMR). This measures the number of people dying from different diseases at any given age relative to the national average. It was the nearest that RAWP could get to a measure of the healthiness of regional populations and hence of the medical demands they would put on the NHS compared with other regions. This formula was applied in England and led to a substantial evening up of the resources going to different regions, with the north of England being the major gainer. Similar formulae were adopted for each of the other countries of the UK. Even so there were recurrent criticisms of the formulae – notably the use of death rates as a measure of need. Then there was criticism of the absence of any measure of the different costs of delivering health services in remote areas or where labour costs were higher. A series of changes were introduced culminating in the significantly new method introduced in the early 1990s and modified by the Labour government of 1997. (For a detailed account of this history see Glennerster et al, 2000.) Because the Conservative government wanted to separate purchasing authorities from actual providers of care, like hospitals, it was necessary to find a way of allocating NHS funds fairly down to quite small units: district health authorities. The Centre for Health Economics at the University of York produced a new more advanced method. It essentially matched up the population characteristics of small local populations and the demands they put on hospitals and community services. It measured how much more demand would be generated by an old person living alone than by a married man in his forties or a young single mother. The population mix then determined how much each small area would need.

Quite separately the formula took account of the fact that in areas of high labour demand the NHS must pay more to get the same quality of staff than in an area with high unemployment, for example. This is called the *market forces factor*. Similar formulae were introduced in the other nations within the UK. The explicit aim was always to give every person the same chance of treatment wherever they lived.

Major advances were made towards this end in the 25 years after 1976. By 2000/01 only three health authorities in England had allocations more than 4% above or below the target set by the formula. This was a much closer convergence than in 1993 let alone in 1976. In a detailed analysis of small area (ward) level data Bramley (1998) concluded that NHS resources were more closely matched to need at that level than was true of other public services. However, these formulae were derived from the observed *demands* put on the service by different groups rather than by *unmet needs*. They measured demands on *services* not health itself. The new Labour Secretary of State in 1997 asked RAWP's successor, the Advisory Committee on Resource Allocation in England (ACRA), to come up with a way to give more to areas where the population suffered from poor health. The aim should be to reduce health inequalities, not just provide equal access to health services. As a result a temporary *additional* allocation was made from 2001 to 2003, called the *health inequalities adjustment*. It is based on a measure called 'years of life lost' for each area. This is the number of years of premature death suffered by a given population compared with the national average expectation of life. The

50 health authorities that had the worst record of premature death from cancer, accidents, suicides, injury and infant deaths – the government's target problems – received additional funding. An attempt is also made to estimate the differential costs of pharmaceuticals prescribed by GPs in response to social deprivation and age factors.

Work by ACRA continued to try to devise measures that would better measure the relative health needs of populations and match resources to them in England. From 2003/04 to 2005/06 allocations to the new primary care trusts will be based on a revised formula and will incorporate the results of the 2001 Census (see **Figure 4.4**).

The 2003 English formula

The key changes were:

- A fresh analysis of the relative costs of treating different age groups was used.
- A revised and simpler measure of the differential *demand* on services made by different social groups was kept. It used variables that could be kept up to date more frequently derived from the area index of multiple deprivation produced by the Office of the Deputy Prime Minister.
- A measure of *unmet need* was added. The Health Survey for England had shown that minority ethnic groups and very low-income groups made *less* use of health services for a given level of morbidity (illness). This new element gave extra weight to those variables that were associated with underuse – ethnicity, health deprivation and low educational levels.

Figure 4.4: **Allocating NHS resources**

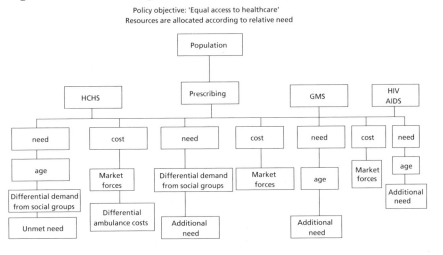

Note: HCHS = hospital and community health services; GMS = general medical services.

- As a result of the above, the temporary health inequalities adjustment was removed, although those authorities receiving it in 2003 have it built into their base allocation.
- The small addition to take the demands of rough sleepers into account has been kept.
- The market forces factor that gives more to areas that have to pay more to attract staff and keep them has been increased and applied to medical and dental staff.
- These allocations will go directly to primary care trusts and their populations are used as the reference point.

Allocating capital resources

So far we have been concerned with formulae that allocate recurrent income. From April 2003 a formula is being used to allocate capital resources for major three-year building programmes. This replaces the old annual judgmental allocations made by the regional offices of the Department of Health. This money for major capital building will go to the new strategic health authorities. Money for minor capital expenditure is allocated on a formula basis directly to NHS trusts and primary care trusts.

The Scottish and Welsh equivalents

Both the Scottish Parliament and the Welsh Assembly initiated their own reviews and as a result have developed methods different both from each other and from England!

The 'Arbuthnott' Review in Scotland decided on four indicators that research had shown were strongly related to healthcare costs and used an unweighted average of these indicators (Scottish Executive, 1999). This was a much simpler but also much cruder measure than the English one. It did not seek to take into account so many factors but did try to consider unmet needs rather than simply differential demand generated by different population types, as was the case in England. The later English review built upon some of its work. The Welsh Review (National Assembly for Wales, Health and Social Services Committee, 2001) relied on epidemiological measures taken from the Welsh Health Survey.

So far we have been describing ways of allocating 'revenue', or current expenditure on salaries and materials, not on buildings. Despite differences in detail each country has adopted a more evidence-based way of allocating resources to meet the distinctive healthcare needs of quite small areas. The depressing fact is that despite such growing sophistication the *health* of people in different parts of the country still varies widely, as it also does by social class (Acheson Report, 1998).

In East Surrey, Kingston and Richmond, wealthy suburbs of London, the average expectation of life at birth is 79. The expectation of a healthy life unaffected by disability or poor health is 67 years. In Barnsley the expectation of life is 76, with only 52 years of healthy life. Much more basic forces are at work affecting health than the amount spent on health services.

On top of these carefully calculated need indicators the Labour government in 1997 introduced a series of special allocations designed to fund particular initiatives driven from the centre. These included money for deprived areas that were experimenting with innovative ways to combat health inequality – Health Action Zones. The major additional funds were grouped in the *Modernisation Fund*. This was made up of separate pots of money for: adult mental health services, primary care improvements, gynaecological cancer, information technology and above all, money to reduce waiting lists. For politicians these pots of money have the advantage that they create headlines when they are announced but they cause local managers considerable difficulty in monitoring and reporting on how each is spent. They may or may not accord with locally perceived priorities.

Raising the money

Rising expectations of the NHS and the constraints on its tax-financed budget have led many to question whether tax funding is the right way to finance the service. Two major alternatives have been advocated and we discuss them below: moving to a social insurance-based system and creating a larger role for private insurance. *Local taxation*, which the Swedes and Danes use very effectively, is not much discussed in the UK but would offer another route.

A less radical option was chosen by the Chancellor in 2002. He increased national insurance contributions by a full percentage point, justifying his action by saying that the extra revenue would go to the NHS. This was just raising taxation by another name and was largely a matter of political presentation. A more radical version of the same idea would be to finance the whole of the NHS with an earmarked health tax. We discussed this in the last chapter (see pages 40–1) as part of a general discussion of hypothecation.

An insurance-based system

There are four quite different elements to Continental European health insurance schemes. Some are more exportable than others. Germany, France and the Netherlands are the most frequently quoted examples.

Employer/employee contributory basis

One common characteristic is that employers and employees contribute a percentage of their wage bill or their own wages to health insurance funds. Historically, this has had some advantages in providing higher revenue. The level of contributions was set in negotiations between employers and trades unions. Governments had relatively little control. The level set in France was not opposed by Parliament and the funds were not in the state's jurisdiction. In a period of growth and little worry about labour costs or unemployment, this produced a relatively unconstrained health budget. The 1990s have changed all that. Governments have moved in to set limits to contribution levels as the amounts raised reached 10% of the GDP and coincided with growing levels of unemployment.

Those who need healthcare most are not employed. Hence insurance-based schemes had to be extended to take in unemployed people, older people and other non-workers. Either existing schemes had to be forced to cover such categories, people who had not paid contributions, or separate tax-based funds were created for such people. With government-set contribution levels and budget ceilings the schemes now look very much like tax-based ones. They have lost their capacity for open-ended spending and are left with a form of tax that is not progressive and makes employing labour look expensive. Much of the advantage these countries enjoy is simply because they spend more on healthcare. There are other aspects of European systems that may be worth emulating.

- *Fee for service:* those who provide services, hospitals, clinics and GPs, are paid for each item of service that they provide, as are dentists and opticians in this country. Some hospitals in the UK were paid that way by GP fundholders under the 1991-97 arrangements. Patients pay their GP directly for each visit and recover a portion of the cost (75% in France) from the insurance funds. The insurance scheme or the sick fund will approve your entry to a hospital and then pay the fee, although typically the user will pay something too. This creates an incentive for hospitals and doctors to treat patients and to do so promptly. These systems have few waiting lists. The more patients providers treat, the higher their income. On the other hand, this can lead to over-doctoring, unnecessary repeat visits or long hospital stays. The system is also difficult to combine with a limited or 'global budget', as the French and Germans are finding. Institutions reach their budget limit while patients are waiting to be treated. Since there is money at stake the institutions tend to break their budget targets. To resolve this tension patients have come to be charged significant sums to curb demand. In France much of these charges are met by the middle class taking out supplementary insurance, as we shall see.

- *Purchaser–provider split and consumer choice of provider:* this is a feature of insurance-based systems but not exclusive to them. Other tax-based systems, including Sweden, have moved some way towards such a pattern. Insurance or sick funds pay a variety of institutions for the treatment that they provide. These may be not-for-profit hospitals run by religious foundations or profit-making providers. They may be independent public hospitals. In Germany 40% of hospitals are not-for-profit organisations, 5% are private for-profit and 50% are independent public agencies. Patients can either choose which provider to go to within the limits set by the sick club that they belong to or their GP can choose, as in France. In Germany and the Netherlands people can choose which sick fund to join and they can change if they are not satisfied. This means that they have a choice of GP, of hospital and of the agency which pays the bills. The Netherlands has a national formula, which readjusts the amount a fund will get depending on the type of members they attract. More potentially costly patients attract more money. This is an attempt to counter cream-skimming (see page 23). This degree of choice and competition between providers seeking custom does not have to be confined to insurance-based schemes. Denmark, for example, has a tax-funded system. Patients can go to any hospital in the country and the hospitals gain more resources the more patients they treat.

In short, insurance-based schemes combine varied characteristics. Some are economically undesirable. Others may well be worth copying and some have been adopted already by tax-funded systems, notably by several county councils in Sweden who are paying hospitals by the number of patients they treat. Tax funding does not necessarily entail a centralised command and control pattern of provision as it has in the UK. Recent government changes (see page 75) recognise this.

Private insurance

A feature of some social insurance-based systems is that they can make use of voluntary private insurance built on top of a basic core of services (Mossialos and Thomson, 2001). The German government permits high earners to opt out of the social health insurance scheme. Spain does so for civil servants. The Dutch government *excludes* a third of the population from compulsory membership of social insurance schemes. Those earning above an income ceiling choose how much and what kind of insurance they want. In Germany high earners have to be a member of a private scheme if they opt out of the social insurance scheme. In other countries like France there is a three-tier system. The social insurance system does not cover a range of services and does not reimburse charges for hospital accommodation or above-scale charges made by many doctors. So individuals and firm-based groups take out additional insurance to cover these costs. Much of the cover is provided by not-for-profit mutuals, which have tax advantages. On top is the third tier of the private profit-making providers. Voluntary and separate private insurance exists in all European countries. In some it is heavily subsidised through the tax system, as in Ireland. There is no tax relief in most European countries and only very limited tax subsidy in Germany and the Netherlands.

The proponents of tax subsidies for private health insurance argue that it would:

- increase individuals' take-up of private health facilities and reduce demand on the overstrained NHS;
- increase the total level of health spending in the UK without the taxpayer having to do so;
- increase the range of choice of private facilities available;
- increase the pressure on the NHS to do a better job by offering a high quality competitor;
- make families more self-reliant and make them think more carefully about their health and pattern of living.

Opponents have argued:

- short-term reductions in demand for NHS facilities would be small, since most private users opt out to gain non-emergency and relatively cheap treatment. Serious cases, long-term care of older people and the long-term ill will remain with the NHS. These make up the bulk of NHS spending;
- major opting out of the NHS could reduce taxpayers' support for higher taxes and lead to a downward spiral: worse service, more opting out, less taxes. Propper (2001) examines the survey evidence for this argument and suggests that those who have opted to use the private sector do not change their support for improved NHS services and higher taxes. Those who opt for private services *are*, however, less supportive of high taxes and NHS spending in the first place;
- the private sector internationally exhibits poor cost control. It would be inefficient to subsidise it;
- it is subject to serious market failures of the kind discussed in Chapter Two.

Local taxation

Both Denmark and Sweden's healthcare systems are tax-based and popular (European Observatory on Health Care Systems, 2001). They are, however, funded primarily from local taxation, an illustration of the argument discussed in the last chapter. In both cases the county council is the unit of taxation and administration. Overall responsibility for the pattern of provision and access lies with the central government. The Swedish local income tax rate was on average 10% in 2000, 8.5% for health services.

On balance

Tax funding and needs-based provision for healthcare ought, in principle, to be more pro-poor than arrangements that rely on taxing employment through social insurance contributions, but that depends on how pro-poor the tax system is! Evidence suggests that the UK has one of the most progressively financed systems of healthcare and one of the most equitably delivered (Propper, 2001). The Wanless Report (HM Treasury, 2001) on NHS funding concluded, on examining the available evidence:

- ... financing through general taxation is generally regarded as being more efficient than other means of financing, ensuring strong cost control and prioritising and minimising economic distortions and disincentives;
- a reliance on financing through general taxation involves the maximum separation between individuals' financial contributions and their utilisation of health services;
- a greater share of healthcare is associated with better health outcomes;
- the general absence of out-of-pocket payments for clinically necessary services ... is equitable and does not discourage people from seeking treatment. (p 57)

Improving choice and efficiency

The size of a health budget is no guarantee of its efficiency or public satisfaction, as is evident in the US. The way revenue is allocated to those providing the service matters not just in terms of equity but in terms of encouraging prompt and effective care.

We have seen that other funding arrangements, including tax-based ones, give users more choice and subject providers to more competition than in the UK. Fee-for-service arrangements encourage prompt response but are not especially cost-effective or equitable. Can governments in the UK devise a way of remunerating those who provide services so as to retain equity and foster a more consumer-friendly service? Certainly both Conservative and Labour governments since 1990 have been trying to do so. The Conservative government diagnosis in its 1989 White Paper (DoH, 1989) was that the NHS suffered from all the elements of government failure discussed earlier in Chapter Three.

The hospitals and community health services were monopolies since inception. Patients had virtually no capacity to exit and to choose alternative providers. The service providers got a set, usually slightly rising, budget, however well or badly they performed. Indeed, high waiting lists usually prompted more money to reduce them. Bad performance was rewarded and actually still is! The solution tried between 1991 and 1997 was to fund two kinds of purchasers, district health authorities and general practices who wished to buy services for their own patients. Districts were the largest purchasers of health services for their populations and were responsible for making contracts with hospitals and other providers on an annual, supposedly competitive, basis. If a hospital performed badly it would lose its contract, so the theory went. Larger general practices could make their own contracts for non-emergency care and a specified range of relatively cheap treatments. The budget they received included a sum that covered the cost of the drugs that they prescribed and, towards the end, community services. This last arrangement, *GP fundholding*, was a more radical departure than district-based purchasing (Glennerster et al, 1994):

- It devolved the budget to those who actually made the decisions to refer patients on to secondary care. Instead of the decision to refer a patient being costless, a GP would have to weigh up whether more could be done in the way of tests or treatment within the practice. Some GPs felt that the intrusion of money into the decision was quite wrong. Others argued that much more could be done more efficiently in primary care. The temptation to refer on and burden hospitals unnecessarily would be curbed and this was in the long-term interest of patients.
- It broke the rigid boundary walls between primary care, hospitals and the community services. It encouraged GPs to consider whether much out-patient work and community nursing could not be better done in a primary care setting. Critics argued that this was not something GPs should decide on their own and it was a more costly solution.
- It capped the amount of drugs that GPs could prescribe. Instead of the decision to write a prescription being costless for the GP they had to weigh whether this was really necessary compared to other treatment, exercise or physiotherapy, for example. It also gave GPs an incentive to use generic drugs. These are not brand names and are cheaper but equally effective. Again many GPs thought that introducing finance into the prescribing decision was quite wrong, interfering with their medical judgement of need.
- GPs had a direct interest in getting patients treated quickly; it meant less pressure on their practices. They shopped around and pressurised hospitals and those doing blood and other laboratory tests to work more effectively and quickly. District purchasers were less aggressive. Because GPs were small agents they had much less concern about the consequences of switching contracts to get faster or more convenient treatment. Districts had to worry about the stability of the whole system, which made them more cautious.

Hospitals complained about the cost of making lots of small contracts and having to keep track of payments made by many small practices.

District health authorities were much more constrained. In many ways the competitive quasi-market was never really allowed to work (Le Grand, 1999):

- Government became so worried that hospitals might close as a result of purchasers switching custom that they forced districts to minimise the amount of contract switching they did. Many simply gave money to the same hospitals for a wide range of functions – a block contract. The outcome was hardly different from the past. The ultimate sanction of cutting off funds from very bad hospitals was almost never applied.
- Neither trusts nor district health authorities were allowed to keep any surpluses they might make, whereas GP fundholders could.
- GPs had a small direct interest in creating a surplus to be used in improving their premises; hospital trusts had no such incentive.
- District staff were deeply suspicious of the 'market' reforms. They were not trained as entrepreneurs. There were no benefits for them in being tough with local providers and there were costs: time, trouble, broken collegial relations.

This experiment generated a vast and interesting literature (for a review of several hundred studies done, see Le Grand et al, 1998). The sober conclusion drawn by one initial enthusiast for such reforms (Le Grand, 1999) was that they had made remarkably little difference, with the partial exception of GP fundholding. There *was*, however, evidence that the incentives built into the fundholding system in particular had:

- encouraged innovation and shifted the focus of some hospital activity towards primary care (Glennerster et al, 1994; Audit Commission, 1996);
- encouraged quicker discharge from hospital (Raftery and McLeod, 1998);
- reduced the growth of the pharmaceutical budget particularly in the early years before the incentives to do so were less (Wilson and Walley, 1995; Harris and Scrivener, 1996; Rafferty et al, 1997);
- reduced hospital waiting times and the number of referrals to hospital (Dowling, 2000; Gravelle et al, 2002; Propper et al, 2002).

None of these changes were huge but they were encouraging. There was also evidence that a halfway house, giving groups of GPs on a wider community basis devolved budgets and decision-making powers, had had some of the same benefits (Glennerster et al, 1998).

Primary care trusts in England

In England the 1997 Labour government tried to keep some of the advantages present in the fundholding scheme while avoiding the high costs of billing and administration and the divisive consequences of some GPs being in the scheme and others not.

Primary care trusts, which now cover populations of 100,000 to 250,000, are the result. They:

- receive a formula-based sum which covers hospital, community and pharmaceutical spending. Traditional boundaries between these service areas can now, in theory, be questioned;
- are responsible for making agreements (contracts) with providers including private ones if they wish, or indeed overseas suppliers; they have the capacity to terminate contracts or shift money to give local providers an incentive to be efficient and provide users with some choice.

However:

- they are very large, cutting the direct link between a small social unit such as a GP practice and the level at which decisions are made about purchasing;
- government again began by discouraging 'competition' or shifting contracts;
- there was no direct link between work done and rewards;
- they may have lost both the entrepreneurship of fundholding practices and the power of larger districts.

The Labour government introduced some powerful central levers based more on bureaucratic sanctions than financial incentives. These included performance indicators for hospitals and other local service providers and a national inspectorate (although it was not called that!) – the Commission for Health Improvement (CHI), and NICE to set national standards.

The early results of giving up the modest efficiency incentives of the 1991–97 period were worrying. The Department of Health produces an annual cost-weighted activity index – roughly the number of people treated in hospital and by the community services weighted by the cost of their treatment. By dividing this by the volume of resources the NHS uses – discounting health price increases – it is possible to produce a productivity index. How much more are these services doing per pound spent? Over the decade before the internal market reforms, productivity was rising by about 1.5% a year. After those reforms, productivity rose by about 2.0% a year. Weak though those incentives had been, they did seem to have made some difference.

In 1997/98 and 1998/99, after the internal market and competition were abolished, NHS productivity actually began to *fall* quite significantly, suggesting that the internal market had been more effective than many thought (Le Grand, 2002a). Labour ministers were forced to take some notice. Delivery, not just higher spending, became imperative. They felt they had to return to some kind of quasi-market system of incentives. (For a revealing interview with Alan Milburn, the Secretary of State for Health, see Timmins, 2002.) In a document produced at the time of the 2002 Budget (DoH, 2002a, chapter 4), the Labour government proposed what was, essentially, a return to a modified form of internal market. The system of block contracts or agreements with hospitals, where hospitals are merely paid to do the best they can for another year, will go. In the case of non-emergency ('elective') treatment, hospitals will be paid for the amount of work they actually do. That is, the kind of treatment where the waiting lists occur and where GP fundholders had used the same approach with success.

From 2003/04 all providers will be contracted to achieve a minimum volume of elective cases necessary to meet government waiting time targets. If they fail, they will lose money. Providers will earn more resources on a cost-per-case treated basis if they outperform these targets. There will be a 'tariff', or price paid, for a completed treatment of a given complexity, which will vary on a regional basis. The NHS calls this treatment category a Health Resource Group (HRG). In the US a similar measure, used for many years, is a Diagnostic Related Group (DRG). Patients will be given greater choice of provider and will be able to choose their hospital, taking the payment for their treatment with them. This will apply initially if someone has waited for longer than six months. By 2005 it is intended that all patients will be able to book appointments when and where they wish. (Robinson and Dixon, 2002, have a good discussion of what levels of choice are open to people in different healthcare systems and what some of the pros and cons are.)

Successful hospitals, as measured by government targets and indicators, will be given more freedom from central control and will be able to manage their own assets such as land and buildings, selling them off and using the proceeds for other purposes, for example. Or they will be able to borrow to undertake new building up to an agreed 'prudential' level. They will be able to create their own staffing structures and pay, within national guidelines. These hospitals and other agencies will then have 'foundation status', which will put them somewhere between a public body and a not-for-profit organisation.

Primary care trusts and patients will be able to choose from a wider range of providers including, in some cases, private providers. From 2003 a new *Commission for Health Care Audit and Inspection* (CHAI) will inspect standards of care and provide detailed information on providers' performance and on the outcomes achieved by different health services in different areas. In many ways this follows the precedent set by schools (see Chapter Six). The new Commission replaces the Commission for Health Improvement, and takes over some of the functions of the Audit Commission and the healthcare work of the National Care Standards Commission.

At the end of 2002, a long negotiated new contract for consultants was rejected by the profession. The pot of money set aside to finance it is to be used to pay surgeons and anaesthetists extra for each patient they operate on. This is a major departure and will begin to copy the incentive arrangements in the other healthcare systems that we commented upon. Finally, to reduce the problem of older people 'blocking beds' because they are unable to find care in their own homes or in residential care, NHS hospitals will be able to charge social services departments for stays beyond a given period.

These are all very significant changes in the way hospitals and other health service providers are paid. Time will tell how effective they will be. Propper et al's research (2003) on the previous experiment with market incentives in the NHS shows how important it is that hospitals and other providers are forced to compete on quality, not just price. If hospitals compete on price alone they may well cut quality. However, we do now have the information for it to be possible for consumers to choose in an informed way with their GP's help. But, as Propper's research shows, competition can produce perverse results. Close evaluation of these changes will be needed.

Local healthcare cooperatives in Scotland

Scotland took a different route and has not returned to some kind of quasi-market. Local GPs have been encouraged to join with other professions to operate a more collaborative service. Local pharmacists are encouraged to provide advice and treatments for minor ailments. Practice nurses undertake a much wider range of care, as they do in England. A failing private hospital has been taken over to provide a dedicated facility designed to take patients from all over Scotland who have been waiting a long time for operations. Similar experiments are underway in England. A comparison of the outcomes of these Scottish and English models should prove instructive.

Taking the changes even further?

In a wide-ranging review of the NHS' problems, a group of senior practitioners and experts from the King's Fund (2002) would have the government go further. They felt that the source of funding for the NHS was not the problem, and nor, if the government's promises to meet the European average were met, was the scale of funding. However, they felt that there was too much detailed central interference and no proper organisational incentives to respond to patients. They wanted to see the creation of an arm's length Health Service Corporation to set national quality and spending priorities, and to regulate and inspect local providers. Hospital trusts and community service providers should be turned into separate not-for-profit public interest companies who would compete for custom and be at risk of closure if they could not attract custom, and did not respond to help or support. This should create enough spare capacity in the long term to give GPs and individual patients real choice of provider. Money should then follow patient choice. They believed that such a shift should be undertaken as a gradual process. Indeed it has already begun.

Overview

- The NHS is a relatively low-cost healthcare system but rising expectations have forced the Labour government to set unprecedented expenditure targets.

- The way the NHS is funded, through taxation, and money allocated to areas according to medical need, is more equitable than is the case in most other advanced economies. The way institutions and individuals are paid, however, has many drawbacks. It gives little incentive to fast or responsive treatment. Indeed some motives are perverse. Here the NHS has much to learn from other systems.

Questions for discussion

1. How does the way that the NHS is *funded* differ from that in other countries? Which systems have some similarities and what are they?

2. How do other countries differ in the way health services are *provided*? How do incentives for those who work in the service differ?

3. How are funds allocated to local areas in England, Scotland and Wales in relation to need?

Further reading

For a review of trends in NHS expenditure and outcomes see **Propper (2001)** and **Le Grand and Vizard (1998)**. For the latest spending figures and a series of both past and forecast spending, see the Department of Health website (www.doh.gov.uk).

For a good summary of the relative international spending levels and what this means for the UK, as well as forecasts of future pressures on the NHS, see the Wanless Reports, both the interim and final versions: **HM Treasury (2001)** and **(2002b)** (www.hm-treasury.gov.uk).

For a comparative overview of financial mechanisms and dilemmas see **Dixon and Mossialos (2002)**; also **Bromley and Stibbs (2001)**. Wendy **Ranade's** edited collection, *Markets and healthcare* **(1998)**, gives a critical perspective on quasi-market type reforms.

For a succinct evaluation of both the Conservative and Labour governments' reform efforts see **Le Grand (1999, 2002b)** in the American journal *Health Affairs*. **Robinson and Dixon (2002)** review the Labour government's most recent innovations and the general case for alternative funding sources in an accessible way.

For a discussion of the arguments for and against using the private sector and private finance see **Propper and Green (2001)**.

A full summary and listing of all the research done on the NHS internal market can be found in the King's Fund review by **Le Grand et al (1998)** (www.kingsfund.org.uk).

The history of resource allocation formulae for health services is contained in **Glennerster et al (2000)**.

Financing social care

Summary

- Social care is difficult to define and therefore to quantify. Social care is necessary when individuals are unable to care for themselves or for members of their families. This may include orphans or children whom parents can no longer look after or are abusing. The courts then have powers to step in to act as the child's protector and arrange other care, usually through the agency of a local social services or social work department. The boundary between 'family' and 'social' care depends on a judgement made by a court and advised by social workers.

- The line between an individual who is 'coping' and one who needs support in order to live with a mental illness is again a judgement call. Much the same is true for an old person who is frail or suffering from short-term memory loss. It is difficult, therefore, to draw a distinction between medical care, social care, housing and residential care and between formal institutional and family care. Indeed, the best social care is a sensitive mixture of all these. It is one of the UK's major social policy failings that it has not devised a pattern of finance that facilitates such a flexible mixture. Each kind of care provider is separately funded. The result is a complex and confusing maze faced by vulnerable people and their families.

- Informal family care forms a large element of provision. This extends not just to direct care but to emotional support for those retaining their independence and support for those doing the caring. Volunteers used by formal not-for-profit organisations also play a larger role than in other services.

- Market failure characterises this field as it does healthcare. However, the force of this argument varies considerably between the groups at risk. While abused children cannot be expected to act as fully informed market agents, there is no reason why many older or disabled people cannot do so if they have sufficient financial resources and information. Markets do, therefore, have a significant part to play in social care.

Box 5.1: **Market failures in long-term social care**

- Many individuals needing social care do not have the *capacity* to use information about the care that they need even if it were available – for example, children, some older people, mentally ill people.
- Others are *debarred* from exercising choice. Those on probation, for example, cannot buy a 'soft' probation officer or decide their own punishment.
- Many individuals or their families will, however, be able to make perfectly good judgements about the quality of care that they need as a disabled or older person. For them choice and markets will work well.
- Unequal power in the market is especially great with a population of highly *vulnerable* people. They will need support in making choices and protection from exploitation.
- *Uncertainty* about the nature of long-term care 'technology' a long time in advance and about future rates of disability make costs difficult to estimate. Both factors make insurers cautious and quote high premiums.
- Long-term care is also open to adverse selection (see page 23). People have long experience of their own family history and medical and social conditions. They may know their likely need for long-term care better than an insurance company, especially when they are old. This makes private insurers cautious and hence premiums are high.
- Most people do not think that they will need long-term care when they are young (economists call this 'myopia'). People tend to take out insurance only when they are old and when the probabilities of needing it are high. The costs are therefore very high.
- It is difficult for residents to change their long-term care home, once established. Such moves are associated with higher death rates which makes exit difficult.
- Moral hazard issues (see page 24) are particularly severe. Since families do most caring, the possibility is that a generous private insurer (or indeed public) would encourage families to rely heavily on it once taken out, abandoning their family roles. This is difficult to predict and makes private insurers very wary of long-term care cover. See Burchardt et al (1999), Royal Commission on Long-Term Care (1999, chapter 5), and Wistow et al (1996).

The cost of social care

Informal care

The largest element in the costs of caring for children, older people or other dependent citizens falls upon the family – mainly parents and spouses, but also other family members. Disproportionately these costs fall on women, and this is particularly true of the care of children. Care of sick or incapacitated people or older people is more evenly spread, although women still do more of the intimate personal care (Parker and Lawton, 1994; Arber and Ginn, 1995). These caring activities give rise to 'opportunity costs' – time that could have been spent earning – as well as the more tangible costs of accommodation, food and heating where the person cared for is in the same dwelling as the carer. There have been many attempts to calculate these 'informal' costs (see, for example, Parker, 1990; Netten, 1991). Now official statisticians are seeking to include these activities in the National Accounts. One approach is to calculate *inputs*, the cost of waged *and* unwaged time, accommodation and food. Richards et al (1996) put the cost of all informal care of older people at £18 billion in 1995, or 2.5% of the GDP (twice the total cost of publicly provided personal social services). The official statisticians are approaching the task differently, attempting to value the *output* of informal care – what it would cost to buy the same level of care in the market. Holloway and Tamplin (2001) (of the Office for National Statistics) estimate the total number of hours children are looked after by parents, relatives, childminders and staff of nurseries, playgroups and schools. Formal childcare provision, publicly and privately financed, has been growing in scale, as has its cost – the wages of nannies have risen! This means that the market value of the care given as parents (and grandparents!) has grown. Holloway and Tamplin put the total value of informal childcare at the equivalent of between 19 and 25% of the GDP. This compares with local authority spending on childcare that amounts to less than one half of one per cent of GDP.

Direct care is only part of the story. Many older people maintain their independence and require neither residential care nor intensive home care. They do so only with difficulty, however. Emotional support from partners and family and neighbours can be crucial in sustaining this independence. The same is true of support given to those who are doing direct caring tasks. The state currently gives tiny amounts of support to carers – weekend breaks or annual holidays in rare instances, for example. This 'support' function is essentially unmeasured, although its economic importance is great.

It has frequently been argued that the supply of informal care will decline as the size of the older population rises. More women are working and working for longer, more are not having any children, divorce rates are rising, fewer older people are living with their children, and kinship obligations are weakening (Allen and Perkins, 1995; Clarke, 1995; Finch, 1995; Grundy, 1995; Evandrou, 1998). More recent trends and analysis have modified this expectation a little (Pickard et al, 2000). Partners are now the main providers of care in old age. More women in the age group 40-65 are married than in earlier cohorts. Men are living longer and there will be fewer widows. More couples are cohabiting and previous studies tended to underestimate the contribution of these partners. Thus the number of dependent older people with partners is expected to rise by 76% between 1996 and 2031. The number of single dependent older people is projected to rise by only 49%. Fears that kinship obligations of children to look after older parents may decline may or may not be true. Such assumptions make estimates of future spending on long-term care difficult to predict (Wittenberg et al, 2001).

We can see from research carried out so far that the cost of *social* care is critically dependent on the effective functioning of family support. If the scale of informal care falls by only a small percentage, the demand for social care could easily double or treble.

Privately funded care

Privately funded care is where families and individuals pay private agencies to look after them at home or to provide nursing and residential care. It also includes payments to a local authority to cover all the costs of their care if they have quite limited capital assets – in England a house valued at more than £19,000 after April 2002, for example. The Royal Commission on Long-Term Care (1999) estimated the total expenditure in the UK on formal long-term care for people of all ages. This estimate included long-term care in hospital, in residential and nursing homes, as well as in people's own homes. In 1995/96 prices, roughly £11 billion was spent publicly and privately (see **Table 5.1**). This sum was equivalent to 1.6% of the GDP. Over a third, £4 billion, was spent by private individuals. Under half of this was paid as charges for local authority services; the rest was spent by individuals on private services. Since then, as a result of the Royal Commission's report, the government began to pay for nursing care, up to a certain limit. In Scotland the government is also paying for personal care (see page 101). From 1 April 2003 the NHS has become responsible for both the fees covering nursing care that were previously paid by private residents and by local authorities. The total cost of this is £600 million. As a result the local authority grant will be reduced and the formula grant paid to primary care trusts will be increased to take account of the estimated additional costs.

Table 5.1: The total cost of long-term care in the UK (1995-96) (£ billion)

NHS continuing care	Local authority social services care	Private expenditure on charges by public bodies	Private expenditure on private services	Total
2.6	4.5	1.7	2.3	11.1
of which:	of which:	of which:	of which:	
long-stay hospital £1.4	residential care homes £1.9	residential care £1.0	residential care £1.2	
community nurses £0.7	nursing homes £1.3	nursing homes £0.5	nursing homes £0.8	
nursing homes £0.2	home care £1.0	meals £0.1	private domestic £0.2	
day care £0.1	day care £0.2	home and day care £0.1	other £0.1	
	meals £0.1			

Source: Data from Royal Commission on Long-Term Care (1999)

Not-for-profit providers

Not-for-profit providers are more important providers than in any other field covered in this book, and their contribution has grown in the past decade. Roughly 40% of the voluntary social services sector's income comes from the state, with the rest split equally between private fees and voluntary gifts. For a review of the sector's coverage and funding in a comparative context see Kendall with Almond (1998). Their summary is worth quoting here:

> Relations between the UK third (voluntary) sector and government have traditionally developed in a pragmatic and ad hoc way.... This sets it apart from much of Northern Europe especially, where the concept of subsidiarity, with deep roots in Catholic doctrine, has played a key role in determining the sectoral division of labour in the delivery of human services. This has long been interpreted by policy makers (there) as providing an overarching rationale for privileging denominational welfare services on the grounds that the churches would be necessarily closer and more responsive to their members than the state. [This assumption is now increasingly

> questioned but] still exerts a pervasive influence on policy which
> is not paralleled in the UK. (p 11; HG's insertion in square brackets)

Kendall et al (2003) discuss why it is that the not-for-profit sector is so well-represented in the social care field compared with other human services in Western developed nations. In the European Union, for example, just over half of total employment in the social care sector is with non-state, non-profit organisations. The comparable figure for both health and education is about half that. They suggest that governing elites have been less engaged with social care compared to, say, education. There has been no high status profession to press its claims as with health. Although the church has been heavily involved, economics also plays a part. Social care is less capital intensive, and small firms can enter the market relatively easily. Varied needs and links with informal carers may be best done by small adaptable organisations. The voluntary sector may be better at engendering trust than either the profit-making sector or the state. The voluntary sector may be good at using volunteers and hence gets a competitive advantage over for-profit providers. For whatever reason, the sector is important here. Nevertheless, the state has to meet the hardest cases.

Local authority social services and social work departments' budgets

These departments remain the last line of support for the most vulnerable, and they have a statutory responsibility for them. Including the revenue they received from charges, gross expenditure by local authorities in 2000/01 amounted to about 1.5% of the GDP, much smaller than health or education. Over the 10 years from 1990, however, the real gross current expenditure on personal social services doubled. Just under half was allocated to services for older people, just over a fifth to children (see **Figure 5.1**). Under a half was used to finance residential care, much of it provided by private and voluntary agencies.

How social care funds are allocated

Local social services departments in England and Wales and social work departments in Scotland receive the bulk of their funds as part of the general process through which local councils are funded. Only about a fifth of local government expenditure is locally financed (HM Treasury, 2002e, Table 6.1). Most local revenue is raised through a tax on property – the Council Tax. Other local revenue comes from charges the councils make for services such as home helps, day care centres and residential homes. Such charges cover about 16% of social services departments' total spending. The bulk of their revenue comes in the form of central government grants, and the largest of

Figure 5.1: **Social services departments' budgets, England (2000/01)**

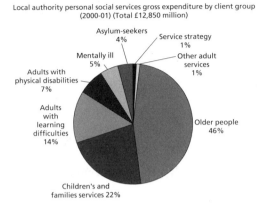

Local authority personal social services gross expenditure by client group
(2000-01) (Total £12,850 million)

Asylum-seekers 4%
Service strategy 1%
Mentally ill 5%
Other adult services 1%
Adults with physical disabilities 7%
Adults with learning difficulties 14%
Older people 46%
Children's and families services 22%

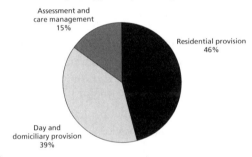

Local authority personal social services gross expenditure by type of service
(2000-01) (Total £12,850 million)

Assessment and care management 15%
Residential provision 46%
Day and domiciliary provision 39%

Source: DoH (2002c)

these was the Revenue Support Grant. In April 2003 this was replaced by the Formula Grant. This, too, is a general grant that adds to local authorities' general revenues and is not explicitly tied to any service. It is, however, calculated in a way that reflects the relative demands different populations can be expected to put on services in their area. The older or poorer a population, the more central government help it gets.

Changes to local government finance in 2003

The 1988 Local Government Finance Act abolished the domestic rating system that had existed even before 1601 in non–statutory form (Cannan, 1898, 2nd edn, 1912). This tax on the value of property was replaced, briefly in the late 1980s, by a Poll Tax, a per head levy. It was so evidently unfair that it gave way to a new property tax on dwellings – the Council Tax. However, rates on commercial and industrial property continued to be levied nationally. Once collected, this revenue was allocated back to local authorities on a crude population basis. A separate set of formulae – standard spending assessments – distributed the largest sum, raised from *general* taxation. This rather pointless complexity was removed in 2003. One formula will now determine how much central government money each council receives in England. (There are separate similar formulae for each of the UK nations. See pages 189-91 for the allocation process between countries.)

The English formula has different elements to it, one for each of the main service areas it covers. (For a simple guide see ODPM, 2002a.) In the past each sub-formula was calculated in a different way. Now each follows a similar pattern:

A basic allocation (per school child or old person)
+ a deprivation top-up
+ an area cost top-up (mainly pay and recruitment differences that reflect local labour markets)
+ other top-ups that reflect a range of local cost pressures, such as rural sparsity, high density and a large visitor or commuting population.

Each local authority's *formula spending share* (FSS) is derived from this calculation. The logic is that every council in the country should be able to provide an equivalent standard of service for its population on the basis of what central government gives it, plus what it can raise from Council Tax, given the value of property in its area. Some areas with high levels of deprivation will have more needs or demands. Poor older people living alone or lone parents will, on average, generate more demands for services. Some areas will find it more difficult to recruit staff because of high demands for labour or because of high housing costs in the area – they will have to pay more to gain the same quality of staff. And there may be other reasons why costs are higher – the area may be remote, with high transport costs. Needs may differ for reasons other than deprivation. Each sub-formula addresses each of these issues in comparable ways. A substantial amount of work was undertaken to try to distinguish a rational basis for a formula in each of the main service areas. Various 'floors and ceilings' have been introduced so that every authority will gain at least some increase in grant from 2003 onwards although some will gain more than others. Thus, the effect of the new formula will be phased in over a period (see www.odpm.gov.uk and www.dfes.gov.uk).

The personal social services

In calculating the personal social services part of the formula there are several distinct elements, each relating to the very different client groups the social services departments serve.

Children

There will be a basic amount per resident child aged 0–17 living in the local authority area

+ a deprivation top-up
+ a foster care top-up recognising the different costs of foster care in different areas
+ an area top-up recognising the pay differentials and other variations in costs by area.

The deprivation top-up is calculated from the following five factors:

• the percentage of children living in one adult households;
• the percentage in Income Support claiming households;
• the density of population;
• the percentage living in flats;
• the percentage with long-standing and limiting illness.

These factors came from a study undertaken by the University of York's Centre for Health Economics. An adjustment is made to take account of the variations in the costs of fostering in different parts of the country.

Younger adults *(mostly with mental health problems)*

A basic amount per adult 18–64
+ a deprivation top-up as more people need such care in poor areas
+ an area cost top-up.

The deprivation element is calculated from:

• the percentage of residents, aged 18–64, claiming Income Support;
• the percentage of households with no family;
• the percentage of households living in social housing flats.

Older people

A basic amount per older person in each authority
+ an age top-up for those areas with a higher proportion of very elderly
+ a deprivation top-up
+ a sparsity top-up for rural areas
+ a low-income top-up
+ an area cost adjustment.

Previously there were separate elements for those in residential care and those in the community. Since policy is to blur this distinction, a single sub-formula was developed by the Personal Social Services Research Unit at Kent University. The factors included in the age and deprivation top-ups are these:

- aged 75–84;
- aged 85+;
- on Income Support;
- receiving Attendance Allowance or Disability Living Allowance;
- living in rented accommodation;
- with limiting long-term illness;
- not a couple or head of household;
- living alone.

Specific grants

In addition to this untied formula grant local councils receive 'specific and special grants' that are tied to particular kinds of spending. These have proliferated since 1997 and include grants to support services for carers, children's services, preventative services, mental health, AIDS and prevention of drug and alcohol misuse (see Table 5.2).

Table 5.2: Central government grants to social services departments, England (2002/03) (£ million)

Total personal social services provision	**11,169**
of which:	
Special and specific grants	**1,444**
of which:	
Carers	85
Training support	58
Preserved rights	570
Performance	50
Children's services	451
Care Direct	10
Child and Adolescent Mental Health Services	20
Young people's substance misuse planning	5
Teenage pregnancy local implementation	16
Deferred payment	30
Mental health	133
AIDS support	17

Source: ODPM (2002a)

Capital spending

So far we have only described revenue funding. For buildings, local councils can borrow money on the open market. However, because central government would have to bail out authorities that got into difficulties if they borrowed too much, the Treasury has always had powers to limit borrowing. This used to be given to one project at a time – *loan sanction*. Then *credit approvals* were given on a service-by-service basis, effectively. Most recently the government has introduced something called a *Local Prudential Regime*! This gives local authorities the right to decide what limit they want to set to their total borrowing for all services and the total debt they wish to carry. Once these are set they must keep to the limit unless circumstances change – such as having much more revenue coming in. Councils will have to set out capital plans saying what building they wish to undertake three years or so ahead and how they propose to finance it. The Chartered Institute of Public Finance and Accountancy will draw up a code of practice to insure 'prudence'. There must also be public consultation on the capital plans. The Audit Commission will oversee it to make sure that councils do not go in for wild spending and building sprees, but this will be a real extension of local freedom and responsibility. Central government will retain the right to curb local capital plans if total capital spending by all local authorities exceeds what the Treasury deem acceptable in economic terms.

In addition to borrowing and repaying out of their own resources, local authorities receive some support from central government to cover capital expenditure. Once given for specific schemes, it is now handed out on a less controlled basis. Since April 2002 each local authority is given a capital finance allocation set by a needs-based formula. This covers all services – 'a single capital pot'.

Personal social services authorities make relatively little use of Private–Public Finance Partnerships, which use private firms to undertake capital development. If they wish to use the private sector they buy services from it.

Perverse funding

We tend to think of funding in positive terms – money that *enables* an organisation to do things. Yet funding can be given in ways that discourage organisations from working together to meet a client's needs. There are all too many examples in the personal social services.

The separate funding and organisations of health and social care illustrates this. The NHS is funded by the central exchequer. Local social services (England and Wales) and social work departments (Scotland) are funded, in part, from local Council Taxes. The longer the council can force patients to stay in hospital the less the demand on local services and the lower its Council

Tax. Since staying in hospital is more expensive, the taxpayer ends up paying more. Local councils have had little incentive to work with the NHS to prevent 'bed blocking' of older patients in inappropriate beds in acute wards. 'Bedblocking', in fact, saves them money at a time when governments are pressing them to hold budgets down and keep Council Tax low. This perverse incentive problem was first commented on by the Guillebaud Committee (1956), and a series of small-scale measures have been taken in the past quarter of a century to counter it. In the mid-1970s the Labour government introduced *joint finance*. This was a sum of money that could be given by the NHS for projects undertaken by local authorities which could speed hospital discharge or help reduce demands on NHS resources. However, these were short-term project grants with the local authority picking up the continuing costs after a period of years (Glennerster et al, 1983). The total sums were small, rising to merely 5% of the total personal social services budget in the 1980s. More recent examples of the same approach with longer-term funds include specific mental health grants. These specific grants to local authorities have to be spent in ways that the local NHS agrees to, and local authorities have had to contribute 30% of the funding.

The 1999 Health Act gave the NHS and local authorities powers to introduce joint budgets to administer, as a single unit, services for people with mental illness, older people or people with disabilities. This should encourage the two agencies to consider how best to allocate resources between them instead of indulging in the competitive 'dumping' of problems on each other.

Four experimental care trusts have been created. They will be able to commission services covering primary care, hospital and other secondary healthcare *and* social care. The power to do so more widely will be extended from 2005. These would enable 'one-stop-shops' to develop – an individual will be able to go to one place with GPs, practice nurses, social workers, care managers, home helps, community nurses and community psychiatric nurses, all in the same building, employed by the same agency and financed from a single budget. Both the NHS and local authorities will contribute to this. It was a model advocated by both the majority and minority reports of the Royal Commission on Long-Term Care (1999) despite their other disagreements.

The government has also introduced a penalty system on local authority social services departments. Where a patient is clinically ready for discharge from hospital but cannot be discharged because of lack of social services cover, the social services department will be liable to make a payment to the NHS to pay for continuing hospital care. This follows a similar system that was established in Sweden in 1992 and is now operating in Norway and Denmark.

Another example of perverse financial incentives occurred in the 1980s. It was a by-product of changes being made to the social security system. What had been exceptional payments to help people who had got into financial difficulty in private residential homes became a virtual right. Thus an older person, who had a low income and no capital, by accident or design, could get the social security system to pay for private home fees up to a given ceiling. The sums involved rose from £10 million in 1979 to £2,500 million in 1992. At a time when local authorities were being urged to support people in their own home, another branch of government was paying large sums to encourage people into private residential homes. The perversity was first criticised by the Audit Commission (1986). A subsequent report by Sir Roy Griffiths (DoH, 1988) recommended that the sums then being spent by the social security system be transferred to local authorities, and that further funding of new places by the social security system would not be permitted. The higher rates of Income Support for new residents entering private homes were abolished in April 1993. The funds that would have been spent on social security were transferred to local authorities, giving a substantial boost to local authority budgets but adding to their responsibilities for this group of older people. A *special transitional grant* was made to local authorities in 1993/94, 1994/95 and 1995/96 which amounted to about £2,000 million. It had to be spent on the care of older people and younger adults in need of care, and 85% had to be spent in the independent sector. In 1996/97 the sum was absorbed into the general revenue support settlement. The Labour government removed the 'independent sector' requirement, although significant use of the sector continued. (For an account of this period see Lewis and Glennerster, 1996, chapter 2.) Residents who had been admitted prior to 1993 had their Income Support rights preserved until April 2002.

Fees and charges

Unlike the NHS and state schools where it is illegal to charge for services, the personal social services have a history of charging. Local authorities must charge for residential care in line with national rules. Local authorities *may* charge for home help services, meals on wheels, day care centres and residential homes, but there is now formal national guidance on this too. They *may not* charge for social work support. Charging for intermediate care for those being discharged from hospital is also to be abolished.

A wide range of justifications has been advanced for charging. Bevan argued that charging for residential care put it on a par with private hotel provision and took away its stigma. Charging for the care of children taken from their parents has been justified as providing parents with a disincentive to abandon their children; most of all, charging provides a way for hard-pressed local authorities to supplement their resources and keep services going that they would otherwise have to cut. (For an excellent historical and analytical discussion, see Judge and Matthews, 1980.)

Improving choice and efficiency

The kind of logic that led to the adoption of a quasi-market in healthcare led to a similar move in the personal social services. It went further and faster. There had always been a larger independent care sector. The 1990 NHS and Community Care Act was to push back the boundaries of state provision and to develop a very mixed market. Social services departments were no longer to be mainstream providers but 'enablers' and purchasers of services from a variety of agencies. This model was to become much more successful than the parallel experiment with the NHS begun by the same Act. Many areas began hesitantly, while others took on the model wholeheartedly (Lewis and Glennerster, 1996; Wistow et al, 1996). By 2002 change was significant. This was partly because there was already a tradition of provider diversity, and partly because entry for new providers is easier – small-scale family businesses can enter the residential home sector. Voluntary organisations, local Mind or other user-led groups no longer face the vast capital risk involved in building a new hospital or medical facility. Knapp et al (2001) provide an overview account of this.

They argue that in the 1990s there were unprecedented rates of growth in the scale of independent services for older people, the beginning of a reversal of a 50-year growth in care home provision as well as substantial contracting out of services for people with mental illness and learning disabilities. Elaborate regulatory procedures had been evolved.

As the authors go on to argue, the Labour government's policy statement (DoH, 1998, 1999) did nothing much to alter any of these changes in direction. The Labour government withdrew the Conservative government's requirement to fund independent profit-making providers. They left local authorities free to choose the provider so long as they could justify *best value*. If anything, Labour favoured using the voluntary sector as a way of developing diversity and choice. The share of places in local authority residential homes for older people fell from 65% in 1980 to only 20% in 2001 (see **Figure 5.2**). If we take the whole range of care provision for older people and physically disabled people, including hospitals and nursing homes, 81% of places were in independent private facilities by 1998 compared with 61% in 1990.

At the same time, local authority funding, as distinct from social security funding, has led to a rise in domiciliary care. Within domiciliary care there has been much more diversity in the intensity and nature of care purchased. Contracts with providers took a more varied form than had ever been the case in the NHS internal market. Block contracts for a standard service are made with some smaller agencies, giving a guaranteed income to pay for a block of services. Other contracts are 'spot' or 'call off' ones that pay for services at an agreed price when needed. They enable care managers to mix and match the services that they use but can be more expensive to negotiate.

Figure 5.2: Residential care for older people, England (1980-2001) (total places)

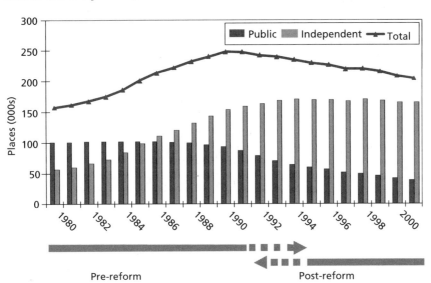

Source: Updated from Knapp et al (2001); personal communication from authors, 2002

Cost and volume contracts guarantee a baseline supply of services and more is paid for on top if needed. The strategies used and how much independence frontline care managers have varies widely. It is too early to reach a definitive conclusion on the impact of these changes, not least because local authorities' capacities to manage this market are still growing. But Knapp et al (2001) conclude:

> After initial reservations and a quite widespread reluctance to embrace the market mechanism, most English local authorities are now using their substantial commissioning powers to shape local markets. Whilst commissioning arrangements could mature further, particularly by encouraging obligational rather than adversarial relations, the situation today is utterly different from 1990. Choice, quality and cost-effectiveness improvements appear to be following. (p 304)

However, the switch of funding from social security to local authorities and the tight control on fees that they were prepared to pay led to a steady decline in the number of places in residential care homes. Local authority pricing policies, the rising standards of care legally required and minimum wage legislation have caused a crisis in the market for residential care (Netten et al, 2002).

The spending on and organisation of social care in other countries

It is not possible to produce a simple international league table for spending on personal social services as it is for health. There is no internationally agreed definition of the field of social care. Many countries do not distinguish between health and social care, treating those with mental illness and people with developmental or physical disabilities within healthcare. Large parts of the services are provided by voluntary organisations on which there is poor or non-existent financial information collected nationally. Some of the childcare functions form part of the court system and are measured differently in different countries.

The dominant feature of many other systems is the extensive nature of not-for-profit, voluntary or intermediate provision, as we have seen already. The term varies between countries but indicates provision by organisations that are some way between state-run organisations and for-profit companies. Even the Scandinavian countries have been moving tentatively in the same direction, although care services there are still primarily delivered and funded by local municipalities (see Anheier, 2000, and Forder, 2000, on which the following draws).

In the 1980s **France** moved to decentralise funding and provision, building a partnership between not-for-profit associations and local government. The total spent on social care was about 3% of GDP, although this includes nursing homes that would count as NHS spending in the UK. Residential facilities for older people and disabled people receive about a quarter of their income from the state and a quarter from users. Altogether about 25,000 not-for-profit agencies provide personal social services. They are 60% funded by the state, 35% from fees and investment income and 5% from gifts. State funding for long-term care of older people comes from two sources: the social assistance system (*Aide Sociale*), administered by local government, and the social insurance fund (*Caisse Nationale d'insurance viellesse*). Not-for-profit associations are purchasers of home care as well as providers working within state-set rules. Newer types of association also act as brokers to help individuals purchase services for themselves. Residential care for older people is funded through two streams: that which funds the accommodation element and the care element which is part of the healthcare system of funding. The individual and the family are deemed responsible for accommodation costs (*obligation alimentaire*). Where the extended family is too poor to do so, the social assistance scheme helps out. From 1995 individuals have been able to draw on financial support to care for themselves. This help is means tested and is administered as part of the tax system.

In **Germany** intermediate not-for-profit welfare institutions provide 60% of services, with local public bodies providing 30% and for-profit ones about 10%. Public financing is shared between local government and the Länder. The funding of long-term care recently passed to a national scheme financed by an addition to the social insurance contribution (1.7% of earnings). This funds the same sick clubs that provide healthcare. They contract with the homes and domestic service agencies that provide long-term care. Alternatively they give cash to individuals to make their own arrangements with carers (Cuellar and Weiner, 2000). Seventy per cent of those entitled to long-term care have chosen this route and 12% have chosen a mixture of in-kind and cash support, even though the cash support is limited to half the value of in-kind services.

Japan has also moved to levy a national insurance surcharge to finance long-term care (Campbell and Ikegami, 2000). The initial addition to the health insurance contribution from 1 April 2000 was 0.9% of earnings shared between employer and employees aged between 40 and 64. Those 65+ will have contributions deducted from their pensions. This revenue will cover half of the long-term care budget and is transferred to local municipalities to organise the care. The other half comes from revenue collected by the prefectures and local municipalities. Individuals or families apply to the local authority for a needs assessment and each level of assessed need approved entitles the applicant to a given budget ceiling of care, to which the individual must contribute 10% and can add more. A care manager decides the combination of services, under that ceiling. Private and not-for-profit agencies can compete with public agencies to be the providers of services.

Scandinavia has a quite different model. **Denmark**, for example, pays for most of its care services out of local taxation and local government provides most of these. Recently there have been experiments with funding private agencies.

In **Spain** and **Italy** social care is very limited in scope, especially residential care. The family continues to provide more care but that too is changing. In Italy roughly 85% of the formal provision that does exist is provided by not-for-profit agencies.

The **US** provides fewer positive examples. The relatively generous provisions for medical care for older people via Medicare do not extend to regular long-term care, although there are all kinds of loopholes such as extended care at home for those discharged from hospital. The separate systems for funding health and long-term care dog the US, as in England (Feder et al, 2000).

Because of the commonly perceived rising costs of long-term care for older people, international agencies such as the Organisation for Economic Co-operation and Development (OECD) have sought to put together firmer comparable data (Jacobzone, 1999). (For an excellent collection of papers outlining recent developments in long-term care services internationally, see *Health Affairs*, May/June 2000.) These figures show a considerable clustering of total spending around the 1-1.5% of GDP level in 1995 (see Table 5.3). All countries expect that figure to rise but differently, depending on their demographic trends. Japan expects its spending to nearly double in the period 2000 to 2020. France and Germany expect something nearer a quarter to a half increase and the UK nearer to a 20% growth. Much depends on whether the trends to a more healthy and active older population continue. Trends in the US suggest that despite an ageing population, reduced levels of disability could lead to a fall in the need for care.

The same resentments and moral hazard problems arise with the means-tested and asset-tested services provided under Medicaid. These include hospital, nursing home and domiciliary care. As in England and Wales these are only available if the individual has little or no capital (Glennerster, 1996). Little major progress has been made towards resolving these problems. Although the private sector has extended its coverage, private long-term insurance is taken out by no more than 7% of the population for the market failure reasons

Table 5.3: Long-term care provision and spending in eight countries (various years) (%)

Country	Projected institutional-isation rate, age 65+ (2000)	Formal home care rate, age 65+ (1995)	% of older popula-tion living alone (1990)	Total long-term care expendi-tures[a]	Public long-term care expendi-tures[a]
Australia	6.8	11.7	26.0	0.9	0.8
Canada	6.2	17.0	27.0	1.1	0.7
France	6.5	6.1	28.0	n/a	0.6
Germany	6.8	9.6	41.0	n/a	0.7
Japan	6.0	5.0	14.0	n/a	0.8
New Zealand	5.5	n/a	33.0	0.9	0.4
UK	5.1	5.5	38.0	1.6	1.0
US	5.7	16.0	30.2	1.3	0.7

Note: [a] As a percentage of GDP.

Source: Anderson and Hussey (2000), reproduced with permission

outlined at the beginning of the chapter (US Senate Committee on Ageing, 2002). Even then it is often inadequate to cover the eventual costs that people will face.

The European Union Economic Policy Committee (EUEPC, 2001) has published estimates of the impact of ageing, and this included estimates of the costs of long-term care in member countries.

The funding and organisation of long-term care in the UK

The recent history of the funding of long-term care in the UK exemplifies many of the general issues discussed in this chapter, and shows how difficult they are to solve. The UK system of long-term care shared many characteristics with other European and English-speaking countries until more recent reforms in the Netherlands, Germany and Scotland. Services for the very elderly and infirm grew piecemeal out of local public assistance systems, with the result that:

- they were organised and funded separately from healthcare while overlapping extensively with it. Indeed, as medical science has become more successful at prolonging life, there are more highly dependent people whose needs fall precisely on the hazy boundary line between medical, nursing and personal care;
- non-medical services are usually financed, at least partially, by local taxes and are run by local government;
- public provision is income and capital tested – free only to those on low incomes with virtually no capital or savings.

Complex funding streams

Locally elected councils fund the bulk of formal long-term care in the UK. They are, in their turn, heavily supported by central government grants supplemented by local property taxes. For people living in their own homes, local councils provide personal care, domestic cleaning and shopping assistance. They also provide meals in the home, social lunch clubs for the mobile and day care centres with social facilities and organised activities. About 5% of older people live in sheltered housing with a warden. This forms part of the housing budget. Voluntary bodies may provide the activities although the local authority pays. In addition, for more dependent people, local councils may arrange for a place in a residential or nursing home. (People are free to make their own arrangements at their own cost, of course.)

As we saw earlier the foregoing services usually carry a charge on a sliding scale depending on the income and assets of the old person. Where a local authority arranges for residential or nursing home care it is required by law to determine what level of contribution the individual should make. Almost all the resident's income, including the state pension, is taken into account in the means test except for a personal expense allowance – 'pocket money'. If the NHS is funding provision in the long term, the state pension is reduced by the contribution to food and accommodation costs that that person no longer has to meet for themselves. However, the individual's capital is not touched, but it is if someone is in local authority care. In 2002, if total savings were between £11,750 and £19,000, residents in a local authority care home had to pay something. With over £19,000 they had to pay the full cost until their assets fell below that limit. A partner owning the house or living in it will avoid such a charge. Since the average value of a house was then about £90,000, that meant most people owning their own house with no spouse were expected to pay for their own long-term care even if it was provided or arranged by the local authority. In 1999 56% of those aged over 75 had assets above £16,000 and the figure will rise as later cohorts own more houses and have higher savings. People can and do try to ensure that they run down or give away their assets before they need long-term care, although there are rules to prevent the most obvious abuses of this.

Housing departments of local authorities and not-for-profit housing associations provide purpose-built accommodation for older people with attendant wardens. Tenants pay rent for such accommodation but in many cases older people will have these rents met through Housing Benefit (see page 170). Very special housing with much more intensive support has proved the most cost-effective way of keeping older people out of institutions (Royal Commission on Long-Term Care, 1999). But it needs a fearsome degree of energy to put together funds from different statutory agencies.

The NHS is the next largest public provider of services. At one end of the spectrum are the geriatric wards in hospitals and some small old hospitals as well as hospices for the terminally ill. Provision under the first two headings has been steadily reduced, particularly in the 1990s. Since 1983 hospital beds available for older people have been reduced by about 40%. Such geriatric provision is meant to be confined to rehabilitation after brief periods in hospital, for example, after a stroke or deterioration due to personal neglect. Beyond that families and local authorities are meant to take over. Protracted wrangles often then ensue. This is made more difficult by the fact that NHS hospital care is free, but on discharge to a residential home or to the patient's home any services provided will carry a charge if the older person has an income or assets above the strict limit.

Private individuals pay for services, whether provided publicly or privately, on a large scale. As we saw earlier, rather more than a third of the cost of formal long-term care services is paid for privately. The Association of British Insurers estimated for the Royal Commission that only 23,000 people in the

UK had taken out insurance as of 1998. The figure had risen to 36,000 by 2002. Thus, where people pay, they do so out of savings, current pension income or by selling assets such as their house.

This was the set of problems that the Royal Commission on Long-Term Care discussed and reported on in 1999. The *Majority Report* concluded that on grounds of horizontal equity as well as efficiency, those who needed long-term intensive personal care should be treated in the same way as those needing long-term healthcare regardless of the public agency providing that care. The boundary line between the two forms of care was impossible to draw clearly. The overlap between health and care agencies' functions was too great to justify fundamentally different funding principles.

So, they concluded, the principles that apply to the NHS, tax-funded services, based on need, free at the point of use, should also apply to long-term nursing and personal care. They defined personal care in some detail – help with personal toilet, dressing, bathing, assistance with eating and drinking, medication and its monitoring, and ensuring personal safety. Funding health and personal care in the same way would enable rational efficient decisions to be made about who does what. It would not only remove arbitrary inequities but enable there to be a common budget and hence a simplified and effective system of delivery from a single point.

The proper place to draw the funding boundary was between care, on the one hand, and food and accommodation costs, on the other. This is a distinction that other countries make, as we saw earlier. When individuals remain at home they are expected to pay for their accommodation and food out of their pensions or other income. They would receive help if they were poor, but for most of the population these would remain personal responsibilities. They are also areas of life strongly affected by personal choice and lifestyle, not by external professional decisions. Those in institutional care should therefore pay for food and rent from their pension just as they would in their own homes. In all these respects this set of proposals would have put the UK broadly in line with Germany's new system of funding long-term care.

The costs of the proposals, the Commission argued, would be moderate. A model devised for the Royal Commission estimated the total economic cost of long-term care relative to the GDP over the next half century. The model's base case assumed that age and gender dependency rates would not change, and that patterns of care would not change. Unit costs would rise at the same rate as in the past. It also assumed existing growth rates in the GDP, no policy changes and existing trends in age, family composition, and family income. On these assumptions, the share of the GDP devoted to publicly funded long-term care services would not change much for 20 years and then rise from 1.0 to 1.1% of the GDP.

The reasons for these apparently low costs were part demographic and part structural. Costs of long-term care and health in the public sector have been kept under strict control in the UK with effective budget capping. The annual costs of care have been rising more slowly than the GDP, about half as fast, in fact, for the past 20 years. More spouses have been looking after their partners and not calling on public or private support. Private contributions to public sector costs have been rising as more people who reach their seventies do so with major and growing capital assets of a house, which means that the state can charge them for the services it renders. These two factors have more than offset the rising public sector costs that could have been expected from a slowly ageing population. However, it is precisely the unpopularity of paying for care from their assets that provoked the political problem the Royal Commission was appointed to address. Moreover, critics pointed out that rising expectations could destroy the model's assumption that costs could be contained as they had been in the past.

The costs of its proposals to extend free care and give extra help to carers, the Royal Commission suggested, would increase the taxpayers' contribution by the equivalent of 0.3% of the GDP by 2051. Later work emphasises the sensitivity of these figures to a range of demographic and other assumptions (Wittenberg et al, 2001).

The *Minority Report*'s objections to these proposals largely centred on cost and on who would benefit. The majority had underestimated the cost of their proposals, it claimed. Rising expectations would force spending to rise faster than in the past. The fact that personal care was free would make people demand more of it. This would let loose a 'Croesian flood of expenditure'. Eliminating the means and asset tests as far as personal care is concerned would financially benefit the middle class most. It is clear both from the tone of the report and from personal communications with the lead author that this was the key motivating argument.

The *Minority Report* merely proposed raising the asset test limit a little to £30,000. It did, however, produce two other ideas. The first was that people could be guaranteed that they would not have to sell their house during their lifetime to pay for care. After they had spent down to the £30,000 limit the state would total up the costs of its funding and recover them from the older person's assets on death. In effect, it would be a loan to the individual or family until death. Another idea advanced in the notes of dissent was for the state to encourage private insurance by providing catastrophic cover. The state would provide cover for those who had already received four years of private care.

The Labour government accepted the *Minority Report*'s view that free personal care was too expensive. Instead it proposed free 'nursing care', and the funding of more intermediate care easing the move from hospital back into the community (DoH, 2000). It is planned to help prevent inappropriate hospital admission and prevent avoidable admission to residential care. Subsequent announcements suggest more than 10,000 places in NHS or local authority funded facilities by 2006. The government did accept and implement the Commission's call to set up a National Care Standards Commission to regulate care provision. This was later merged with the functions of the Social Services Inspectorate to form the *Commission for Social Care Inspection.*

The decision to fund nursing care in whatever setting it was provided, but not personal care, posed a fresh set of problems. The government defined nursing care as "registered nursing time spent on providing, delegating or supervising nursing care in any setting" (DoH, 2000, para 2.9). Payments are also based on the levels of need – three levels of need in England provoking payments of £35, £70 or £110 a week initially. In Wales there is a single band. This requires an assessment of all those who might qualify. The Royal College of Nursing has criticised this arrangement, arguing that many who are not registered nurses have been trained to perform this kind of care. People looked after by non-nurses would have to pay. As we saw earlier, from April 2003 the NHS in England took over the payment of these nursing costs in private homes whether currently paid by local authorities or the residents. The Scottish Parliament took a different line in its 2002 Community Care and Health (Scotland) Act. It was implemented by order of the Scottish Parliament from 1 July 2002 – residents in care homes are assessed by a social worker to see if they qualify for free care. 'Free' means that a contribution is made by the state to the cost of that care. This was set at £145 in the case of personal care and £210 if the individual was receiving nursing care. The rest of the expenses are considered to be 'hotel' costs, that is, for accommodation and food. Local authority supported residents lose the Attendance Allowance and Disability Living Allowance care components after 28 days (Care Development Group Report, 2001).

A report by the New Labour think-tank, the Institute for Public Policy Research (Brooks et al, 2002, chapter 5) argues that the government's attempt to avoid the logic of the Royal Commission's recommendations has led to a greater mess than before. Long-term care illustrates the way in which perverse and complex funding systems can make sensitive services difficult to achieve.

Overview

- Much of the cost of long-term care is borne by families and partners who provide care themselves. Families also buy care both privately and from local authorities. Older people may sell their house.

- Funding of statutory care for a range of client groups is shared between the NHS and local authorities. Much provision is undertaken by not-for-profit and for-profit agencies – a mixed economy of welfare.

- Social services departments, funded partly locally, remain the main source of last resort care and support for children, older people, people with disabilities and people with mental illness.

- The extent to which individuals and families have to pay has been reduced by state funding of nursing care in England and nursing *and* personal care in Scotland, following the Report of the Royal Commission on Long-Term Care.

Questions for discussion

1. What are the main sources of finance for the care of young children and the long-term care of older people?

2. Describe and assess the moves to a more mixed economy of care in the personal social services.

3. What are the main sources of market failure in the case of long-term care?

4. Assess the arguments against extending state support for the costs of personal care. What does Scotland's experience tell us?

Further reading

For an introduction to the economics of social care see **Knapp (1984)**.

For an account of social care policy, spending and outcomes, 1974-95, see **Evandrou and Falkingham (1998)**.

For changes in funding policy in the early 1990s, see **Lewis and Glennerster (1996)**. For an overview of the decade see **Knapp et al (2001)**.

For the best account of long-term care funding see the **Royal Commission on Long-Term Care (1999)**, including the appendices and note of dissent.

For a critique of the government's policy with costed options for alternatives see **Brooks et al (2002, chapter 5)** and the accompanying statistical models (**Falkingham et al, 2002; Wittenberg et al, 2002**).

six

Financing education

Summary

- The production of human capital depends as much on the investment of parental time and skill in children as it does on formal schooling. That is most true when children are very young (Sparkes and Glennerster, 2002). Long hours of work by both partners or by lone parents may increase family income but disinvest in children (Ruhm, 2000). The finance of education should therefore be properly conceived of as involving far more than how we finance schools or universities.

- Education is an investment in an individual's future earning capacity. The additional earnings gained by those who stay on at school and enter higher education are substantial. UK graduate women earn twice that of their non-graduate contemporaries. Thought of as a return on such investment, the rates of return are higher in the UK than in other advanced economies (OECD, 2002b). This raises the whole question of whether those who benefit from this investment should repay some of the cost.

- What constitutes a 'good' education is disputed. Some parents demand a religious education segregated from others with different religious beliefs. Some require strict discipline, single-sex schools and traditional teaching methods. Others require more freedom and co-education. Many argue that methods of funding must preserve and promote parental choice.

- Some argue that equal opportunity for all children to develop and for social cohesion require that children should not be segregated but learn to live with diversity. Funding mechanisms should foster these goals.

- These different views about education's role in society lead to opposing views about how it should be funded, which go far beyond the debates about efficiency. Nevertheless, familiar issues of market failure and government failure apply as well. Market failure (see **Box 6.1**) is less evident in higher than in school education: 18-year-olds are capable of making informed choices.

- The UK spends rather less than other countries but does not lag as far behind as it does in healthcare. Despite this, the performance of primary school children in particular has risen sharply in the 1990s (Glennerster, 2002), and that of secondary school children compares well with those in other advanced economies (OECD, 2001b). The improvement coincided with significant changes to the incentive structures facing schools.

Box 6.1: Market failures in education

- Children are not perfectly informed consumers. Parents' interests may conflict with those of their children (for example, to encourage children to leave school early to reduce the family's costs and increase family income). Most parents do have aspirations for their children, but are very unequally endowed with the capacity to act on their children's behalf. This may lead to under-consumption of education. The government thus requires school attendance, sets a national curriculum, tests children to inform parents how well their children are doing compared with expected levels of achievement at a given age, and inspects schools.
- In rural areas the local school may be the only school that parents can practically use. It becomes a local monopoly. Working-class parents in urban areas often only consider the local school, making it an effective monopoly.
- Education is, in part, a public good – the benefits of knowledge spread across the globe. The wider community benefits from an educated populace beyond the private gain. Without it debate is less informed, social cohesion and law and order more difficult to achieve. There is no reason why an individual should consider these consequences in deciding how much to spend on educating their child.
- Education not only produces beneficial side-effects – it can separate communities. It may be bought merely to gain an advantage over others in the race for jobs or status – it is a 'positional good' (Hirsch, 1977).
- Although an individual graduate may have a potentially high income, private banks are reluctant to lend large sums of money without security. A poor student will not own property nor have rich parents to reduce the bank's risk. Under-investment results (capital markets are imperfect).
- However, given good information about the quality and content of courses, older students can make efficient choices.
  For a range of key papers on the economics and finance of education see Marshall and Peters (1999).

The cost of education

The UK spends a little more than 5% of its GDP on its educational institutions, which compares with 5.8% across all the advanced economies in the OECD (see **Table 6.1**). The author's figures (Glennerster, 2002) put total UK education spending at 5.6% of GDP in 1998 as it includes higher estimates of *private* spending. The UK had once spent much more of its income on education.

The post-war peak came in 1975 when, it is fair to say, the school population was higher (Glennerster, 1998). Then the total spending on education reached

Table 6.1: **Expenditure on educational institutions as a % of GDP (1999)**

	Public	Private	Total
Austria	4.5	1.4	5.8
Belgium	5.3	0.3	5.5
Canada	5.3	1.3	6.6
Denmark	6.4	0.3	6.7
France	5.8	0.4	6.2
Germany	4.3	1.2	5.6
Greece	3.6	0.3	3.9
Ireland	4.1	0.4	4.6
Italy	4.4	0.4	4.8
Japan	3.5	1.1	4.7
Netherlands	4.3	0.4	4.7
Norway	6.5	0.1	6.6
Spain	4.4	0.9	5.3
Sweden	6.5	0.2	6.7
UK	**4.4**	**0.7**[a]	**5.2**
US	4.9	1.6	6.5
OECD country mean (unweighted)[b]	4.9	0.6	5.5
OECD average	4.6	1.1	5.8

Notes: [a] This excludes household expenditure on education such as home tuition and fees of profit-making enterprises included in HG's higher figure in Table 6.2.
[b] Including some small OECD countries not included above.

Source: OECD (2002b)

6.8% of the GDP, mostly in the public sector. Public spending fell to 4.5% of GDP in 1998 but has risen since to 5.3% (see **Table 6.2**). The broad figures of national spending can be translated into spending per pupil in schools. From 1995-2000 there was little change. Thereafter it rose significantly (see **Table 6.3**).

Of current public education expenditure the majority goes on schools. That is almost equally divided at the moment between primary and secondary education. Nearly a quarter goes to higher and further education institutions. Only about 5% goes to students in the form of loans or, in the past, grants (see **Figure 6.1**).

Comparisons with other countries' 'spending' are difficult. Official exchange rates are not good guides to actual price differences for goods in the shops let alone the price of education – mainly teachers' salaries in each country. OECD figures (see **Table 6.4**) go some way to answering the question. They use figures that reflect the relative costs of goods in the shops but not the general relative income levels in different countries. However, relative income levels in Central and Northern Europe are not strikingly different, and the relative priorities between levels of education are interesting. The UK is relatively high spending at pre-school level, but less generous for its primary schools. Even taking account of somewhat higher average salaries in the US their emphasis on higher education facilities and staff is striking.

Table 6.2: UK education spending relative to GDP (1975-2003) (%)

	Public	Private	Total
1975/76	6.5	0.3	6.8
1979/80	5.2	0.5	5.7
1989/90	4.8	0.5	5.3
1995/96	5.1	1.0	6.1
1996/97	4.9	1.1	6.0
1997/98	4.8	1.1	5.9
1998/99	4.5	1.1	5.6
1999/00	4.5	–	–
2000/01	4.8	–	–
2001/02	5.0	–	–
2002/03	5.3	–	–

Source: Glennerster (2001b)

Figure 6.1: Public expenditure on education: where it goes (2000/01)

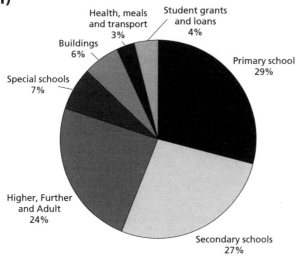

Source: Glennerster (2001b)

Table 6.3: Funding per pupil (1995/96-2003/04), real-terms index

	1995/ 96	1996/ 97	1997/ 98	1998/ 99	1999/ 00	2000/ 01	2001/ 02	2002/ 03	2003/ 04
England[a]									
Primary index	100	99	97	102	107				
Secondary index	100	99	97	98	102				
Scotland[b]									
Primary index	100	99	98	98	101	104			
Secondary index	100	99	97	97	100	101			
UK[c]									
All schools index	100	100	100	102	106	113	120	125	129

Notes: [a] School-based expenditure per pupil.
[b] Budgeted school running cost per pupil.
[c] Revenue funding per pupil.

Source: Glennerster (2001b)

If we compare these relative spending levels with pupil performance in international studies, there is little or no correlation. The US does relatively poorly, Japan very well. So does the UK (OECD, 2002b).

How education funds are allocated

There are three distinct funding systems that allocate public money to different kinds of educational institutions in the UK:

- schools
- colleges of further education
- universities.

These patterns also differ between the constituent parts of the UK.

Table 6.4: Annual expenditure per student in different countries, by level of education[a] (1998) ($)

	Pre-school	Primary	Secondary	Tertiary (further and higher)
Australia	–	4,858	6,850	11,725
Belgium	3,035	3,952	6,444	9,724
Denmark	4,208	6,721	7,626	10,657
France	3,901	4,139	7,152	7,867
Germany	4,937	3,818	4,918	10,393
Greece	–	2,176	2,904	4,260
Ireland	3,386	3,018	4,383	9,673
Italy	5,133	5,354	6,518	7,552
Japan	3,154	5,240	6,039	10,278
Netherlands	3,848	4,162	5,670	12,285
Norway	11,699	5,920	7,628	12,096
Spain	2,789	3,635	4,864	5,707
Sweden	3,396	5,736	5,911	14,222
UK	**6,233**	**3,627**	**5,608**	**9,554**
US	6,692	6,582	8,157	19,222
OECD country mean	3,847	4,148	5,465	9,210
OECD average	3,746	4,229	5,174	11,422

Note: [a] Measured in terms of exchange rates that measure what $1 would actually buy in each country – 'purchasing power parity'.

Source: Data from OECD (2002b)

Schools

Private schools are primarily financed from the fees parents pay (Glennerster and Wilson, 1970). Local education authority (LEA) schools are funded in a two-stage process. Central government contributes roughly three quarters of the cost, with the rest made up from the local Council Tax. This is part of the same process that funds personal social services (see pages 85-7 for a longer description). Each local authority then allocates money to schools on a formula basis that is largely determined by central government. We describe each in turn.

Central government allocations

Local authorities receive a general grant that reflects their relative needs. Those with more school children and older people receive a higher grant. A formula is used which has components for each major service. Education has the largest weighting. The research underpinning the education component in England can be found on the Department for Education and Skills' website (www.dfes.gov.uk/efsg). This determines education's Formula Spending Share in England. Similar formulae exist in the other countries of the UK. There are two basic elements to the formula: one that relates to schools, and another that covers LEA administration costs and youth service costs. The schools element has a similar structure to that for the personal social services:

Basic allocation + deprivation top-up + sparsity top-up + area pay cost top-up

The main school formula has three sub-blocks:

- *Under fives:* the aim is to ensure that all three- and four-year-olds have pre-school provision by 2004. There will be a basic per pupil entitlement assuming part-time enrolment for three-year-olds and full-time for four-year-olds. Those with universal provision are funded on the basis of the numbers in school and those working their way to it are funded on a population basis.
- *Primary:* as with under-fives there is a basic entitlement of so much per primary child plus top-ups we discuss below. Basic primary numbers are those at school aged 5 up to 10 (not having reached 11 by 31 August).
- *Secondary:* the basic element relates to the number of pupils aged 11-15 plus extra for 16-year-olds who are not in sixth forms. (Those doing sixth form courses are funded separately by the Learning Skills Council.)

On top of these basic entitlements based on pupil numbers there are top-ups, or adjustments, to take account of special circumstances and different levels of need:

- *Additional Educational Needs:* following much criticism (for example, West et al, 2000) of the very limited weight given to the extra demands put on schools coping with very deprived children, or those whose first language is not English, work was undertaken to measure the impact of such features of the school population. The resulting index takes account of the numbers on Income Support in the authority's area, the numbers receiving Working Families' Tax Credit (and its replacement) as well as those coming from 'low achieving' ethnic groups. Only when these measures cross a threshold do authorities begin to receive Additional Educational Needs money.

- *Sparsity and area costs:* in the case of primary schools, an addition is made to take account of the extra costs of running primary schools in sparsely populated rural areas where it is necessary to keep small primary schools open. Research suggested that there were no significant costs associated with secondary schools in such areas. Additions are also made to take account of the higher salary costs that schools face in areas of high demand for labour. They must appoint at higher up the salary scale to be able to appoint at all. Whether this will prove anything like enough to meet the shortages experienced in places like London is open to doubt.
- *High cost pupils:* this block refers to children in special schools or in ordinary schools with special needs ('statemented' pupils) or in pupil referral units. The formula to determine the sum available is related to numbers on Income Support and the incidence of low birth weight babies in the area, the two factors most strongly correlated with high cost pupils.

LEA allocations to individual schools

So far we have been concerned with the way LEAs receive their money. The 1988 Education Reform Act introduced a fundamental change in the way individual schools received money from a local authority, and the freedom of action that they had. Traditionally local authorities had given schools very limited financial freedom. Governing bodies appointed staff to posts agreed with the local authority which then paid the staff. Schools were equipped and maintained by the local authority. This had a number of undesirable consequences:

- schools in favoured suburban locations tended to retain staff who thus rose up the salary scales. The total spending on such schools was higher than in poor areas with a younger staff and a high turnover;
- head teachers, senior staff and governors had little opportunity to manage the school's resources and decide priorities between staff, equipment and buildings. The LEA set these;
- those who provided services such as building maintenance were detached from the school and communications were often poor, simple repairs taking months to achieve.

Various local authorities (Inner London and Cambridge, for example) had experimented with devolving budgets to schools, holding governors and heads to account for their spending. Under the 1998 Act all local authorities were required to devolve most of their resources (85%) to schools' governing bodies – Local Management of Schools (LMS). Staff, parents, members of the local community and some political appointments from the LEA were represented on the governing body. The formula used by a LEA to allocate funds to a school had to be approved by the central Department for Education and Skills but it mainly reflected the numbers and ages of pupils with some small element of social needs (free school meals usually) and extra for children with special needs.

When the Labour government was elected in 1997 they kept to this basis for funding LEA schools and indeed, required further delegation – at least 90% of the LEA school budget – keeping the rest for central support to schools. This was called *Fairer Funding*. The one major change they made was to abolish grant-maintained schools – schools that had been permitted to leave their LEAs and become funded directly by central government through the *Funding Agency for Schools*. Approximately a thousand schools (out of 24,000) had done so. Such schools were permitted to join church schools in their somewhat more distant relationship to LEAs – church schools receive all their current expenditure from their LEA, an arrangement that dates back to 1944 (Gosden, 1976). The denominations contribute 10% of the cost of new buildings (it used to be 50% in 1944) and in return they have denominational members on the board of governors.

The Labour government also increased the number of special pots of money set aside and directly available to schools; this practice was not new. In the last year of the Conservative government in 1996/97, 2.6% of school spending came from these central initiatives. By 2001 it had reached 5% of school spending. The largest element is the *Standards Fund*. There are grants for school improvement, literacy and numeracy hours, extra funds to raise the achievement of pupils from minority ethnic groups and to promote social inclusion by tackling drug use. Education Action Zones in deprived areas receive another pot of money, some of which reaches schools. The Excellence in Cities programme targets inner-city schools. Each of these initiatives requires bids from schools and separate accounting and reporting if successful. However, headteachers had come to welcome LMS, and these central pots of money tended to work against their greater freedom (Glennerster et al, 2000).

A new allocation was introduced as a result of the 2000 Budget. This was a direct grant from central government to all LEA schools depending on their size and whether they were primary or secondary schools. The sum involved was quite small – £40,000 for an average secondary school – but it has since increased and could be a precursor of funding coming directly from central government to schools rather than via the LEA postbox. Such a system would at least be more transparent than the present two-stage formula plus a multiplicity of special funding. The public might then have a chance of understanding and debating how much schools are getting from central government.

Private schools have, in the past, also received funds direct from government. This was true of the direct-grant grammar schools between 1902 and 1976, and it was also the basis of the assisted places scheme in the 1980s. Some places in private schools went to children of poorer families, with the government contributing to the fees on a means-tested basis (Glennerster and Wilson, 1970; Glennerster, 1998).

In November 2002 the Department for Education and Skills and the Cabinet Office (2002) produced a report on the complex range of services for families with young children, and the inconvenience that arises from schools' restricted opening hours. Schools have not been permitted to provide non-educational services such as childcare which was the province of social services departments. Legislation will now enable them to provide pre- and post-school care services, to employ other agencies to do so, and to charge for these services.

Colleges of further education

Colleges of further education used to be funded and controlled by LEAs. During Mrs Thatcher's period in office they became independent organisations directly funded by central government through their own funding council. It is important to note that this income was supplemented by the fees students paid, and colleges are financed according to the number of students they attract. Different kinds of course attendance and success rates determine the level of grant. Such colleges are primarily concerned with instruction and hence issues of funding research do not arise. Many students combine work with learning and are given time off work to train or take evening courses.

Higher education

The costs for higher education are of four kinds:

- the costs of instruction – teaching, equipment and buildings;
- the costs of research which also contributes to the quality of teaching, particularly in the case of postgraduate work;
- the opportunity costs students face in not working, especially when taking full-time courses;
- students also face direct costs of living away from home – food and accommodation.

Each of these costs is funded differently. Until the 1980s universities received a block grant which they could use for teaching and research. All were funded on the principle that higher education teaching and research were part of a single product and all universities were equally funded to do both. The exception was the finance of particular projects, paid for by those wanting the research done, pharmaceutical companies or governments, for example, or research councils such as the Economic and Social Research Council. From the Second World War on, and particularly from 1962, students were paid a maintenance grant sufficient for them to live off if their parents were poor; the grant was less if parents were rich.

The rapid expansion of higher education from the late 1980s put paid to this comfortable world which greatly benefited the relatively well-off who went to university. In the 1960s as much was spent on a university student as on an ordinary pupil throughout the whole of their school life (Glennerster, 1972; Glennerster et al, 1995). When this pattern of finance reached its peak of generosity in 1962, 4% of the school-leaving population went to university. By 2002 the percentage of 18- to 30-year-olds in England going on to higher education was to rise to 43%, and the target was actually 50% (DfES, 2003). Successive governments have been forced to accept that a rapid expansion of higher education was incompatible with such generous funding. It would have meant spending several times more on universities than on schools to fund expansion according to the old pattern. This was neither politically feasible nor socially equitable. The state could not support research at all the universities in the UK at the high levels that would be needed for all of them to compete with leading universities abroad. If some world-class institutions were to survive, there had to be some concentration of research funding. Such were the arguments that drove the Conservative government in the late 1980s. Hence:

• the funding of teaching and of research was separated;
• maintenance grants were to be abolished and replaced by loans.

Universities now received money from the Higher Education Funding Council (HEFC) in two streams. As long as their teaching standards are deemed adequate in the Teaching Quality Review process, institutions are paid for each home and European student they accept up to a ceiling imposed by the HEFC. Students on different courses attract different sums, medicine and science several times as much as a social science or humanities student. Every university receives the same teaching grant for each home student in the same subject. Overseas students attract no grant.

In addition, some universities receive extra money related to the number of staff for whom they make returns to a HEFC-appointed Research Assessment Review panel. The work of these departments is graded from 1 to 5★. A new grade of 6★ is to be added. The highest grade reflects a judgement that most of the work of that department is of international significance. Lower grades reflect a view that most of the work is only of national significance or of little significance at all! Departments then get a sum of money related to the grade gained for each member whose work was returned. For example, in social policy the sum of money received in 2002/03 for each member of staff for research was:

Grade 5★   £29,865
Grade 5   £20,853
Grade 4   £11 033
Grade 3a   £3,365

During the early 1990s universities were able to take as many students as they liked. In spite of the fact that they were paid less for each student above their set target, student places increased sharply. The cumulative effect of government funding policies in the 1980s and 1990s was to *halve* the average real expenditure per student. In the US in the same period real-per-student expenditure *increased* by nearly half (Glennerster, 1998).

The Conservative government, in its 1990 Education (Student Loans) Act, took the first step towards a policy long advocated by economists. The government would cease to fund institutions and instead enable students to borrow and hence pay their own way through higher education. (This argument is set out in Friedman, 1962; Glennerster et al, 1968; Barr, 2001b; and in the Dearing Committee Report, 1997, para 8.13.) The Labour government's reform proposals (DfES, 2003) will take the process a long step further.

The economists' case

Economists argue the following points:

- The main reason for market failure in higher education is the failure of the capital market to lend to students who have high potential earnings but low current assets. If the government put that right there should be no reason for other state intervention.
- State funding of universities is pro-rich in its outcome, endangers academic freedom and is inefficient in its application. Treasury limits on spending force universities to ration places, which is inefficient and inequitable. The greater the competition to enter university, the fewer students from poor homes succeed in entering.
- On average students reap a high private rate of return on their investment in higher education (Blundell et al, 1999). Graduates are more likely to have a job, earn more and earn for longer. This is more the case in the UK than in any other advanced economy. The average male recipient of tertiary education in the UK earns a private rate of return on the costs he incurred, including earnings foregone, and after tax, of *17% a year*! (The woman's equivalent is 15%.) This compares to 12% for all other leading economies, with the nearest returns being in the US, with just under 15% (OECD, 2002b). The reason British graduates do so well, relatively speaking, is the shortness of the degree courses and the scale of public support.

- Some of the benefits of higher education are shared with the rest of the population (an externality see pages 19-20). Thus part of higher education should be funded through general tax revenue, but only part.
- An additional role for the state is therefore to lend to any student who gains a university place and to recover *some* of the costs of tuition at a time when students can afford to pay, and at a rate reflecting their income.
- The best form of loan is therefore an *income contingent loan* (one related to a person's capacity to repay). This would not deter those who might enter low-paid jobs or bring up a family. Loans should be made by a private company, with the repayments collected through the tax system. This means the expenditure does not count as part of public spending (escaping Treasury control), but defaults on repayments would be low (Barr, 2001b).
- Students should make decisions between courses facing fees that reflect the relative costs of providing them. Expensive engineering courses may not give the student any better career prospects than a cheaper maths or social science degree. Hiding this in a flat fee or no fee produces an inefficient choice.

Critics argue that economists are ignoring many young people's fear of being in debt. Those from working-class homes are most risk-averse, and face more risk of failing at university (Scott et al, 2001; Naylor et al, 2002). Loans, rather than maintenance grants and free tuition, pose higher barriers for working-class students. The sociology and psychology of student finance really do matter. Maybe, economists reply, but what matters most, surely, is widening access. Narrow access gates harm working-class students most. And hard economic and political reality means that relying on taxes to generate the revenue will result in narrow gates.

The Conservative government appointed the Dearing Committee which reported just after the new Labour government took office in 1997. It recommended a range of options but largely followed the logic set out above.

'New' Labour's policy: phase one

'New' Labour was faced with a difficult choice. They had promised not to spend more than the Conservatives for two years. The universities were, however, critically short of money. Student loan repayments would not bring in more revenue on any scale until well into the future. The Treasury refused to change the way public expenditure was calculated, so loans would count as public spending. The government went for a compromise. Universities needed funds immediately, but the government could not help, having tied its own hands. So richer students would have to pay. Home undergraduates from 1998 were required to pay a fee if their parents' income was over a given sum, half if it were lower, nothing if lower still. The top fee was originally £1,000;

£1,100 in 2002/03. Students whose parents'residual income' was over £30,502 had to pay the full fee; at less than £20,480 there was no fee at all. In England 42% of students were not required to pay any fee. The universities got the extra money but the policy proved highly unpopular.

The Scottish Parliament rejected the policy, arguing that it restricted access. It did not, however, reject the idea of asking graduates to repay fees after they had graduated. The fees were essentially translated into a loan which students would repay, together with one for maintenance (see **Box 6.2**). The Northern Ireland and Wales Assemblies also rejected the fees policy (see Callender, 2002 for a critique of Labour's phase one policy; also see the Report of the House of Commons Education and Skills Committee, 2002).

The Labour government did follow Dearing and the economists' arguments when it came to the costs of maintenance. The levels of aid available were increased but those who accepted funds to cover maintenance would have to repay them on an income-related basis through an addition to their income tax in later life.

In practice, the Labour government's policy satisfied neither side in the argument. Glennerster (2002) argued:

- up-front fees endangered access so fees had to be low and means tested. The total revenue was therefore only £350 million in 2001/02, rising to £400 million in 2003/04. This was tiny in relation to total spending on higher education of £10 billion. The policy was inequitable *and* ineffective;

Box 6.2: **The Scottish model**

Following an inquiry by the Cubie Committee a compromise scheme was worked out:
- Tuition fees for eligible Scottish and EU students were to be paid by the state.
- Scottish students studying elsewhere in the UK will be liable to a means-tested contribution to the fees.
- For new students under the age of 25 Young Students' Bursaries are available. For 2002/03 the maximum bursary is £2,050. It will also apply to Scottish students studying outside Scotland.
- There are zero real interest loans available on a means-tested basis. They will be repaid when earnings are over £10,000 a year at a minimum of 9% of earnings over that figure.
- A 'graduate endowment', that is, a graduate tax, will be payable by students from the April following graduation. It was set at £2,000 for 2001/02 and linked to inflation. There will be exceptions and only half of all graduating students are expected to have to pay.

- fees were uniform, not varying by subject, hence losing the efficiency gain that would come from presenting students with the differential cost of each subject;
- the loan to cover maintenance repaid through the tax system was economically efficient but:
  - it was given with a nil rate of interest. Students repay a sum of money increased for inflation but not a rate of interest. The Treasury therefore count most of the spending as public expenditure and hence keep it constrained;
  - because it is advantageous to borrow money this way it is a subsidy to the rich. To prevent excessive borrowing by the rich the loan is means tested on parents' income. This denies much of the point of the scheme and complicates it;

(The last two criticisms also apply to the Scottish version.)

In October 2001 the government accepted that some revision was necessary, and a review was announced. This resulted in a White Paper published in January 2003 (DfES, 2003).

The 2003 White Paper on Higher Education Funding

This radical and controversial plan for higher education funding in England goes a long way to meet some of the criticisms made above of the current system, but raises more of its own. It is driven by the need to put a lot more money into higher education both for expansion *and* to improve the quality of teaching and research. Despite a historically generous award of public funds of 6% per annum in *real terms* between 2002/03 and 2005/06 it would have still left universities lagging far behind the top universities abroad, particularly those in the US. There was no political likelihood of getting more taxpayers' money into the system, nor was there a case in equity for doing so given other demands. The government could have simply given up on the struggle to maintain world-class universities and risked at least some leading institutions becoming entirely private, catering only for those capable of paying very high fees. Instead it has targeted more state resources at the very peak of the system, but has also allowed universities the freedom to charge variable fees to be repaid *after graduation*. Students who go to the 'top' universities earn over 40% more than those in the least advantaged universities. A significant premium exists even when we take these students' higher grades into account (Naylor et al, 2002). Since they gain so much from their extra privileged education why should they not contribute more to their universities' costs, the government argued.

Recognising that these higher fees, even if paid after graduation, might deter some applicants from disadvantaged backgrounds, the freedom to charge higher fees carries a duty for these universities especially to recruit more such students. If they do not do so, in the future they will lose their freedom to charge more. Paradoxically, therefore, this freedom to charge higher fees may actually improve the social class mix of the top universities. Critics argue it will not – it will do the reverse. Only time will tell.

Freeing universities to vary their fees, up or downwards, as well as between subjects, makes good economic sense for the reasons outlined above. To improve applicants' information the government will work with the National Union of Students to publish more about courses and their quality.

Specifically the White Paper proposed:

- abolishing the up-front payment of fees from 2006 onwards;
- paying universities 20% more for each student they take who comes from a deprived background;
- permitting universities to charge between nothing and £3,000 a year for particular courses. There will be a cap on this sum until the end of the next Parliament, probably 2010. These 'graduate contributions' can be deferred until after finishing the course and repaid through the tax system like the maintenance loan. Repayments will be linked to capacity to pay. There will be no real rate of interest and repayments will rise with inflation;
- the government will continue to meet the full £1,100 cost of tuition fees for students with family incomes up to £20,000, and part of the fees for families with incomes between £20,000 and £30,000 a year;
- the income threshold above which ex-students will have to repay their maintenance loan, and eventually the new contribution, will be raised from £10,000 to £15,000 in 2005. Income over this threshold will be 'taxed' at 9% until the 'contribution' is repaid. If people want to pay earlier they can;
- student teachers are exempted from the present tuition fee and the NHS pays for the tuition fees for nurses, midwives and allied health professionals from September 2003. Students on social work courses will have their fees met by the Department of Health. Arrangements are still under discussion for after 2006;
- from 2004 a student from a lower-income family will receive a grant of £1,000;
- universities will only be permitted to raise fees if they make an agreement with a new 'access regulator' showing how they will improve access for young people from more deprived areas and schools;
- the present loan system covering maintenance costs and repaid through the tax system will continue. Richer students will still have their loan capped at 75% of the full loan (although the present complexities may be simplified);
- students of whatever age will be encouraged to give part of their income to fund higher education institutions from which they have benefited through

the tax system. Corporate giving will also be encouraged. There will be a time-limited scheme in which government will match gifts made by individuals and firms. It will, in the long term, encourage the growth of endowment funds for universities;
• there will be more research funding much targeted by creating a new 6★ grade.

For a critique see Barr (2003) and NUS (www.netlondon.com/education/organisations/nationalunionofst).

Improving choice and efficiency

The changed funding of schools, that occurred after the 1988 Education Reform Act, incorporated many features that economists had advocated for years:

• devolved managerial control of a school's resources to the school itself in the form of its governing body that includes parents, teachers and members of the local community;
• national standard setting and a national curriculum with public information about a school's performance for parents and community representatives to judge it by;
• a financial incentive for staff to raise standards since only if the school attracted pupils would it receive funding for them;
• national guidance on how best to achieve literacy and numeracy targets (this idea, experimented with before 1997, was made general by the New Labour government).

This had all the elements of a *quasi-market* (see pages 30-1). It had many elements of a voucher scheme but only operating within the state system. Funding pupils, not schools, is an idea with a long pedigree (Paine, 1791/92, 1969; Friedman, 1962; Maynard, 1975; Coons and Sugarman, 1978; Chubb and Moe, 1990).

Many of these reformers would have taken the idea further. They argue for the state giving parents the equivalent of a sum of money for each child, which they can spend at any school, public *or* private. The parent could then add to the value of this voucher, thus being able to send their child to a 'better' school, costing more than the state, or the voting public, was prepared to pay. Parents with a higher preference for education, not quite able to afford it without state support, could therefore match their preferences to the better-than-average education that they desired for their children.

Taken together, these two elements would create a full-scale market in school education. Economists argue that this would both expose state schools to more competition than a quasi-market and widen the range of choice for parents, for example, not to follow the national curriculum. There are, however, critics of both quasi- and full market arguments:

- Working-class parents, in particular, do not see schooling as a market. They do not identify with 'choice', preferring to go to their local school, and expecting it to be good. They do not exert their exit power. The middle class do. Hence this efficiency lever is exerted in ways that benefit the middle class (Gerwirtz et al, 1995; Ball, 2002).
- Schools seek to compete for students who will add to their performance table position. These league tables do not reflect the difficulties some schools face – they measure intake and not output. Hence schools will cream-skim (see page 23). Selecting bright or hard-working pupils is an easier way to improve performance than improving the efficiency of the school (Glennerster, 1991).
- There are insufficient spare places in good state schools or capacity to expand for a real market to exist.
- To extend the voucher scheme to private schools would mean an increase in public expenditure to subsidise those already opting for private education, who, on average, have high incomes. Money could be better spent improving state schools.
- Enabling parents to 'top up' vouchers and move to private schools would extend the range of unequal opportunities in schooling, and lead to a greater degree of social and ethnic separation.

Some of these arguments amount to differences in values and objectives for the education system. There is also conflicting evidence about the effects (Gerwirtz et al, 1995; Whitty et al, 1998; Noden, 2002). Gorard and Fitz (1998), surveying schools in Wales, found that social segregation initially rose after the quasi-market changes were introduced, and then fell significantly. This is the opposite to the predictions. One explanation is that headteachers in some deprived areas faced with poor results actively sought to widen their catchment areas to 'improve' their intake; they 'counter-cream-skimmed'. Work in the Centre for Analysis of Social Exclusion at the London School of Economics and Political Science is suggesting that this may be true. It turns out that linking polarisation to the arrival of quasi-markets may be spurious. It may have more to do with changes in the economy, with the selection of pupils for grammar schools and with housing allocations than with school choice (Goldstein and Noden, 2003: forthcoming).

If this evidence on cream-skimming is inconclusive, then that on educational outcomes is more consistent.

For the 30 years prior to 1995, the only absolute measures we have of all pupils' performance at school in England derive from samples taken for international surveys of mathematics and science achievements. We do have school leaving exam results – GCSE and A levels – but these reflect pupils' decisions to stay on at school as much as school performance, and the exams themselves have changed their nature. The Maths results for 13-year-olds in the surveys since the mid-1960s suggest no improvement took place, in fact, even a small decline. This was not untypical of other OECD countries. More had been spent on schools with no improvement in outcomes in most school systems over a 25-year period – a decline in schools' productivity. Gundlach et al (2001) put this down to the absence of incentives and competition in state school systems. Between 1988 and 1995 English schools became subject to the range of incentives we have described, and the results are striking (Glennerster, 2002):

- there has been a steady and quite large improvement in the number of pupils reaching the target level of attainment set in English, Maths and Science at ages 7, 11 and 14. In Maths 45% of pupils reached the Maths achievement targets expected of 11-year-olds in 1995. By 2002 the figure was 73%. In Reading the figures went from 49% to 80%;
- the poorest performing schools improved more than the average and top schools;
- the schools with the most poor pupils (over 40% on free school meals) improved more than the average schools.

Even entering various caveats about the figures it is difficult not to accept that something significant had occurred. Pinning this entirely on the quasi-market is hard given a simultaneous battery of changes. But it is plausible to suggest that each element was necessary and interconnected. Would schools have responded to target setting if it were not combined with the sanction that parents could identify schools that did poorly and remove children and therefore finance? A comparison with the NHS' failed attempt to link standards with such incentives is instructive.

There is also more direct evidence. Bradley and Taylor (2000) and Bradley et al (1999) looked at the exam performance and attendance records of all English secondary schools from 1993-97. They standardise for intake and the special situations of schools, and measure their relative efficiency in exam performance. The results are clear. Those schools that faced most competition from nearby schools improved their performance most. The greater the competition the more the improvement, and the longer this persisted, the more they improved.

The evidence suggests (as does that from other countries) that the quasi-market has actually increased efficiency. It may have done so at the cost of encouraging selectivity, although the evidence is weaker. It is possible to counter this disadvantage by increasing schools' financial and other incentives to accept more difficult or slower learners.

Incentives in higher education

The same principles are being applied to the funding of higher education in England, as we saw earlier. Students will face fees that cover, some at least, of their tuition costs, and fees will vary between universities and subjects. Students will be able to make informed choices, and universities may respond to their preferences and demands more readily! Productive and allocative efficiency of higher education in England may improve. The outcome will be instructive to watch.

The finance of education in other countries

Schools

The ways in which other countries fund their schools differ fundamentally. At one extreme, **France** still has the most centralised pattern of funding and organisation. The French Ministry of Education and Culture largely funds all stages of education through regional *Academies*. Since 1982 the Ministry, the regional and the local authorities, have jointly supervised schools. The Ministry determines the main decisions, including the allocation of teachers to schools. It determines the curriculum, the nature of the schools and the national system of testing children in core subjects at ages 8 and 11. Teachers are centrally paid civil servants.

At the other extreme, the **US** resisted any federal role in the finance of local schools until the War on Poverty in 1965 included some federal aid to schools with high numbers of poor children. Federal aid remains limited, at about 10% of total school spending. A recent reform by President Bush enables parents whose children are in persistently poor-performing schools to take this federal funding with them if they transfer their children to a school of their choice – a limited voucher experiment. District school boards raise a separate education tax levied on property, supplemented by state level funding. US schools remain traditionally administered, with limited delegation of funds to schools and limited school choice. Where you live still largely determines to which school you go, although school choice experiments are taking place in various states and cities (Ladd, 1996). School districts are small, so parents exercise choice by moving house, to suburbs, for example. Hoxby (2000) shows that schools in areas with small school districts where parents have more geographical choice are more efficient – they get better results with less resources. This bears out the English evidence that we have already discussed. The US constitution forbids federally funded religious schools of the kind that we currently have in the UK. As a result, parts of the US have a large private sector – nearly a fifth of the school population. Much of it consists of Catholic schools and schools in urban areas with poor public provision.

The **Scandinavian** and **German** patterns of funding are essentially based on local taxation, with limited national or federal intervention.

Belgium and **the Netherlands** have had a quasi-market in schooling since the Second World War. The reasons were not to do with efficiency but to enable the different religious and ethnic groups to have their own schools. A total of 70% of schools in the Netherlands are private. Parents can sign their children into any state-approved school that individuals or religious bodies are able to set up. The school receives a sum of money for each child enrolled. Studying the effect in Belgium, Vandenberghe (1996, 1998) concluded that there was evidence of the cream-skimming of academically able children. There are no studies of the efficiency consequences.

New Zealand embarked on a quasi-market reform at the same time as the UK (in 1989). Schools were given delegated budgets, and parental choice was allowed, but only part of the budget was devolved and not the biggest element – teachers' salaries. Again there is evidence of cream-skimming, and a growth of more and less successful schools. For a discussion of these comparisons see Le Grand (2003).

Higher education

The Dearing Report (1997, Appendix 5) provides a descriptive account of higher education in a wide range of other countries, including finance and cost structures. The EU website has country-by-country descriptions (www.eurydice.org). Barr (2001b) gives a more analytic and comparative account focusing on recent efforts to reform student and institutional finance.

At one end of the spectrum are European countries such as France, Germany and Italy, who have traditionally had free, or virtually free, higher education with the right to a university place if a young person passed the entrance qualification hurdle, the *Baccalaureate* or the *Abitur*. (It is, in practice, more complex than this. The *Zeugnis der Allgemeinen Hochschulreife* entitles the holder to admission to all subjects at all higher education institutions. Nevertheless restrictions apply to particular high demand courses like medicine.)

Over 90% of those who gain the *Baccalaureate* in **France** go into higher education, at least for a period. However, support for students' living expenses is poor. In France there is financial support available based on a means test of parental income, but the income limits are low as are the sums offered. Less than a fifth of students receive grants.

In **Germany** the majority of 'full-time' students work to pay their way through college, with parental help. Limited support is available from the federal government to students from poor families. In both countries courses last longer than in the UK and many students drop out – roughly a quarter in their first year in France, with only a quarter completing their first stage diploma in the two years expected.

The rapid expansion in entry that has resulted from increasing numbers gaining the *Arbitur* and *Baccalaureate* has not been matched by increased funding. This has led to overcrowding and large teaching groups. German institutions are mainly funded by the Länder. The grants are based on the number of students and a range of other indicators which include incentives to take more women, graduate students and to encourage students to complete more quickly. In contrast, in France, most university funding comes from the Ministry for Education. Universities negotiate a contract with the Ministry setting out expected student numbers and staffing by grade and function. University staff are paid directly by the Ministry. In both countries the finance of both students and higher education institutions is facing serious and unresolved problems.

Sweden and **the Netherlands** have evolved a mixed pattern of much more generous student support and incentive-based funding of institutions. In the Netherlands there is a mixed pattern of student funding. Every student gets a basic monthly sum to help with expenses – travel, books and study resources, tuition fees and medical expenses. On top of that students with poorer parents get a means-tested additional payment. Both elements are initially given as a loan with interest set at the market rate. If the student fails their studies they have to repay it. If they gain their qualification within the given time limit they do not have to repay the whole of the sum. In addition students can borrow more from the government at an interest rate set at about 2% above the rate for long-term government bonds. Repayments for all the loans begin two years after the student leaves university and are income-contingent. Those on low incomes repay less or nothing. Any outstanding debts after 15 years are wiped out (see Barr, 2001b).

In **Sweden**, too, there is a mix of grants and loans to cover living expenses. Grants meet the minor part of living costs, loans the remainder. Loans are repaid at 4% of a graduate's income over an income threshold. Unpaid debt is forgiven at the age of 65! There are no fees. Institutions in both countries are funded directly by government, but on a performance-related basis, for example, completion rates within a given period.

Australia was the first country to adopt the idea of a graduate tax (Glennerster et al, 1968). In order to finance an explosion in university places, the Labour government introduced what it called a Higher Education Contribution in 1989. This was essentially a flat fee of A$2,000 a year. It was equivalent to about a quarter of the average cost of tuition. Students could pay the fee on entering university and get a discount or defer the payment. It could be repaid after graduation through the tax system. The sum was linked to later inflation but there was no interest payment. By 1995 the extra revenue was providing 10% of funding on higher education and will rise to 20% in the near future. The loan facility does not cover living expenses; it is merely a deferred fee. Considerable research on the scheme suggests that it did not affect the social class balance of entry, any disincentives being offset by the effects of expansion (Chapman, 1997).

In 1996 the scheme was changed. Fees were increased from 25% of tuition costs to 37% on average. They varied by subject so that students in agriculture paid 26% of tuition costs and law students 80%. A separate category of private students was introduced, paying 100% of tuition fees, increasing an institution's incentive to give preference to students from rich families. These later changes were unpopular and led to an enquiry like that of Dearing (Commonwealth of Australia, 1997). It argued that institutions should have the freedom to set fees for the courses that they ran, but that no student should be required to pay 'up front'. Income-contingent loans should be available to cover any fees charged. Further changes are expected.

New Zealand followed Australia with important variations. Fees covering about 25% of tuition costs were introduced, but were set by the universities. A loans scheme covered both the fee and living expenses, and there is a maintenance grant for students with poor parents. The loans carry a virtual market rate of interest. This scheme came nearest to what academic economists would recommend. However, the scheme was further modified in 2000 in ways that economists found less effective. Full-time students, and low-income part-time students, were able to repay at a low nominal rate of interest. This will substantially reduce the income from the scheme and increase the exchequer cost of higher education.

The **US** is different from all the above examples. It has many private and largely privately funded universities. They vary from an internationally famous institution such as Harvard, which does attract federal research money in significant amounts, to small liberal arts colleges that attract little or none. Tuition costs are met from fees and scholarship funds financed from gifts often by old students. Then there are large state universities which are public institutions with significant state funding. Nearly half of all higher education institutions in the US are in the public sector and charge low fees to students from within the state. Out-of-state students and those from overseas pay higher fees. All the major institutions have extensive scholarships available to poor students, able students and good football players! Generalisations are therefore difficult. Tuition fees cover about 20% of the income of public universities and between 10 and 40% of private ones. Loans are available from various sources including the federal government, but are nearly all of a 'mortgage' type. They have to be repaid whatever the student's later income. The loans have an interest rate subsidy. They are not repaid through a tax system but merely rely on legal measures to collect. There are high default rates. The system is not strong on equity but it does accommodate large numbers of students and good facilities funded by high revenues.

Overview

- The UK spends slightly less than other advanced economies on education, but used to spend significantly more as a share of its GDP. The amount spent by parents privately has risen. State school education is now to get a major increase in funding.

- State schools are funded mainly through grants paid to LEAs and partly from Council Tax. Cash reaches individual schools as a result of parents choosing the school. This quasi-market, combined with the national curriculum and literacy and numeracy hours, has increased school productivity.

- The funding of higher education has changed in controversial ways, with the tax system being used to administer an income-contingent loan to cover maintenance in England. Fees have to be paid on a means-tested basis by about 40% of university students. This is set to change.

- Funding of higher education in other countries is also under discussion and major change can be expected there too.

Questions for discussion

1. Who produces and who finances education in the UK? How does the picture vary in other advanced economies?

2. Describe the ways in which funds reach schools, colleges of further education and universities.

3. In what respects is the finance of schools in England like a quasi-market?

4. How, if at all, would you reform the finance of higher education: (a) in England, (b) in Scotland?

Further reading

For a detailed account of UK education spending from 1973/74 to 1995 see **Glennerster (1998)**; for an update see **Glennerster (2002)**.

For a collection of accessible academic papers on the economics of education, human capital theory and the use of market incentives see **Marshall and Peters (1999)**.

For a lucid discussion of attempts to reform higher education finance see **Barr (2001b)**.

For an account of the history of needs-based funding of schools in the UK see **Glennerster et al (2000, Chapters 5 and 9)**.

For an influential advocacy of devolved school budgets see **Chubb and Moe (1990)**.

seven

Financing income security

Summary

- In developed capitalist economies a regular income from work is the primary means through which individuals purchase their most basic needs and sustain their dignity. Yet, over the life cycle, most individuals will not be able to rely on the job market to sustain them for significant periods.

- The level of education and training required for the modern labour market means that most people will begin their careers in their mid-twenties. The average age of leaving the labour force has, however, been falling in most OECD countries. The trend reversed in the US in the mid-1980s and may have halted in the UK in the mid-1990s. It is now age 62 in the UK and in other advanced economies (OECD, 2001c). At the same time life expectancy is rising. In 2000 the expected lifespan at birth in the UK was 75 for men, 80 for women. By 2030 both will be over 80. Work will thus provide income for less than half of an individual's life unless working life is extended.

- Many people experience poverty for at least part of their life. One in three people in Britain are 'poor', or slip below half-average earnings, once in four years. (For a review of evidence see Burgess and Propper, 2002.)

- Those who have good long-term jobs are able to save for their own retirement. Those with good health records and qualifications can make their own arrangements for sick pay or for bridging any gaps between jobs. 'Poorer' people find the insurance and banking markets fail to help. Even higher-income groups will find securing a relatively stable income through life difficult. Some risks can be insured against privately, but many cannot (see **Box 7.1**). Apart from the family the state is the only agency that may be able to provide support. It may also fail.

The state's role: income replacement or poverty relief?

There is a fundamental difference in objectives between those who believe that the state's function should be confined to preventing poverty, and those who argue that its role is to replace previous earnings in times of hardship, even if those earnings were quite high. Those who hold that the state's role is only poverty relief argue that it is no business of the state to determine how far individuals should replace their income in old age, for example. Sustaining your living standard at either 80% or 50% or 30% of your previous lifestyle is a matter for individual choice and employer–employee collective bargaining. Most Continental European pensions and social insurance arrangements assume that it is part of the task of any pension or insurance scheme to sustain a person's living standards when earned income ceases or is interrupted. That goes for state schemes too. Some who favour private schemes also believe that individuals may have to be coerced into saving enough to replace their incomes.

This was neither Beveridge's view nor that of those who created the early pension schemes in Australia and Denmark. Beveridge believed that the state's role should be confined to erecting a platform at, or just above, the poverty line. The rest was for individuals to decide. Others argue that even that gives too large a role to the state. Governments should support only those who fall below the poverty line, and should only make up their income to that level. Different countries' income support systems reflect these varied views often inherited from the original founding schemes. **Figure 7.1** illustrates these differences.

Figure 7.1: **Alternative principles of state pension schemes**

	Universal state provision	Required membership of approved private schemes plus income tested residual pension schemes
Replace earnings in work	Germany, US, France Sweden, Italy UK: 1978 State Earnings Related Pension Scheme (SERPS)	Chile, Australia and Sweden for supplementary schemes UK: Conservative 1997 plan
Provide a minimum income in retirement	New Zealand, the Netherlands Denmark UK: 1942 Beveridge Plan	Australia, the Netherlands Denmark UK: 1908 Lloyd George scheme 2003 Guarantee and Pension Credit (but not compulsory membership of private schemes)

Source: Adapted from Agulnik (2000)

Down the left-hand side of the matrix we can distinguish two distinct objectives: *replacing earnings in work* up to, say, 60% of previous net income, or *sustaining a minimum income.*

The first has been the basic intention of the state schemes in Germany, the US, France, Sweden and Italy, although adopted at different dates. Chile and various other South American states also adopted the principle. But they achieve it by requiring their population to take out private pensions that will give a replacement income of a given level. This puts them in the second column. This model is accompanied by a standby means–tested pension for those whose required contributions to a private scheme are insufficient to achieve a pension above the poverty line.

The second basic option is to *confine* the state's role to sustaining a basic poverty income. New Zealand provides a universal state pension that is sufficient to raise all older citizens above the poverty line, at least in theory. Australia, again in theory, does the same, but taxes away the basic pension from the top income groups.

It also now requires employers to contribute to an occupational pension scheme for their employees. Hence it occupies two boxes.

The UK began with a means-tested state pension in 1908. In 1948 it moved to adopt a flat rate pension which, in theory, although never in practice, was to lift all pensioners above the poverty line. In 1978 it added a State Earnings Related Pension Scheme (SERPS) on top. It began to scale this down in 1985.

In 1997 the Conservatives proposed ending any state scheme, relying on compulsory private provision and Income Support. This was a fairly close copy of the Chile model. In 2003 the UK has a very small income-related state pension for the poorest groups, the remnant of the Beveridge pension, and a means-tested pension funded out of taxation. In short, it has relics of policies in all four boxes.

The case for insurance markets

Despite their weaknesses private insurance markets have significant advantages:

- Most people are 'risk-averse' to some extent. They want to be protected from the consequences of a sudden fall in income or big necessary expenditure, which will affect their accustomed lifestyle, such as their house burning down. They will be prepared to buy insurance so long as the value of security to them outweighs the cost.
- Some people are particularly risk-averse: they choose high pensions or high fire premiums. Others are less risk-averse. For the state to determine how much fire or life insurance is to be taken out would be inefficient. The risk-averse individual would feel underinsured, the optimist overprotected.

Markets enable us to match our risk preferences and their cost. This is the way house insurance works. The same, it can be argued, applies to pensions. People should be free to decide whether to spend a riotous youth and a relatively poor old age, or to spend savings on their children and grandchildren and not on a luxurious retirement.

- Competition between insurers will provide a range of choices to suit varied needs in retirement or job lifestyles. State schemes tend to be uniform.
- Failure to insure may bring costs to others. Failure to insure yourself as a driver for injuries to others in an accident may mean that the injured cannot recover damages. Hence the state requires such 'third party' cover. This does not mean that the market cannot work. The state requires a market in such insurance. It can do the same for pensions or sickness benefit and in many countries it does so increasingly. We can be required to save up to a given amount for retirement but use competing pension providers.

Thus the scope for the market in income security is significant and contested. It is, nevertheless, limited. The lifetime poor do not have the purchasing power to make the insurance market work.

The cost of income maintenance

Public spending

The public income maintenance or social security budget distinguishes two kinds of expenditure: that which is financed out of general taxation and that which is funded out of national insurance contributions. The distinction has large elements of history and mythology attached to it.

A wide range of benefits, but primarily pensions, are paid out of a separate government fund in the UK called the National Insurance Fund (there used to be several but they were amalgamated). These benefits are listed in **Box 7.2**. The income to this fund comes primarily from those at work – employees' contributions – and from their employers. The self-employed pay a combined contribution. These rates are set so that the combined cost of benefits is met by the total contributions in that year. Unemployment and sickness are difficult to predict so the fund has a surplus – or contingency – to cover this risk (see **Table 7.1**). Contributory benefits can only be received if a person has been paying for a defined period.

Box 7.1: **Market failures and Income Support**

Unemployment

Nowhere in the world does the private sector provide insurance against unemployment. Brief cover for those who have mortgages is an exception. Full cover would be too risky for any private insurer because:

- risks of one person being unemployed are linked to others' risks. A slump would bankrupt an insurer;
- some individuals, such as the low-skilled, have a very high risk of lengthy unemployment. Their premiums would be high, their capacity to pay low;
- individuals have considerable influence over whether they get a job (moral hazard).

Long-term sickness

No private insurer or employer will give sick pay for an unlimited period:

- the cost over a lifetime would be high, the contributions small;
- moral hazard, delaying returning to work, is high.

Pensions

There is good information on people's life expectancy, retirement is relatively brief, and there are few problems with adverse selection. People who retire early receive lower pensions. Over half the UK population has a private pension of some form. Thus the market works, at least for some. But even here it does not work perfectly:

- Decisions about how big a pension you want, and in what form, have to be taken far in advance. People have difficulty thinking 30 or 40 years ahead and predicting their own preferences. They may give greater weight to current spending and not appreciate the need to save (myopia, as economists call it). People simply may not be able to appreciate their needs in retirement until they experience it. Evidence from the US health and retirement study suggests that a large minority of Americans save nothing and do not even think about retirement until they reach it (Lusardi, 1999).

   Contrary to assumptions of standard economics, people typically do not have clearly defined preferences, they lack information that would be necessary for a full analysis of the implications of various decisions regarding work and saving, they lack the mental capacity to analyse even the data that are available to them, they are heavily influenced by social networks and they tend retroactively to justify as optimal the courses of action that they happen to select. (Aaron, 1999, p 2)

- Inflation is unpredictable and all pensioners in an economy suffer from it simultaneously. Thus private schemes do not offer complete inflation proofing. In some countries, like the UK, limited inflation proofing is required.
- Private schemes depend on the valuation of stocks and shares at the time pensions are paid or annuities are bought. The stock market can be volatile.
- Occupational (that is, employer-based) schemes are designed to tie individuals to their company and reduce labour mobility.
- Just because contracts are so complex individuals may be at a disadvantage and be exploited or defrauded. Enron shares were held in the pension portfolios of Enron employees. When the firm collapsed so did employees' pension rights. Tough and complex regulations are now in place in the UK after the 'Maxwell' scandal in which the employer used his workers' pension scheme to try to save the firm from bankruptcy. But regulatory safeguards are also expensive to administer.

Box 7.2: National insurance contributory benefits

Contribution-based Jobseeker's Allowance (Unemployment Benefit)
Incapacity Benefit
Maternity Allowance
Widow's Payment
Widowed Mother's Allowance
Widow's Pension
Bereavement Payment
Widowed Parent's Allowance
Bereavement Allowance
Retirement Pension (Category A on your own contribution; Category B on spouse's contribution)
Graduated Retirement Benefit
Note: These benefits are only available to those who have built up a contribution record.

National insurance contributory rates (2003-04) (% of earnings)

Weekly earnings	Employee	Employer
Below £77 (lower earnings limit)	0	0
£77-£89 (primary and secondary thresholds)	0	0
£89 (upper earnings limit, £585 in 2002)	11	12.8
Above upper earnings limit	1	12.8

Table 7.1: The UK National Insurance Fund (1999/2000) (£ billions)

Receipts

Opening balance[a]	12.625
Contributions from employers and employees	51.852
Transfers from general taxation	0.853
Grant from Consolidated Fund (compensation for loss of income from employers when sickness benefits became payable by them)	0.625
Income from investing surplus	0.724
Other receipts	0.127
	66.206

Expenditure

Incapacity Benefit	7.206
Maternity Allowance	0.040
Widow's Pension	1.020
Guardian's Allowances and Child's Special Allowance	0.002
Retirement Pension	41.157
Pensioners' lump sum payments	0.126
Other payments	0.019
Administration	0.847
Transfers to Northern Ireland	0.230
Redundancy payments	0.174
Jobseeker's Allowance (contributory)	0.475
	51.297

Surplus	14.909

Note: [a] Surplus from previous years to cushion effects of a sudden rise in unemployment.

Source: DWP (2002a)

In some respects these benefits are like a private insurance scheme and it is sometimes claimed that as a result contributors have a 'right' to benefit in contrast to tax-funded and means-tested benefits. However:

- a right to benefit is wholly dependent on political decisions. In the 1980s Margaret Thatcher's government abolished wage-related sickness and Unemployment Benefit altogether and steadily reduced the relative scale of other benefits by linking them to prices not earnings;
- many non-means-tested benefits, like Child Benefit, are funded out of taxation (see **Box 7.3**);

Box 7.3: Tax-funded benefits

Non-contributory benefits (received as a right of status or condition)
Invalid Care Allowance
Disability Living Allowance
Attendance Allowance
Industrial Injuries benefit
Category D Retirement Pension (aged 80 or over)
Child Benefit
Guardian's Allowance

Means-tested benefits
Income Support
Income-based Jobseeker's Allowance
Housing Benefit
Tax credits

- the sums paid in, in any one year, equal payments. The surplus is not enough to secure future years' pensions if the government were to go bankrupt or decide not to collect any more contributions or workers voted not to pay as much. The scheme is a Pay-As-You-Go (PAYG) scheme (see more below);
- the payments are compulsory. A contribution implies a voluntary payment, and these are not. So to economists the payments are a tax. In the UK pension scheme workers can voluntarily contract out into a private scheme and reduce their contributions to the state scheme, which makes it less of a tax.

Tax credits

Since 1997, notably under the Chancellor Gordon Brown, support for the incomes of poorer families has increasingly taken the form of tax credits. These reduce a worker's taxation or supplement their income if that worker is not paying tax (see page 144). They are steadily reduced once a worker's income passes a set threshold. This has been part of a general strategy to *make work pay*. They have the same effect as a means-tested cash benefit but are administered through the Inland Revenue.

The first tax credits introduced by Gordon Brown in 1999 were the Working Families' Tax Credit (WFTC) and the Disabled Person's Tax Credit (DPTC). The WFTC replaced a cash benefit (Family Credit) which performed the same task but had a sharper rate of withdrawal, or 'taper', and was worth less.

The Child Care Tax Credit (CCTC) enables those with children who are working to claim help with meeting their 'relevant' childcare costs, as defined by the regulations, and up to a ceiling (in 2002 the limits were 70% of actual costs up to £135 a week for one child or £200 for two children).

From April 2003 the tax credit scheme has been extended to those on low pay with no children or disabilities, over the age of 25. The whole scheme becomes the Working Tax Credit (WTC) with a base amount supplemented by extra sums for couples, lone parents and for the costs of childcare. The taper is set at 37% – that is, the credit is reduced by 37p for each extra pound earned above the ceiling until it ceases. The calculations will be based on annual income. From the same date a new Child Tax Credit (CTC) brought together all the assistance given to families with children through the old WFTC, DPTC, Income Support and the Jobseeker's Allowance. It does *not* depend on the employment status of parents and is paid direct to the main carer – usually the mother.

Clearly such tax credits cost the government money. The big argument has been how to calculate and express it in the National Accounts. It can be seen as tax-not-collected – a *tax expenditure* (see pages 9-10). Or it can be seen as the cost of a cash benefit. After long debates with the Office for National Statistics (ONS) and the Organisation for Economic Co-operation and Development (OECD), it was agreed to count the expenditure as "negative taxation to the extent that credits are less than or equal to the tax liability of the household, and as public expenditure where credits actually exceed that liability" (HM Treasury, 2002a, p 216).

Thus when a family receives a cash payment and is not paying tax the sum counts as public expenditure. Where the family's tax bill is reduced it does not count as public spending. This makes it extremely difficult to track what is happening or what these massively important changes really cost. A line does appear in the budget putting a figure on the cost of the two elements, but in tracking public spending trends this sleight of hand needs to be watched. In 2002/03 the cost of tax credits to the Exchequer was estimated at £1.6 billion, or only a little more than 1% of the total social security budget.

Tax allowances

This is not the end of the taxpayer's involvement in Income Support. Those who pay into private pension schemes can reduce the level of income on which they pay tax. The older they are the higher the rate of tax relief. Up to the age of 50 people can contribute up to 17.5% of their earnings into a retirement scheme and reduce their taxable income accordingly. Aged 61-74 they can pay 27.5% of their earnings and gain relief. This costs the Exchequer a significant amount but it does not appear in the budget. About a fifth of all pension expenditure is financed through tax relief.

Finally, we have individual's own contributions to income smoothing through private insurance and retirement schemes. Over a quarter of all pension funding is of this purely private kind. In Table 7.2 we bring together all these forms of funding for the year 1999/2000 drawing on the work of colleagues in the Centre for Analysis of Social Exclusion and using the categories explained in Chapter One derived from Burchardt et al (1999).

Spending in other countries

The UK's public spending on child support, and particularly on pensions, is low compared with most other advanced economies. Its benefit levels are low in relation to average earnings or past earnings, but a relatively high percentage of its potential workforce are employed. Partly because state benefit levels are low and partly because of tax incentives, spending on private pensions is higher than in most other countries. The average income of a 65- to 74-year-old in the UK is about 65% of those aged 41-50. In other countries studied by the OECD the figure was nearer 80% in the mid-1990s (OECD, 2001c). The sources of pensions vary widely between countries (see Table 7.3).

How social security funds are allocated in the UK

Unlike the previous services that we have discussed, there is no process of geographical allocation. Individuals claim on the basis of their contribution record and situation. When they are sick they need a doctor's certificate. If they are over retirement age and have ceased regular employment they must present their birth certificate. They may apply for Income Support as a lone parent or young person, and provided that they can prove that their income is below support level, they should be entitled to benefit. Thus, unlike health or education departments, the Department for Work and Pensions does not have a fixed budget – a *departmental expenditure limit* (see page 187). Its budget is demand-led, determined by the number of people who qualify in any one year. Nevertheless, the Treasury does have some hold on spending because it has an important say in the decision about where benefit levels are set. These are fixed with agreed statutory rules in mind such as up-ratings, with inflation measured at a given date. But these rules change with political pressure. There have been major reviews of benefit rates and social security expenditure at least once or twice a decade since 1945, and many more smaller adjustments. In each budget, estimates of social security spending are presented to Parliament based on assumptions about levels of unemployment and numbers who will be eligible for Income Support given the predicted state of the economy.

Table 7.2: Funding Income Support, UK (1999/2000) (£ billions)

Category	Pensions only description	Amount	% of total pension spending
Public provision, finance and decision	Basic state pension	35.9	43.5
Public provision and finance, private decision on membership	SERPS (now second state pension)	4.5	5.4
Private provision, public finance, private decision	Contracted-out deduction for occupational pensions	6.5	22.2
	Tax relief	9.4	
	Incentive rebates for personal private pensions	2.4	
Private provision, finance and decision	Occupational pension contributions, employer and employee	19.9	28.9
	Personal pensions	3.9	

Category	All income security	Amount	% of income security
Public provision finance and decision	Basic state pension	35.9	
	Other social security	49.6	
	Child support	0.2	
	Total	**85.7**	**64.1**
Public provision and finance, private decision	SERPS (now second state pension)	4.5	3.4
Public provision, private finance, public decision	Payments by mostly ex-husbands via Child Support Agency	0.3	0.3
Private provision, public finance, private decision	Contracted-out deductions and tax relief	18.3	13.7
Private provision, finance and decision	Occupational and private pension contributions	23.8	18.5
	Other private welfare insurance eg permanent health insurance mortgage protection for unemployment and securers	0.9	
	Total	**133.6**	**100.0**

Source: HG's calculations

Table 7.3: **Combination of public and private pensions, international comparison (non-working males aged 65-69)**

	% who are:		Pension income as a % of average disposable income of working-age population	
	Beneficiaries of public pension	Beneficiaries of private pension	Public pension	Private pension
Canada	99.8	60.7	41.0	30.6
Finland	100.0	3.3	95.2	–
Germany	100.0	16.4	79.3	4.6
Italy	97.5	5.2	75.0	4.2
Japan	99.3	12.8	65.2	2.5
Netherlands	95.0	82.7	50.2	52.5
Sweden	100.0	88.2	87.8	25.8
UK	99.0	80.7	27.2	36.6
US	96.8	54.4	39.6	27.8

Source: Data from OECD (2001c)

The present structure of UK pensions

The basic state pension

This is funded from compulsory contributions made by employers, employees and the self-employed, as described above.

The Pension Credit

From April 2003 this subsumed the old Minimum Income Guarantee for pensioners and adds to it. Those on modest incomes in retirement have their incomes made up to a guaranteed minimum. But instead of losing all the value of any modest extra income above the basic pension, for example, from an occupational pension or the second state pension (below), they keep part of it up to a ceiling. The credit tapers off at the rate of 40%. This is, essentially, a means-tested supplementary pension with a longer taper.

The second or additional state pension

This replaced SERPS in April 2002. Employees and employers who have not contracted out of the scheme fund it. It is particularly designed for low-paid employees and women who will be deemed to have a minimum level of earnings in calculating their pension whether or not they contributed. In 2002/03 this minimum income was £10,800. This amounts to a subsidy to the lowest paid and tapers off as individuals earn more. Those who used to be members of SERPS have their pension calculated on the amount of pension accrued up to April 2002 on the old rules, plus any earned from that date under the new rules.

Occupational pensions

Employers have to include employees in the second state pension scheme unless they are members of a salary-related, or defined benefit, occupational scheme – or employees may be in a money purchase scheme to which the employer contributes. (Here what you get as a pension depends on what the fund is worth when you retire – a defined contribution scheme.)

Personal pensions

There are two kinds of such pension. *Approved personal pensions* are where employees are contracted out of the second state pension. Employers rarely contribute to such schemes. *Group personal pensions* are pensions that belong to the individual but are arranged for the firm's workforce.

Stakeholder private pensions

These are private pensions targeted at those on low incomes. Employers who do not provide occupational pensions or fail to contribute otherwise must offer a stakeholder pension. They do not have to contribute. Charges for administering such schemes must be kept to 1% of the fund value. Other restrictions are imposed and membership is voluntary.

Additional Voluntary Contributions

On top of the above schemes, all of which carry some element of compulsion, there are Additional Voluntary Contributions (AVCs). These are added to an occupational scheme and they attract tax relief as described earlier.

The private pension industry complains that the UK system is now too complicated even for pension consultants to fully understand. This is especially unhelpful given the points Aaron (1999) made about ordinary people's difficulty in the face of complexity.

A way out of the maze?

A precondition is to face up to a harsh fact. A population that is living longer *and* working fewer years, as ours has been, must either save more out of current earnings, be taxed more heavily, or work longer to sustain income in retirement. The government has spelt this out in a consultative paper (DWP, 2002b). It finds that, under the UK's relatively voluntary approach, perhaps 3 million people are seriously underprovided for in their retirement. A further 5-10 million may need some more savings to earn an adequate pension. The government assumes that half to two thirds' previous pay is 'adequate' given the reduced obligations of those who are retired and what the average household receives. It concludes that the UK should continue with its basic voluntary approach to pensions supported by targeted help to the poorest. But to encourage saving it should simplify the Byzantine tax rules that cover private pensions, simplify the rules that govern private pensions and give more information to people about their likely pensions. Compelling people to save a given percentage of their income for old age is rejected, but is to be kept under review. Specifically, the White Paper proposes:

- giving individuals information about their future pensions – state pensions first, other pensions as soon as practicable;
- it rejects increasing the state retirement age, preferring to concentrate on encouraging more people to work until they are 65 in the first instance (raising the full pension state retirement age might have given a strong signal which would have helped achieve this result);
- increasing the incentives to stay on at work. Tax changes covering private schemes, higher pensions and lump sums for those who delay retirement;
- simplifying the tax rules and regulations that govern private and occupational schemes;
- appointing a Pensions Commission to keep the question of compulsory private pension contributions under review. If possible people should be left free to choose how much to save for retirement;
- it was not enthusiastic about retaining defined benefit final salary schemes (see page 152). They were not suited to those who moved jobs frequently and were employed by small firms. However, it did admit that if a shift from defined benefit to defined contribution schemes (see page 152) led to a significant reduction in employers' contributions (as it has done), this would "pose a serious problem" (DWP, 2002b, p 52).

In short, the government has set itself the task of simplifying the rules governing private pension schemes. It has not sought any simplification in the interaction of public and private schemes. This is something many reformers would like to see happen but all the main alternatives have their problems. To introduce a dominant state scheme with a high replacement rate on the style of the, now reformed, Swedish or German pension schemes, to which all would be forced to belong, has its problems. It would take a long time to mature and involve high contribution rates. If it were made compulsory for all, it would destroy many existing funded private pension schemes as people would not be able to afford belonging to both. Some kind of opting-out would be necessary. Hence the scope for subsidising the pensions of the poor from the contributions of the rich would be small. Whatever its intrinsic merits, the path UK pensions have taken in the past 20 years rules out this route.

Another option is to return to a contributory flat rate state pension set at Income Support level or to introduce a citizens' income at that level for all who reached some set age. This would take all older people off means-tested pensions, although many would still be on Housing Benefit and hence subject to a means test. It would be very expensive, but it would enable the government to phase out both the second state pension and the Pension Credit. It would remove the disincentive to save. The Institute for Public Policy Research report (Brooks et al, 2002) suggested raising the full pension retirement age to 67 for both men and women to pay for such a policy. People could retire earlier but on a reduced pension. It has been suggested by the Pension Policy Institute that the normal retirement age when you get your full state pension should go up to 70.

A third option is to abolish the state pension, to force all people to belong to private-funded pension schemes and to keep the Minimum Income Guarantee. This would be done gradually, applying to all pensioners retiring after a given date. This was the scheme proposed by the Conservative Party in 1997, and it was not popular!

The final option would be to adopt an Australian model, with a flat rate pension at Income Support level for about two thirds of the population by taxing it away from the upper-income groups. This pension could take the form of a tax credit. This still has some savings disincentive effect but probably not that great. On top there would be compulsory membership of private or occupational pension schemes to which employers would have to contribute. For the moment such radical alternatives seem off the government's agenda. If the pensions issue deepens they may be forced back on.

Public assistance

The oldest systems of Income Support were what we today call *public assistance*. They began in medieval Europe, Lyon in France and in the cities of Germany.

These were local responses to the movement of poor peasants into the cities and were locally funded. Similarly English Poor Relief began as a local parish endeavour which came to be centrally regulated from the early 1600s. It was still locally administered, in part, right up to 1948, although central funding grew, notably with the mass unemployment of the 1930s. The 1948 National Assistance Act established what is still an unusual model internationally. The central state set a national minimum income or safety net. Any resident unable to work for a good reason had a right to have their income raised to a given level consistent with the nature of the family unit. A 'wage stop' prevented that income exceeding previous wages. The scheme was administered nationally through local offices of the National Assistance Board. Its modern variant, Income Support, is administered by the Department for Work and Pensions. Crucially it was, and still is, financed by central government out of general taxation. (There is a small local contribution to the housing element as we shall see in the next chapter.) Most other countries retain often very large elements of local administration and significant amounts of local funding.

In the **US** the 1996 welfare reforms largely turned responsibility back to the states. The federal government gave the states a set amount and required limits to the length of time welfare recipients could receive benefits. Beyond that states were left with the responsibility of providing for the poor. Not even at the height of its interventionist phase did the US federal government require states to support poor men, or women without children.

In **Continental Europe**, including Scandinavia, locally administered, partially locally funded, public assistance is still the norm. Generous contributory social insurance schemes can coexist with very ungenerous local public assistance. Often the giving of social work support and cash income go together as they did in pre-1948 Britain. For a categorisation of public assistance schemes see Gough et al (1997).

Under the pressure of rising unemployment, concern over social exclusion and pressure on local tax revenues, central governments in Europe have become more involved.

In **Germany**, *cost-of-living assistance* is a form of income guarantee to meet an individual's basic needs if other forms of income, including from the wider family, do not make this possible. The federal government sets out what basic needs should be met but the Länder set the actual cash figures that vary between Länder and are lower in the east, for example. The national law of 1961 creates what is essentially a national system locally administered – the exception is Bavaria (non-residents and asylum-seekers are not included but come under a different programme). Local government taxation meets the cost of this income support scheme.

In **France** a complex, if generous, pattern of social insurance schemes left many excluded, the origin of the term 'social exclusion'. Once again it was locally administered and financed public assistance that took the strain. The

Socialist government in 1988 introduced a nationally funded cash assistance scheme called the *Revenue Minimum d'Insertion* (RMI). The cash benefit element of this programme is funded nationally but the element that seeks to reintegrate people into the labour market is largely financed at departmental (regional) level. Local authorities have to pay 20% of the cost of local programmes.

A significant local involvement is still evident in **Scandinavia**, although reduced by work incentive schemes in recent years. Despite generous social insurance schemes, Scandinavia has a very localised system of public assistance. In Norway the finance of assistance is the responsibility of local authorities. They set benefit levels in relation to the local cost of living and determine eligibility. There has been an element of 'work testing' since 1991 when some attempt at a national framework was attempted, but its extent, in practice, varies between local authorities.

There are, in short, big differences in the way countries finance their public assistance programmes and the UK's nationally funded, defined and administered, safety net remains unusual.

Pensions in other countries

The UK is also highly unusual in the way it finances pensions, at least among advanced economies. This difference is set to grow. We have already seen that privately financed pensions are more important than in most other advanced economies. The Netherlands is the only other European country to rely as heavily on private pensions. The Labour government intends to reduce the state's role even further – the goal is to reduce the share of pension income financed by the state from 60% to 40% by the middle of the 21st century. The actual share of the GDP spent on pensions could fall slightly – in every other European country it will rise significantly (see **Figure 7.2**), on present policies.

Care should be taken with such predictions. They tend to ignore the risks to the state budget if private pension schemes fail, and often exclude means-tested Income Support for older people. Most other OECD countries are trying to reduce pension promises and future state budgets. The UK debate is about whether state provision should actually be *increased*.

Strategies of reform internationally can be grouped into four types (Disney, 2000):

- *changes to the basic 'parameters' of state schemes:* the age of retirement, the nature of indexation (a shift from wages to prices for example); and the replacement rate;
- *introducing actuarial 'fairness' between the generations.* It makes a cohort's pension level dependent on its not increasing the burden on the next generation. Sweden's recent reforms are an example;

Figure 7.2: State pension spending as a % of GDP (2000 and 2050)

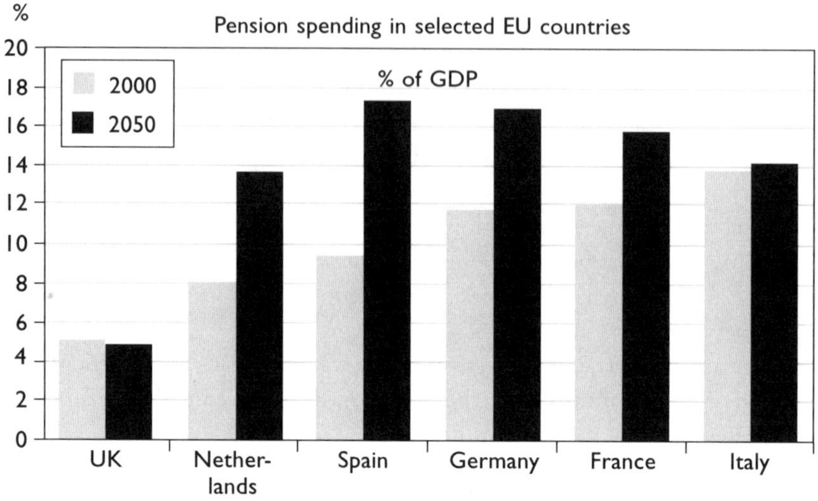

Pension spending in selected EU countries

Legend:
- 2000
- 2050

% of GDP

Source: HM Treasury (2002g)

- *'clean break' privatisation:* beyond a given date, or for a given cohort, no more contributions are made to the state scheme and required contributions are made to approved private schemes. Chile is the obvious model here;
- *partial privatisation:* individuals may be required, or encouraged, to contribute to approved private schemes on top of contributing to the state scheme. The recent Swedish and German reforms are of this kind.

Countries' pension schemes still vary widely.

The **Netherlands** has a system that is perhaps nearest to that in the UK except for two features that are much in its favour. First, it is simple, and second it has a more generous minimum. It has a flat rate pension that depends on a person's years of residence in the Netherlands, paid from taxation, not on a contribution. Women thus qualify by virtue of citizenship, just the same as men and those unable to earn. The level set for long-term residents takes citizens above the poverty line. Beyond that the state essentially requires workers to be members of private occupational schemes which are of a defined benefit nature. **Ireland**, too, has a tax-financed basic pension. **Canada** is similar to the UK in some respects. It has a flat rate state pension but topped up with an income-tested addition and an earnings-related public pension. Occupational and private pensions play a big role.

Denmark has a basic pension that is tax-financed, with compulsory membership of defined contribution schemes built on top for those who are members of collective agreements between employees and employers.

At the other end of the spectrum are those countries with compulsory membership of wage-related state pension schemes. The purest model, perhaps surprisingly, is the **US**. In 1935, under President Roosevelt, the Social Security Act began a federal pension scheme which was gradually extended to nearly all the US population. It excludes federal and state employees. The benefit formula redistributes contributions towards those on low pay. It is financed entirely from employer and employee contributions and is currently running a substantial surplus in order to help pay for additional pensioners in the next half century. Full pension age is gradually being raised from 65 to reach 67 by 2022. Despite being accused by critics of being in crisis, the US pension scheme is probably one of the most secure. It is also moderately generous for the average and below-average paid worker. President Bush has proposed permitting individuals to contract out of part of the scheme if they invest in private pensions. This would involve *reducing* the federal pension if the scheme were to stay in balance. The President's Commission (2002) proposed various alternative schemes. Little progress in gaining congressional support was evident at the time of writing. For those with a poor or non-existent contribution record there is a means-tested federal system of income support for older people, but it is *not* generous.

Sweden and **Germany** have wage-related contribution and benefit schemes which date from the 1950s. Both countries have been concerned by the cost of their schemes. **Sweden** discussed ways of reducing the commitments to future pensioners who are living longer and requiring a steadily increasing contribution rate from current workers. An agreed scheme followed four years of inter-party discussion. A 'notional' defined contribution scheme has been introduced which calculates how much pension is affordable, given the agreed maximum contribution rate of 16.5% of earnings. Given the life expectancy of each age group of retirees, that replacement rate may have to be steadily reduced. Each individual's contributions are recorded in an account that nominally earns interest. The scheme remains PAYG, so in fact these are 'credits' that are transformed into a pension entitlement by a figure that factors in changes in life expectancy, GDP growth, salary and years of employment. The pension will be fixed in a way that will keep the scheme in balance. If life expectancy goes up and GDP growth slows, the pension will be less than for previous generations. On top of the 16.5% contribution of earnings to the state scheme, a further 2.5% *must* be paid into a funded scheme. Most choose an approved private-funded scheme but people have the option of contributing to a residual state-funded scheme. The **German** reforms of 2001 are similar, except that the additional contributions to funded schemes are voluntary, encouraged by subsidies from the government, particularly in the case of the low paid. In fact the reform is being reassessed as relatively few people opted to pay more! The pay roll tax is to be capped at 22%. The standard state replacement rate is to fall slightly from 70 to 67%. The hope was that private provision would raise the total pension provision back to 70%. This was not happening by late 2002. The private schemes had to comply with a wide range of regulations to attract tax relief.

Chile forms the pure privatised model. State pensions in Chile were fully privatised in the early 1980s. Workers had to belong to a private funded scheme of a defined contribution type. They were given government bonds in compensation for lost pension rights. This means that all the risks of future economic uncertainty fall on the individual. Workers had to contribute 10% of their earnings plus a commission charge to a privately run scheme. There is no redistribution to poorer workers within the scheme, and pensions are indexed to prices not to growth in earnings.

Nevertheless, the transition to a new system was, and could be more, costly for the government. The current pensioners have to be paid. Taxes have to be raised from workers already contributing 10% of their wages for themselves. If future private pensions fail, the government will have to pay a means-tested tax-funded minimum income. Many people do not pay the 10% as they are in the informal economy. Some, including the World Bank (1994), sing the praises of this scheme. Others are more doubtful (Diamond, 1996; Barr, 2001b).

Australia, like Chile, has compulsory membership of funded schemes. Employers are required to contribute to their workers' schemes. The compulsion began at 3% of earnings in 1992 but by 2002 had reached 9%. Compulsory saving is, however, built on an extensive tax-funded basic pension: the Age Pension. It is funded from general taxation and is subject to an 'affluence test'. It is withdrawn from high earners.

New Zealand has a universal flat rate pension financed out of general taxation that is not separately affluence-tested but is taxed as part of a person's income. The pension is set at two thirds of the average wage. A proposal to replace this pension with a Chile type scheme was heavily defeated in 1997 in a special referendum.

France is an example of another widespread problem, as is **Greece**. Although pensions for the wider public have been somewhat scaled back, those for public servants remain generous. Attempts to reduce them have led to massive public sector strikes. While full pensions in the private sector accrue after 40 years, for the public sector it is 37.5. The public sector pension is calculated on the worker's best 10 years. In the private sector it is 25. Similarly, retirement ages are 60 and 65 respectively. Attempts to encourage private sector pensions have not been very successful. President Chirac's new government in 2002 was pledged to make some progress with pension reform (*Economist*, 8 June 2002).

Japan, with its rapidly ageing population and generous pension provision that derives from the period of its youthful workforce, faces the most difficult adjustment of any of the advanced economies (Takayama 1992; Endo and Katayama, 1998).

In short, pension finance is one of politics' hottest potatoes worldwide.

Improving choice and efficiency

Arguments about consumer choice and economic efficiency in income support systems are partly analogous to those in health, the caring services and education. Will competition between pension or sickness benefit schemes promote more efficiency and consumer choice than relying on a single national pension scheme? Is market failure significant? The efficiency debate ranges more widely in the case of social security. Does the very existence of generous income support weaken the incentive to work and to save? If it does, it has a major impact on the whole economy. The economic stakes are higher.

Work incentives

The view that generous levels of state support to the poor lead to individuals not working is not new. The debates about the old Poor Law from 1770 to 1834 were about precisely this. The workhouse test – the notion that the workhouse should be a less attractive option than living on the lowest wage that the market offered – came directly from the new liberal economists of the time. This idea runs through the 19th and 20th century debates. The fact that it often resulted in harsh regimes for the poor does not mean that the fear was misplaced. By the 1980s research was suggesting that relatively generous income support schemes, with lax ways of encouraging employable people back into work, were a major contributory factor in producing high levels of *long-term* unemployment (Layard, 1997).

The much wider dispersion of incomes that occurred in the 1970s and 1980s contributed to the problem. Between 1975 and 1999 the real value of wages of the poorest 10% barely changed. The rewards to the top 10% meanwhile steadily rose. For the lowest paid, work became increasingly valueless compared with Income Support (McKnight, 2002). Faced with the dilemma governments could:

- drive people back into work by keeping benefits low and withdrawing benefits if welfare recipients did not take up work;
- accept that a rising number of people on Income Support was a price worth paying for social cohesion;
- try to lift the floor of low wages by raising the minimum wage and by supplementing wages through the tax and benefit system.

Different countries in the 1990s tried different combinations of these strategies (Evans, 2001; Lødemel and Trickey, 2001). The UK government tried to tighten up work requirements for those on benefit and took measures to 'make work pay' through introducing a National Minimum Wage as well as tax benefits that supplemented low wages. Although relatively few people may have been 'forced' into work by specific schemes, labour economists suggest that these measures, and others, reduced the level of long-term unemployment and the point at which the economy tips into inflation. In the 1980s the UK economy had to be given doses of deflation with interest rates raised, when there was still nearly 10% unemployment. By 2001 the economy seemed able to run in a non-inflationary way, nearer to 5% unemployment (Nickell and Quintini, 2002). In so far as this was the result of changing the Income Support system and 'making work pay', then the macroeconomic benefits have been huge. Atkinson has argued for many years that the structures of benefit systems are critical determinants of individual jobseeking behaviour (Atkinson and Micklewright, 1991). Yet, as McKnight (2002) shows, it is still the case that work is *less likely* to lift the poor out of poverty than it was before the economic changes of the 1970s. Those countries that have been most successful in limiting poverty have done so by active measures to correct their low wage labour markets – education, training and wages policies. There is a limit to what Income Support alone can do.

Saving incentives

Economists argue that individuals seek to smooth their income through their lives. People save in order to insure themselves against income shocks, such as sickness, and expected losses of earned income that occur when age prevents them competing effectively in the labour market, when their skills and health have declined (Modigliani and Brumberg, 1954; Burtless, 1999). In making their lifetime income plan people take account of what the state is doing. If the state provides a decent pension this reduces the need to save – the income smoothing has been done for them. Individuals will take some account of how well the state has performed. Where it has done a bad job, as in the UK, individuals will be more prone to save or to pay into private pension schemes. If the state administers its pension scheme on a PAYG basis, with contribution income equalising pension spending in each year, as most schemes do, the state will not be saving. Hence, the level of savings in the economy will be lower than if the state had not provided pensions. If savings levels are low, economic growth rates will be low because savings finance investment. The classic statement of this view and international evidence in its favour derives from the American economist Martin Feldstein (1974, 1980). It underpinned the case for a general shift from state to private pensions. A furious debate followed. Other economists have concluded that it is not that simple!

- Even in theory, increases in savings will only occur during the build-up period of private pensions. When the schemes are mature the running down of the pension fund by pensioners will equal the new savings of workers.

- More saving for retirement may lead to less saving for other things. People may have a current income target that does not change much. Private pensions merely change *for what* people save. Evidence seems to support this view (Lusardi, 1999).
- More saving in an economy does not necessarily produce higher investment.
- The transition from a PAYG to a funded system has problems. If past pension promises are simply withdrawn, and pensioners suffer a large income loss, savings overall may rise. But if governments feel unable to do this, taxes will have to rise to pay pensions while the current generation of workers start to contract out of state schemes and pay into private ones. Higher taxes may reduce the savings of the working population.

Given these problems it is not surprising that the evidence for a rise in savings with new funded pensions is weak. "Taking the evidence as a whole, there is no robust confirmation that a switch from PAYG to funding increases saving in any country except the USA; and the US evidence is controversial" (Barr, 2001b, p 103). Evidence from the UK (Disney et al, 2001) suggests that incentives to join private pension schemes have increased the rate of saving but not by much – perhaps 0.2% by the end of the 1990s. It is also spread differentially across income groups. Only 40% of those in the lower-income groups were saving 'enough' for a reasonable pension; 75% of the higher income groups were.

To fund or not to fund?

The arguments for and against funding go beyond the savings issue to the political economy of pensions. Most state pensions schemes are PAYG, although they do not have to be. Private pension schemes are funded. There has to be sufficient money invested in a fund to secure the future pensioners some kind of pension. A defined benefit scheme means that the fund must be big enough to secure a pension that is set, for example, in relation to the final salary of the member. Or it may be set in relation to an employee's lifetime earnings. A defined contribution scheme merely requires that a given percentage of an individual's salary is paid into the fund. What comes out as a pension will be whatever the fund managers secure from their investments in stocks, shares and government bonds (see **Box 7.4**).

In the early years of state pension schemes there was much to be said politically for PAYG. At first only a small part of the population was covered. Then new types of workers were included. The growth in the number of contributors was larger than the growth in the numbers drawing a pension. The growth in the economy was also larger than the growth in the pension population. Income

Box 7.4: **Defined benefit and defined contribution schemes**

Defined benefit schemes have benefits which are specified independently of both the contributions payable and the investments of the scheme. A typical scheme might pay a proportion of final salary on the basis of duration of employment, for example, one sixtieth of final salary for each year of service. Following the 1995 Pensions Act all defined benefit schemes are required to offer limited price indexation up to a maximum of 5% per annum on rights accrued after April 1997, and most public pensions schemes index benefits to Retail Price Index. Just under half of private sector defined benefit schemes operate a 'clawback' mechanism which makes an adjustment to payments to take account of the value of the basic state pension (Government Actuary's Department, 2001).

Defined contribution schemes have predetermined contributions, with benefit levels dependent upon total contributions achieved, investment returns within the fund, and annuity rates at the time the individual's fund is converted into a pension. Each individual has an account, usually funded, which builds up in value until retirement when it is used to buy an annuity.

To the individual, the advantages of defined benefit schemes are commonly understood as increased predictability of benefits and insurance from investment risk, which lies in the first instance with the employer offering the benefits. However, defined benefit schemes often suffer from a lack of portability between jobs, as such schemes are frequently designed to improve workforce retention in the first place. In addition, workers face the risk of premature employment termination which can significantly reduce the value of benefits based on final salary values. Defined contribution schemes are generally more portable, but usually expose the individual to significant investment and annuity rate risk. Some companies operate hybrid schemes with both defined benefit and defined contribution elements.

Approximately 46% of all employees, including those working part-time, were in occupational schemes in 1995. This figure comprised 52% of male employees and 39% of women (Government Actuary's Department, 2001). Historically, coverage for men remained above 60% from the early 1960s to the early 1980s before declining to the 1995 level. Coverage among female employees has risen slowly from around 20% in 1963 to its present level. Of the 6.1 million members of private sector occupational schemes, three quarters were in defined benefit schemes, 18% were in defined contribution schemes and the balance were in hybrid arrangements in 1995. Virtually all public sector schemes have defined benefits (more recently there has been a significant shift to defined contribution schemes).

Source: Brooks et al (2002, p 32), reproduced with permission

rose faster than pension pay-outs. Politicians could agree to growing pensions without imposing higher contributions, and this proved a highly popular game! (See **Box 7.5** for a good description of the process and also some caveats.)

As the size of the older population grew and economic growth rates declined, the balance changed. State pensions now have to be financed by growing contributions from the working population in most countries.

Would funding be a solution to the ageing issue? Again the answer seems to be no, or at the very least, only partially so. The essential task of a pension scheme is to give the non-earning population a claim on the resources produced by the earning, working, population. That remains true whatever the funding mechanism. In PAYG schemes the government simply taxes the working population. It may be politically difficult – workers want to retain the rewards of their labour. However, exactly the same problem arises with a funded scheme. The non-earning section of the population has to capture the production of those in work in just the same way. In funded schemes that process is achieved by scooping the profits of the firms in which the pension fund has invested. The workers in those firms must forgo the rewards of their labour to pay the last generation. They may object as workers just as they may object as taxpayers. Successful resistance brings wage inflation, price rises and real pensions decline.

So far we have assumed a closed economy, with no international investments. One attraction of a funded scheme is that it can invest in the output of young countries, but that has its own risks, as the South East Asia crisis showed. Barr (2001b) has a whole chapter in which he debunks ten myths about the advantages of funded schemes. Recent experience in the UK shows that private pension promises are not secure. Poor returns on the stock market and rising expectation of life are reducing expected levels of private pensions. During the 1980s and 1990s, when stock markets were rising, firms took 'contribution holidays'. They ceased contributing because the rising capital value meant that the fund could pay pensions without the employers contributing. Falling capital values and recession have placed firms in a difficult position. It is doubtful if such 'holidays' should actually be permitted. Firms have also taken the advantage of switching from defined benefit to defined contribution schemes in order to reduce their commitment (*The Guardian*, 26 June 2002). Both private funding and state PAYG therefore have their risks. Neither painlessly solve the financial problems of an ageing population.

The UK government has not done well in keeping its pension promises. One way to hedge bets against the risks of private market and government failure is to go for a mix of both. In the end individuals may produce their own solutions. As pension incomes fall relative to past earnings they may work longer to sustain their living standards. All advanced economies will become short of labour as low birth rates feed through into falling labour supply. From the late 19th century on, the coming of pensions and their

Box 7.5: The 'Ponzi Game' nature of unfunded social security

A good deal of analysis of the relative merits of funded and unfunded social security has rested on the scheme satisfying the so-called 'Aaron–Samuelson' condition, named after seminal articles by Aaron (1966) and Samuelson (1958). Samuelson considered an economy where goods were perishable and where people sought to retire from producing their own consumption goods later in life. His point was that individual lifetime utility could be maximised if a 'social contract' could be arranged, so that each generation paid a 'pension' to each preceding generation, such that the implicit return on the contract was equal to the rate of population growth. Since the return on storing perishable goods was negative and population growth was likely to be positive, such an 'unfunded' scheme would be socially optimal. Aaron's generalisation of this 'rule' linked the equilibrium 'return' on unfunded social security to the rate of growth of earnings, being the sum of earnings growth per head and the growth of population. The mechanical application of the 'condition', in a world with capital, would simply compare the rate of return on capital (the return on a funded scheme) with the return on an unfunded scheme, as derived above. Where the latter was high, an unfunded scheme was superior to each generation simply relying on its own saving.

Samuelson's paper bears careful rereading, not least where he discusses the issue of how such a 'social contract' can be maintained. It is extremely hard to think of practical mechanisms by which such contracts can be replicated and implemented by successive generations, without imposing assumptions about the nature of transactions costs (Esteban and Sakovics, 1993), or the behaviour of agents (Hansson and Stuart, 1989). The key point of unfunded social security is that the financing of accruing liabilities is left to future generations. In that case, it bears much the same character as the schemes of Charles Ponzi, an originator of the use of chain letters to raise money.

In particular, if the initial generation in an unfunded scheme obtains a 'return' on its contributions in excess of the Aaron-Samuelson 'rule', later generations will have to accept lower returns to preserve the stability of the scheme. But it is tempting for subsequent generations to attempt to maintain the high initial rates of return by legislating overgenerous benefit accruals for themselves, the liabilities for which will in turn be passed on to subsequent generations. The only constraint on this ratcheting up of programme liabilities is where a generation believed that a subsequent generation will simply renege on future commitments made by a prior generation. Ageing, by making such reneging behaviour more likely given the extra burden it imposes on workers, may actually make pension reform more likely.

Source: Extract from Disney (2000, pp F12-13), reproduced with permission

> *Some caveats to this description*
> There are two basic reasons for the danger in such games. They are based on unsustainable promises and they are voluntary so that once things go wrong people bail out. PAYG state pensions schemes do not have to be unsustainable if they are responsibly managed and they are compulsory. That compulsion, however, depends on electorates' support.

increased size led to people being able to afford a shorter working life. This trend may be reversed – as life grows longer so may working life.

To target or not to target?

At first sight it may seem obvious that with a limited tax capacity the most efficient strategy is to concentrate those tax resources on the poorest. This should enable government either to support a more generous poverty line or alternatively spend money on, for example, the NHS. What use is the present basic pension to the Duke of Westminster? There are, moreover, fewer spill-over benefits than derive from poor and rich children being educated together, for example. However, there are macroeconomic drawbacks to targeting:

* *Disincentives to saving:* if individuals know that if they save for retirement much of the private pension or income from savings will reduce their state pension they may rationally choose not to save, especially if their private incomes would be low and virtually wiped out by loss of state pension. Targeting or means testing is seen as a penalty on those who have worked and saved hard.
* *Failure to apply either from complexity, ignorance or stigma:* official estimates put the non-take-up of the Minimum Income Guarantee at between a fifth and a third of pensioner households. The amounts not being taken up are significant.
* *Weakened political support for generous pensions:* if most pensioners are not receiving a state pension, political interest in keeping it generous may fade. The fact that the UK basic pension is so low may be related to the fact that most pensioners now have other income. Once in this situation a climb back to a high compulsory state pension is all but impossible.

These objections are not conclusive. The amount of savings lost may be quite small if the range of incomes involved in the 'savings trap' is small. All households can be forced to contribute to pension schemes, as in Australia and Chile. Some measures can be taken to protect the savings of poorer households. Income derived from savings can be exempt from tax, up to a point. That is what the new Pension Credit is designed to do (see page 140).

However, the economists' worries about savings disincentives, pension companies' concerns about losing customers, the sheer complexity of the system and popular feelings of injustice combined to lead the government to begin to rethink its pension policy (Brooks et al, 2002; *Financial Times*, 16 June 2002).

Pensions for carers

One of the major drawbacks of all contribution-based schemes, public or private, is that many people do not have the opportunity to build up enough contributions to earn a decent pension. This particularly applies to women who, traditionally, give up work for a period to bring up children and enter less secure and lower-paid employment. Some state pension schemes do, however, count years spent on caring duties as if the person were contributing. After 1975 people caring for young children acquired pension rights for doing so – contributions are credited to those with caring responsibilities in the new second state pension in the UK and Sweden does the same in its pension scheme. It has been argued that such an arrangement should be extended to private and occupational pension schemes in the UK paid for by the Exchequer (Falkingham and Rake, 1999). The state would pay a given sum into a person's pension scheme for each year they drew Child Benefit or a Carer's Benefit.

Because of job changes and minimal employer cover, young people are saving very little for retirement. Older workers are retiring early. These are worrying trends if pensions for a longer life are to be adequate.

Overview

- Fundamental differences of opinion that exist about the purposes of state income support affect the design of social security systems in different countries and in the UK over time.

- The UK has one of the lowest projected levels of state spending on pensions, one of the most complex patterns of pension arrangements, and relatively low incomes in old age. There is a serious case for reform.

- Funded private pensions do not provide an easy way out of the dilemma. As expectation of life has risen, so working life has decreased. This is unsustainable. A higher pension age, however pensions are funded, seems a precondition for a viable old age.

Questions for discussion

1. What is the case for insurance markets as a way of smoothing income through time? What are the market failures in pensions and unemployment insurance?

2. Should the role of the state be confined to poverty relief? Should the state require individuals to save for contingencies such as sickness and old age?

3. How has it come about that the UK has by far the lowest state expenditure on pensions of any advanced economy?

4. What are 'contributory benefits' and 'non-contributory benefits'?

5. What is the case for and against funded-pension schemes? To what extent are public PAYG pensions schemes a 'Ponzi Game'?

Further reading

The best presentation of the economic theory underlying insurance markets is **Barr (1998, Chapters 8-10)**. **Barr (2001b, Chapters 6-9)** contains the key arguments about funding versus non-funding, privatising pensions and pension reform.

The best up-to-date accessible review of UK pensions with policy proposals is the Institute for Public Policy Research study **(Brooks et al, 2002)**.

Hills (2003) reviews the case for continuing any form of national insurance.

The government's Green Paper **(DWP, 2002b)** on pensions contains a lot of useful material and analysis.

The **World Bank (1994)** review, even if you do not agree with its conclusions, contains a clear description of the world's pension schemes and has been a hugely influential document. Other international reviews well worth reading are:

, The Brookings Institution study edited by **Bosworth and Burtless (1998)**;

, **Disney's (2000)** paper;

, The **OECD (2001c)** review has a lot of useful comparisons;

, The Child Poverty Action Group's annually updated *Welfare benefits handbook* is an indispensable reference guide through the complexity of UK income maintenance benefits **(CPAG, 2002)**.

Financing housing

Summary

- Shelter is one of the most basic human needs, but it is provided primarily through the private market.

- Nevertheless the state does play a major role in its regulation and finance.

- The state regulates standards of housing that is permitted to be built, the level of occupation and amenities in existing properties for public health reasons. It determines where housing can be built and at what density. Governments give tax advantages to those buying houses in most countries, although no longer in the UK.

- The state directly subsidises the cost of housing for poor people by some of the following methods:
  - limits the rents that can be charged by private landlords;
  - subsidises low interest loans to those building houses for poor or needy households;
  - helps poor families pay their rents through tied cash benefits.

Housing policy evolves

There are conflicting pressures in the evolution of housing:

- Shelter is a basic human need but housing is also a consumer product about which households have very different preferences. Some prefer tranquil countryside, others busy cities. Place and neighbourhood are a major part of the choices people want to make. Views about living in a particular place, if widely shared, put a scarcity value on the property and area concerned. Those possessing housing in desirable areas resist new development. Markets and choice may be the best way to resolve these pressures.
- The absence of decent shelter in a safe environment leads individuals on a downward spiral of dependence and social exclusion (Hills et al, 2002).
- In times of war, economic or environmental crisis, the acute shortage of housing leads states to take exceptional measures to ration access to shelter and control its prices.
- A range of market failures apply to housing, as they have to other services we have studied (see **Box 8.1**).

These conflicting pressures can be seen in action in the history of housing policy. In the UK during the 19th century private builders and developers responded to the great movement of citizens into the new industrial centres. By the end of the 19th century 93% of all housing was provided by private landlords for rent. The market worked, after a fashion, just as it has today in the developing world: people set up their own rudimentary shelters in the shanty towns that surround cities like Mexico City, Buenos Aires and Cape Town. In a developing country the best thing for the state to do may be to ensure clean water supply and refuse disposal, leaving the informal housing market to cope as best it can. In the 19th-century UK, the market certainly responded by providing accommodation, but the lack of sanitation and overcrowding in industrial cities led to epidemics that threatened the whole of urban society. The public health acts were then set up to require minimum standards of building.

Local councils could, and still can, condemn and demolish 'slums' that were considered unfit for human habitation. Such demolition powers were used on a large scale until the 1970s – such action has a devastating impact on the private housing market, which could no longer operate at the bottom end. The poor could not afford new housing, built to these new higher standards. Overcrowding of existing property grew worse. The Victorians looked to philanthropy to step in and provide what the market would not. To some extent it did, but to nothing like the extent needed.

The 1890 Housing the Working Classes Act gave local authorities the power to build but not the funding to enable them to subsidise the costs of building

Box 8.1: **Market failures in housing**

- Overcrowded and insanitary housing poses a health risk to a population far beyond the immediate occupants. (See 'negative externality', pages 19-20)
- The clustering of poor accommodation in an area may not make it worthwhile for individual owners to improve their property. Property values do not increase because of the negative spillover effects of the bad property and bad 'signals' the area as a whole gives. Improvement of the whole area by collective action can spark a virtuous circle of revival.
- Requiring high standards of housing to avoid public health risks may result in rents that exclude poor people from any access to housing. The state must step in to make housing affordable.
- Unregulated builders may produce urban sprawl, leaving city centres almost empty and crime-ridden. The assets of an urban infrastructure are wasted and journeys to work are long. Planned cities can reduce these economic and environmental costs but again raise the price of housing (Rogers and Power, 2000).
- Once the state has stepped into designate areas that can be developed and has built access roads, its actions create 'development or betterment value'. They raise the price of the land so designated. It is argued that these profits should be returned to the community (Uthwatt Committee, 1942).
- Left to itself, the market polarises communities. It excludes the poor from areas where the middle-class or the rich wish to live. This produces poor ghettos in which crime and disorder may flourish and be seen as a 'public bad' that public policy may wish to prevent. It also excludes public service workers from living where they have access to their jobs.

so that the poor could afford the rents. Some local authorities did manage to do so by dubious means, but little building took place. It was not until the housing shortage produced by the First World War that the inter-war government began to subsidise house building, partly through the local ratepayer, but largely from the central exchequer. Gradually withdrawn as the housing shortage was deemed solved, subsidies were reintroduced after the Second World War. Local authorities were used as the vehicles for subsidy partly because the Treasury did not trust private and not-for-profit agencies not to profiteer and waste public money. Also, not-for-profit housing associations did not respond on a large enough scale. The 1945 Labour government concluded that local authorities were the only agencies large enough to undertake the huge post-war rebuilding programme. They were given priority in the allocation of scarce building resources and built three quarters of all new dwellings in the immediate post-war period. The state turned to massive slum clearance and redevelopment in the 1960s. By the late

1970s councils and new town development corporations owned and rented nearly a third of all dwellings in the UK. This was the largest state housing sector outside Eastern Europe. Governments in Western Europe had mostly taken quite a different route. Cheap housing had been provided, too, but by not-for-profit housing agencies. These received various kinds of state support including the capacity to raise low interest loans subsidised by the state (see pages 163-5).

From producer subsidies to consumer subsidies

In the UK between 1919 and 1972 local authorities were paid so much per year for up to 60 years for each house that they built. This helped pay the interest on the sum borrowed to build the house. These interest payments were the largest element in the annual cost. Councils differed in the extent to which they charged a common rent regardless of the tenant's income or means tested the rent. But most tenants paid relatively low rents whatever their income. (For a discussion of the history of state intervention and subsidy, see Bowley, 1945; Nevitt, 1966; Merrett, 1979; Donnison and Ungerson, 1982; Holmans, 1987; Malpass, 1990).

The result was a complex system of subsidies attaching to particular properties built over many decades. In 1972 the Housing Finance Act swept all this away and left the basis of the system we have today. It replaced *producer subsidies* by *consumer subsidies* (Walker, 1998). Poor tenants are now helped to pay their rent in full, or in part, on a sliding scale depending on the household's income. Moreover, such assistance – Housing Benefit – is available not just to council tenants but to all tenants. We discuss the efficiency and equity of this later. Similar housing assistance schemes are also to be found in other countries.

Rent control and regulation

Another mechanism, used during and after each world war, has been rent control. This limits the rent that can be charged by private landlords on poorer properties, which has short-term benefits preventing landlords from charging high scarcity rents at a time when no new houses are being built. However, the controls become difficult to remove. The rents landlords could charge fall below the level at which they bring a profitable return on property owners' capital. The supply of new rented accommodation for the poor dries up and it becomes profitable to sell the rented property to owner-occupiers or developers. It was partly the long periods of rent control in the UK that destroyed private landlordism. The 1980, 1988 and 1996 Housing Acts effectively abolished rent control. There remains a system of state-regulated renting which gives tenants rights to make agreements that last, mostly for short periods. During that time they cannot be evicted without good cause.

A new tenancy means a new market rent must be agreed. Reasonable rents are set for those receiving Housing Benefit by the local housing officer as we shall see, but this is as much to protect the taxpayer as the tenant. (For an account of these developments see Marsh and Riseborough, 1998.) Another reason for the decline in the rental market was the tax subsidy given to those buying their own homes. That this came about is an object lesson in the force of unintended consequences, and interest group politics rather than the outcome of economic debate.

A subsidy to the rich

Owner-occupation began to expand in the 19th century with the invention of building societies. They were originally formed from self-help groups who formed a club, contributing regularly to a fund from which they would buy or build houses for themselves. Its job done, the society was then closed down. People then realised that the society could continue on a longer-term basis, as a 'permanent society'. It could borrow from local savers and lend to local people. Strictly hedged with legislation after various scandals, the local building society became the normal means of collecting small savings to finance house purchase. In the low interest rate period between the wars, owner-occupation boomed in the better-off areas of the South. The societies were given relatively favourable tax treatment compared with other financial institutions, but the real tax advantages of owner-occupation did not begin until the 1960s.

Originally, owner-occupiers were small in numbers and the tax system simply adapted the existing rules to them. They were assumed to be paying themselves a rent – the level of rent other people living in similar houses would pay. They were taxed on that notional rent, just as a private landlord would be. It made good economic sense, and was a system followed in many other countries. Both the owner-occupier and the private landlord could offset interest and other costs against gross income, just like any business. Thus the owner-occupier received tax relief on the interest they paid to buy a house – just as a private landlord or other business would, on the cost of their investment. The system lasted until 1963. Not having the benefit of weekly economics classes, owner-occupiers could not see the logic of paying income tax on income they never saw. This notional income was set in 1936 values and was never changed after the war, so its real value fell. So did the real value of the revenue the Treasury received. As the number of owner-occupiers grew, the pressure to abolish the tax grew. In 1963 the Conservative Chancellor responded. There had been no revaluation of houses so the revenue was small, administratively cumbersome to collect, and unpopular to boot. The Labour Party did not object.

What about the other side of the equity balance, the right to set off the interest paid on mortgages against tax? That remained in place. At the time all interest payments could be set against tax, even for consumption purposes. When that relief was finally abolished in 1974/75, loans for house purchase were again exempt. The combined effect of these incremental moves was a growing tax subsidy to owner-occupation.

Another major subsidy also arose by accident. The Labour government introduced a capital gains tax in 1965. It was a tax on the difference between the purchase price of a capital asset and its selling price. Owner-occupied housing was exempt. There is some justification for this. For the most part you need to buy a new house when you sell your old one. However, it also encourages people to 'trade up' – to buy as expensive a house as they can, and then to sell and buy a larger and more expensive house as their incomes rise. This both reduces their tax burden and enables them to reap a capital gain on retirement when they move into a smaller house or other form of tenure.

House purchase thus became a combined form of pension, life assurance and tax avoidance.

By the late 1980s this tax subsidy to middle- and higher-income groups had grown in size until it equalled what was spent on Housing Benefit.

For those paying the high marginal rates of tax then in operation the advantage was substantial. An individual could reduce taxable income by the amount of interest paid on their mortgage. If the tax rate on that marginal income were 50%, it effectively meant that the interest rate was halved.

Early attempts to cut the scale of the subsidy were taken in 1976. The Labour government set a limit to the value of the mortgage that could attract tax relief – £25,000, then quite a high mortgage. Raised by the next Conservative government to £30,000 it was subsequently held constant while house prices rose substantially. Then, once Mrs Thatcher had departed office, the Treasury managed to take the next step by confining the benefit to standard rate income tax payers – excluding those on the higher rate. Eventually Kenneth Clarke began to reduce even this relief. Gordon Brown finally abolished it altogether in 2000. Thus, what had been the largest pro-rich tax advantage of all tax reliefs had been gradually removed over a decade (see **Figure 8.1**).

It was a remarkable achievement whose full history has still to be written. The success of the Treasury had more to do with the perceived economic disadvantages of the policy than its pro-rich features. Its disadvantages, as the Treasury saw it, were that:

• it encouraged investment in housing rather than manufacturing or other economic activity and helped to explain the UK's very poor industrial investment record. This was the view of two very influential economists (Atkinson and King, 1982) and became a standard Treasury view;

• it was seen to have encouraged the house price boom and bust of the late 1980s. The Treasury only woke up very late to the huge effect on consumer demand that rising house prices had. People appreciate their growing wealth and hence their capacity to spend is enhanced. They can borrow against their high property values. When prices fell people were caught with debts that they could not pay off. Houses were worth less than their mortgage debt. This helped prolong the recession, as people cut spending. The Treasury decided 'never again'.

The costs of housing

The costs of housing are largely born by households, particularly since the demise of mortgage interest relief. The cost of mortgage repayments, house repairs and maintenance takes a large share of people's incomes, often a third or more. This is especially true in people's youth, while they are bringing up children. When the mortgage is repaid that share falls away sharply and the house becomes a net asset. It is used as a form of insurance against the costs of long-term care, an asset that can be cashed in as a pension investment. Thus owner-occupation has become a kind of personal welfare state and not just a form of shelter. Exclusion from this status restricts individuals' life chances and self-determination, although it also carries risks.

The National Accounts (see **Table 8.1**) show that on average households' housing costs make up about a fifth of their spending. The cost of owner-occupation is measured by the rent that owners would pay if they were renting the property. The rest is the sum that householders pay maintaining and furnishing their houses. A little comes from Income Support but overall public spending probably finances roughly 10% of all housing costs. Nevertheless, about a quarter of all households receive direct support for their housing costs, mainly through Housing Benefit. These are the poorest families.

Costs to the state

The cost to the state of housing has changed substantially since 1980 (see **Figure 8.1**).

Table 8.1: UK housing expenditure of households (2000) (£ billion)

Rents paid by tenants	24.5
Imputed rents (owner-occupiers)	52.6
Repairs and maintenance	9.6
Furnishings, household equipment	36.5
Total	**123.2**
Of which state support for (Housing Benefit)	(11.6)
All household expenditure	587.8

Source: ONS (2002a)

**Figure 8.1: Public expenditure on housing (1973-2001)
(£ million, 1995/96 prices)**

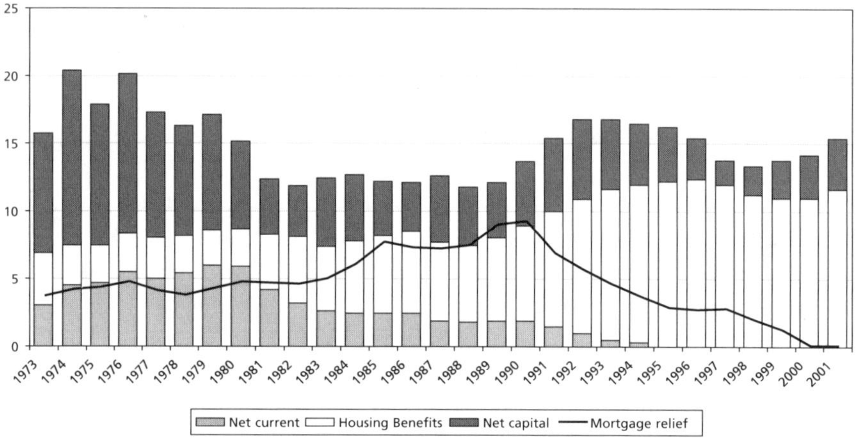

Source: Updated from Hills (1998)

In the mid-1970s direct subsidies to councils to help them reduce their rent levels formed an important part of total public expenditure on housing – 'net current spending' in **Figure 8.1**. Today they have all but disappeared. In the 1970s Housing Benefit was a small part of public housing costs; it is now the main part. New capital expenditure by local authorities and housing associations was a large component too. It then fell sharply to the mid-1990s under the Conservative government. Since 1997 it has risen somewhat, but is well below the post-war years.

The 1980 Housing Act gave council and state sector tenants the right to buy their home at below the market price. This reduced the scale of property owned by local authorities but they were restricted from using the resulting capital receipts to build more than a very few houses. Their building programme has remained tiny despite the Labour government removing this restriction in 1997. Many local authorities are in the process of transferring much or all of their housing stock to existing or newly created housing associations. They still have powers to nominate tenants to fill vacated or new dwellings, but the management and finance of the property is taken over by a separate agency.

Housing associations are now the main providers of new social housing (see **Table 8.2**).

Until the 1970s local authorities were effectively monopoly landlords for the poor. Prospective tenants had little choice of dwelling. The political incentives were to build more homes and minimise rents. In the short run, raising rents to cover maintenance and repairs was unpopular. In the long run, not to do so was disastrous for living standards. Housing management was given low priority (Power, 1987). Cross-party support for extending the

Table 8.2: Housing investment

a) New housing completions in the UK (1977-2000)

	All dwellings	Local authorities	Registered Social Landlords	Private Enterprise
1977	323,836	146,444	23,096	155,296
1980	241,999	88,534	21,476	131,989
1990/91	198,074	16,550	19,342	162,182
2000/01	179,160	915	24,612	153,633

b) Value of housing construction (2000)

New housing	£ million
Public	1,313
Private	8,633
Total	9,946
Repair and maintenance	
Public	6,552
Private	10,354
Total	16,906

Source: ONS (2002b)

range of social housing providers on the Continental model grew. The 1974 Labour government set up The Housing Corporation which was to fund housing associations to provide new or refurbished rental accommodation at affordable rents. This approach appealed to later Conservative governments.

A separate housing association grant was introduced based on an entirely new principle. It involved giving associations a *capital sum* at the beginning of a new scheme sufficient to reduce the loan repayment charges to such a point that poorer tenants could pay the rent. The local rent officer would set a reasonable rent for that new property. The Housing Corporation set a sum that it expected to be spent on management and maintenance of the property. It also set cost limits to the building or renovation of the property. The total capital cost was, therefore, tightly controlled; so, too, were the other regular expenditures. It was possible to work out how high rents would have to be to cover the interest payments and other regular expenditure. A capital sum was then given to the association sufficient to reduce its debt, and therefore its interest payments, to a point where the weekly costs of the association equalled the rent set by the rent officer. The grant was called the *housing association grant* (HAG).

As it turned out, the system had a fatal flaw. It assumed that the fair rent fixed at the outset would hold for the life of the project, or at least it would only be raised sufficiently to meet rising management and maintenance costs.

In the long run, this meant that housing association rents would fall behind fair rents generally. If rents were raised in line with other prices and rents in the economy, the housing association would be making a surplus on that property. This led to various attempts to recover the surplus or redirect it. Other experiments in attracting private capital were tried in the 1980s.

The next significant change to the system came in the 1988 Housing Act, which applied to new schemes after 1989. It reversed the old procedure: grants were now fixed as a proportion of the total capital cost, and private loans were meant to cover the rest. Government has assumed that private loans form an increasing share of the total. Rents are fixed not by a local rent officer, but by the housing association itself, taking into account the costs it has to face, which include the costs of repaying its loans.

The organisation of state finance

Supporting local authorities

Unlike the rest of local authority expenditure, housing activity concerned with the ownership and maintenance of its stock has to be accounted for separately. A *Housing Revenue Account* (HRA) has to be created in ways determined by central government (ODPM, 2002b). It comprises:

Income

- rents
- charges for services like heating
- interest on capital gained from sales but not spent
- central government subsidy
- repairs

Expenditure

- maintenance and management of the stock
- small-scale capital expenditure
- rent rebates to tenants
- loan charges on borrowing to build or improve the housing stock. These are limited to borrowing up to a credit ceiling.

General funds from the Council Tax payer cannot be used to subsidise rents. Central government subsidy is only given where the account comes into deficit for reasons government considers legitimate. It sets what it considers to be appropriate sums to be spent on maintenance and interest. It also sets rent guidelines. If, having set these, the account is still in deficit, the government will give a subsidy to meet the difference. During the early 1990s it steadily raised the level of rental income expected. This raised the income of the HRAs moving many into surplus and avoiding any subsidy.

However, since so many council tenants were on Housing Benefit which paid 100% of these rising rents, Housing Benefit expenditure shot up. Moreover, rent guidelines bore no relation to the different types of property that tenants occupied. There was no rational relationship between the rents local authority tenants were paying and those paid by housing association tenants for the same kind of home. Yet both were paid for by central government. Tenants had little opportunity to choose between properties on the basis of price and quality.

Following a consultation Green Paper (DETR, 2000) the government has now set in place a new way of calculating rents for both the local authority and housing association sectors. A target rent will be set for each property (DETR, 2001). It should reflect the quality, size and location of the property and the average capacity of people in the area to pay.

The target rents will be:

- 70% of the rent for the sector:
  - multiplied by the relative level of wages in the county compared to the national average;
  - multiplied by a factor taking account of the number of bedrooms;
- 30% of the rent for the sector multiplied by the relative value of the property compared to the national average.

From 2002/03 rents of local authority property will rise by 1% more than inflation each year until the rents reach the guideline. For housing association property where rents are usually higher, the pace of increase will be slower – half a per cent a year. This should move rents in the sectors closer to one another and remove all HRA deficits.

Local authority capital spending

- A local authority can use up to 25% of the receipts it gains from selling council houses to build new houses and any surplus of rents over expenditure.
- The major repairs allowance from central government must be used to improve its stock.
- Central government meets two thirds of the costs of facilities for disabled people and makes grants for the repair and renovation of run-down estates.
- Most funding for capital spending is raised in loans. A borrowing limit is set for the whole council in question for all its services – the 'single capital pot'. The cost of repaying the loans falls on the HRA.

Housing associations

These will continue to be helped with an up-front sum of money which is determined and given by The Housing Corporation. It sets total cost indicators, which vary by the type of property and purpose. Sheltered housing attracts a higher figure. A portion of that cost is given as grant and the rest has to be raised as a loan on the open market or in some cases from The Housing Corporation or from a local authority. The rents must cover the costs of maintenance and loan interest and must now come within the new guidelines. (For a discussion of the history of funding mechanisms see Hills, 2000.)

Housing Benefit

This regime now dominates the state's goal of making 'decent' housing affordable to all (Hills, 1998). It is part of social security law and largely financed by central government but is administered by local authorities.

Housing Benefit can be received by anyone who is paying rent, whether to a local authority, a housing association or a private landlord. 'Rent' may cover approved service charges. There are excluded groups such as students, those subject to immigration control, being in a residential care home or with a close relative. The amount of benefit is determined by an income test – the household's financial needs after rent. This is called the 'applicable amount', as with the rest of social security. There are the same capital or savings limits. For those with incomes and capital below these sums Housing Benefit has, in principle, covered all a tenant's rent, excluding ineligible charges. However, the rent level must be reasonable for the tenant's needs. The local housing officer will set a limit to be used to calculate benefit. In the past each rent claim has been assessed in relation to a specific property. The maximum rent paid has been the smallest of three estimates:

- the actual rent;
- a rent on the property determined considering the size and type of property;
- the local market rent for an appropriately sized dwelling – 'the local reference rent' or the 'single room rent'.

If income rises above the 'applicable amount', the benefit is tapered off at 65% of the rise in income. (For the full complexity, see CPAG, 2002.)

The government (DWP, 2002c) has proposed moving in stages to a new way of administering Housing Benefit to meet some of the criticisms discussed below.

Improving choice and efficiency

Critics have argued that the old system caused serious distortions and administrative difficulty (for example, Kemp, 1998, and Hills, 2001b). Four million tenants rely on Housing Benefit, but:

- *administration* is near collapse in many areas. The Department for Work and Pensions sets the regulations but does not have to administer them. This has tended to produce high complexity not tempered by an appreciation of the difficulties. Tenants have had to reapply regularly for benefit, for example;
- *fraud* is costly to avoid in a highly regulated and means-tested system in which landlord and tenant have an incentive to collude;
- *poor take-up* results from the system's complexity and means testing;
- *steep tapers* create the worst work disincentives in the whole social security system. Nothing has been done to limit this;
- *full payment of rent* for many means there is no incentive for the tenant to exercise any choice of cost versus quality or for landlords to be efficient.

Removing these obstacles to choice and efficiency would involve the following:

- Creating an equivalent set of subsidies and guidelines across all social housing sectors. This would enable tenants to choose and move landlord without perverse financial effects.
- Moving local authority housing to similar organisational independence and decentralisation that housing associations enjoy. This is already happening.
- Using the planning system to ensure mixed development in order to reduce the sharp divisions between areas and tenures. This would both encourage more genuine choice and exit routes for tenants to new tenures and positive spillover effects in community cohesion and sustainable public services (Hills, 2001b).
- The limits to rents paid by Housing Benefit have caused hardship for some without increasing choice. Kemp et al (2002) suggest that rent limits should be removed. Housing Benefit would be paid on only, say, 80% of the rent. Tenants would pay the difference but social security rates should be increased too, perhaps by 25% of the average rent in the area. This would bring Housing Benefit more in line with housing allowance schemes in other countries. They tested out how such changes might work in the UK. Kemp et al argue it would increase tenants' choice and independence and alleviate some of the inefficiencies we have discussed, but it would cost more.
- At present the Housing Benefit 'taper' is added on to other means-tested benefit tapers to produce a very high marginal tax rate (see page 44). There is a case for merging Housing Benefit and other tax credit arrangements by inventing a housing credit that would cover poorer households' actual housing

costs, or give them a lower flat rate sum. (For a discussion see Kemp et al, 2002.) Although attractive in principle this would also be costly.

- Homeowners on Income Support can get limited help with housing costs but cannot receive Housing Benefit. A housing tax credit could be extended to poor owner-occupiers.

A gradual reform of Housing Benefit

The aim is to move towards a standard housing allowance, which will vary according to the size of family and the area in which they live. But the same sized family living in the same area will have the right to the same basic sum if they have no other income. There will be no property-by-property assessment, as there is now. The government plan (DWP, 2002c) is as follows:

- In 2003/04 there will be 8-10 'pathfinder areas' in England, Scotland and Wales, chosen to introduce and experiment with the new scheme.
- A flat rate housing allowance will be introduced for private rented property in those areas. If the approach is successful it will be extended to social housing later.
- The allowance will be set in the same way as the local reference rent (see above). It will be roughly the average rent for that sized property in the area. If tenants can find cheaper property they can pocket the difference. If they want better property they can pay more for their housing and less for other things.
- Where at all possible the sum will be paid to the tenant.
- Rules that have required frequent reapplication for benefit will go as will the need to reapply when someone gets a job. There are other simplifications.
- The aim is to have completed this change throughout the country by 2010.

The finance of housing in other countries

David Donnison (1967) long ago reminded us:

> Government's first interventions in the housing field are not necessarily prompted by the need to protect public health and provide homes for heroes. The story may have begun, or been carried forward, by attempts to bring about agricultural reforms and assist poverty stricken regions (as in Italy), to combat depression and mop up unemployment in the building trades (as in Sweden), or to rebuild a war-shattered economy and erect a defence against Communism (as in West Germany), or to attract key workers to growing industries (as in several east European countries). (pp 82-3)

All advanced economies have ways of intervening to assist the very poor in their claim to some kind of shelter. In Europe the agencies that have evolved to fill this function have been private agencies, most often not-for-profit or not-much-profit, supported in some way by the state.

Germany deliberately tried to avoid what were seen as Britain's housing failures, but drew on the cooperative housing models that came from Britain. Housing cooperatives were given a legal framework as were companies with limits to the scale of dividends that they could distribute. These grew in scale in the inter-war period. Afterwards a huge housing programme was carried through largely engineered by *tax* policy not direct subsidies (Power, 1993). Private landlords could write off the capital costs of new building against tax over eight years, as they could the current costs of maintaining and managing the property. This encouraged both building and high levels of maintenance. In addition social housing landlords received a subsidy from government in the form of low interest loans and in return had to accept nominated tenants in housing need.

The government also encouraged owner-occupation from the mid-1950s through a series of low interest loans and guarantees. This brought owner-occupation within the reach of lower-income families. Tax incentives encouraged owner-occupiers to build a house with a rental flat attached, or forming one floor of the building. This both reduced the costs to the owner and widened the scale of the renting market for newly married couples, students or single people.

Local authorities are funded by the Länder governments to subsidise social landlords, nominate tenants and regulate the market. It was this German model that appealed to many reformers in the UK.

As rents were increasingly freed from controls, a system of means-tested housing allowances was introduced in the 1960s. Despite the diversity, choice and high standard of much German housing, it has not escaped the problem of some estates becoming the refuge of the most disadvantaged.

France developed a pattern that shared some of the same characteristics (for a good summary see Power, 1993). The French state never saw its role as providing housing. Some liberal employers took the early lead in providing 'model' housing developments. The decisive move came in 1912 with a law that gave local authorities and the departments the capacity to create arm's-length housing organisations to provide low-cost housing with state subsidies. This set a pattern. After a slow start and the growth of shanty-towns around some French cities that resembled those of the developing world, the French state promoted a vast building programme that outdid many of the errors of the 1960s in the UK. But the agents were the housing associations who were given massive inducements to build.

These *habitations à loyer modéré* (HLMs) have become the main vehicles for French social housing. They are financed by several streams of income and by borrowing. There are state grants to meet the costs of renovating old property, direct subsidies, subsidised loans and rental income which derives from the state for tenants who receive housing allowances. The central state's local representative – the *Prefect* – has the right to nominate tenants, as do employers and local communes. A national law laid expectations on HLMs to make provision for all local residents including those from minority ethnic groups. Private landlords benefit from the housing allowance scheme which, since 1948, has helped preserve the sector. Owner-occupation for low-income families was encouraged by making the housing allowance available to owner-occupiers. The government subsidised the building of low-cost homes for owner-occupation and made grants to borrowers who also received low interest loans.

In **Scandinavia**, social housing similarly relies heavily on social housing companies sponsored by local authorities, trades unions or other bodies. Again tenants' capacity to pay rent is supported by a system of housing allowances.

The **US** has never had a significant public or social housing sector, while at the same time giving massive tax support to owner-occupiers. Both mortgage interest and property taxes can be claimed against federal income tax at a cost of about $60 billion in 1998. The benefits go largely to the higher-income groups – 44% of the tax relief went to the 10% with incomes over $40,000 a year (Katz, 1999). A small scheme of housing vouchers, not that different from UK Housing Benefit, was introduced and expanded by the Clinton administration.

Overview

- The range of housing interventions by the state is wide. They range from building standards, green belt policy, finance of social house-building, and the finance of consumers to rent control.

- The tax subsidy of owner-occupation became the largest component but, partly because of its economic consequences, it was phased out.

- Housing Benefit targeted on the poorest social housing tenants, and some private ones too, faces families with a significant poverty trap, work disincentives and little encouragement to exercise choice.

- Other countries' more mixed systems of tenure and housing finance have some advantages.

Questions for discussion

1. What have been the state's most important interventions in the housing market since 1914, and what have been the consequences?

2. Why did the state shift from subsidising producers of housing to subsidising consumers? What has been the effect?

3. How does the UK system of housing finance differ from that in the rest of Europe and the US?

Further reading

For a strong theoretically based history of the state's changing role up to 1977, see **Merrett (1979)**. For the period 1974 to 1997 see **Hills (1998)**.

Discussion of policy on private renting, owner-occupation and housing finance more generally is covered in **Marsh and Mullins (1998)**.

For possible agendas of change see **Hills (2001b)** and **Kemp et al (2002)**.

The complexity of Housing Benefit and who is eligible is to be found in **CPAG (2002)**.

nine

Rationing scarce resources: managing rising expectations

Summary

- All societies find some way to ration scarce resources. Markets do so, but in periods of extreme scarcity societies adopt political rationing. The same is true of highly valued resources such as healthcare.

- Political and administrative rationing of social welfare resources range from central decisions about funding to local unrecognised allocations of professionals' time.

- Financial rationing in the UK is highly centralised and powerfully concentrated in the process of public expenditure control exercised by HM Treasury. The evolution and constitutional basis for this power is analysed in this chapter.

- An increasingly controversial rationing process allocates the taxpayers' funding between the nations of the UK.

- The chapter concludes with a discussion of the results of the recent Comprehensive Spending Review.

Users of public services seem increasingly dissatisfied, despite the fact that the quality of services has improved markedly since 1950 (Glennerster and Hills, 1998). The level of consumer expectations seems to be rising faster. Discontent may be put down to a malevolent press or professions who continuously talk of 'crisis' as a way of gaining more resources from the Chancellor. The NHS has been in 'crisis' in this sense ever since it was created. However, there is a more structural explanation for this continuing dilemma. Claus Offe (1984), the German Marxist sociologist, comes closest to capturing it, although there is an equivalent New Right explanation. In a pure market economy the price mechanism manages individuals' expectations. They may desire a Mercedes or a holiday in the Bahamas but they know that their capacity to afford such luxuries is determined by their own worth in the labour market. They do not blame the government. In health or education, where no price is charged, expectations are not managed downwards by the market. Supply and demand have to be managed by the political process. In this chapter we describe the realities of the way in which scarce resources are managed and allocated in a non-market system. The dilemmas should not blind us to the fact that *all* scarce resources have to be rationed – the market is just as much a rationing device as the ways in which societies seek to ration collectively. Scarcity is a social product, just as is the 'market'. If we decide that only so many resources can be devoted to road improvements and that there shall be no limit to car usage, the result, that a particular child dies, may appear as an accident. In fact, it is the consequence of a first order choice about the road and rail budget and the level of taxation on cars – a 'tragic choice' (Calabresi and Bobbitt, 1978).

Rationing

Lévi-Strauss (1969), the French anthropologist, saw this clearly in his discussion of the nature of scarcity in early societies. In the absence of socially accepted ways of allocating scarce resources, there will be conflict. The scarcer the resources the worse the potential conflict. So even simple societies devise their own means of rationing scare resources – land for food and shelter as well as access to sexual relationships. These are the means of acquiring children, status and support in old age. He goes on to describe ways in which these scarce resources are rationed – by taboo and stigma, tradition and status. More complex societies, he argues, evolved markets as ways of coping with the complexity of rules that would otherwise be involved, but there are some resources that are still deemed too problematic to leave to the market. In times of danger and extreme scarcity, for example in wartime, we resort to food and clothes rationing. We had ration books and little bits of paper torn from them, which entitled you to meat and eggs, or in my own memory, a little bag of sweets.

The economist thinks about rationing in a rather different and often scornful way. The very term 'administrative rationing' is used in the US as a completely unacceptable limitation on consumers' freedom of access to healthcare, ignoring the fact that the market rations healthcare in the US by excluding a quarter or more of the population from insurance cover. However, the economic concept of rationing has its virtues, for it concentrates our attention on some of the key dilemmas.

Figure 9.1 is an adaptation of an undergraduate economics student's supply and demand curve. In a pure market the higher the price the more services the suppliers of healthcare will provide. The higher the price the less consumers will demand. At some point the two match. There is no need for 'nasty' bureaucrats to have anything to do with deciding who gets what. But what happens when the state enters and taxes people in order to supply healthcare? The supply curve is now a political decision, dependent on how much tax politicians believe people will pay. If the service is provided free, there is no reason why the public should demand less than they would from private doctors who suddenly offered their services free. The demand curve, in short, remains the same. Thus a gap emerges between what people demand and what the taxpayer is prepared to fund. The taxpayer may be prepared to buy more than would arise in a free market, but the total falls short of the demand for services that are free at the point of use. Economists call the gap that results the *queuing* or *rationing gap*. It exhibits itself in waiting lists – people 'pay' by waiting.

Figure 9.1: **The economic concept of rationing**

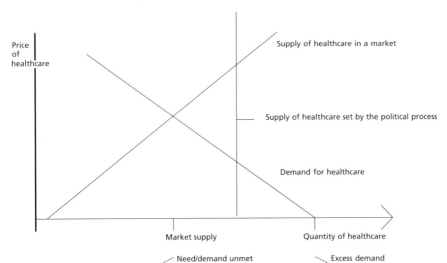

There is some truth in this analysis, but it needs modification. There is not a highly elastic demand for all health services. People do not rush to have their legs amputated for fun, or even go to the dentist for sheer pleasure when these services are free. There are feelings of respect for doctors' 'busy lives' and fear of being diagnosed as sick, which sociologists have charted. However, it is true that these inhibitions which reduced the rationing gap in the past are being eroded. The social distance between a patient and a doctor or between a parent and a teacher has shrunk. Culturally imposed reticence in demanding services is disappearing. Patients deem themselves consumers; they do not expect to wait.

Calabresi and Bobbett (1978) distinguish four kinds of rationing: the market, political allocations that are accountable to public discussion, pure lotteries, and the unaccountable customs and practices of professionals and bureaucrats. All interact. Since 1950 the extent of accountable political rationing has increased (Klein et al, 1996). Arguably most rationing still takes place at the front line in unrecognised ways (Parker, 1967; Judge, 1978; Lipsky, 1980; Aaron and Swartz, 1984). It is possible to think of rationing varying from full political accountability, openness and explicitness across to being hidden and, indeed, almost unrecognised in nature (see **Figure 9.2**).

An example of an explicit and open decision is a public announcement that a given sum will be spent on the NHS over the next three years in the Comprehensive Spending Review. Another that Viagra will only be available on the NHS to a given class of patients based on a reasoned discussion of the

Figure 9.2: **Types of rationing**

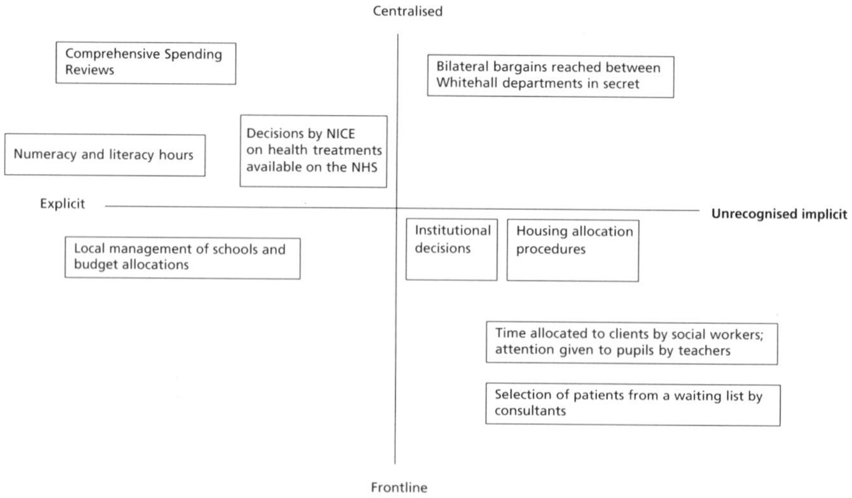

Note: NICE = National Institute for Clinical Excellence

research evidence. An inexplicit or hidden decision is one that is taken by a consultant not to give priority to an older patient with a kidney problem but rather to a young mother.

It is also possible to rank the level at which such decisions are taken from one that applies nationally to one that may be idiosyncratic to a particular hospital, consultant, or classroom teacher. Critical decisions may be made by receptionists (Hall, 1974), and not by professional staff at all. Much service rationing does take place in this bottom right-hand quadrant of **Figure 9.2**. However, such decisions are powerfully constrained by decisions taken at the central level about budget allocations or targets and performance indicators.

Since 1976, as public spending has become more contested, so the whole process of public expenditure control has become more open. Rules that constrain teachers' and social workers' freedom of action have grown. The national curriculum and guidelines about how to deal with children at-risk are examples. Healthcare has been less affected until recently. But the National Institute for Clinical Excellence (NICE) and clinical audit (see page 74) are all examples of pushing allocation decisions to the upper left-hand corner of **Figure 9.2**.

In the bottom right-hand corner are decisions that a school teacher makes about how much time to devote to which pupils in the class – the slow readers, or the fast ones with pushy middle-class parents, to boys or girls, to Maths or Reading or Drama. From studies of classroom activity we know that potentially disruptive boys gain most attention. With the coming of the Literacy and Numeracy hours on the national curriculum these decisions have become more centralised. So long as the evidence about how to spend this time is well-based, there is a case for such centralised guidelines. However, teachers fear other objectives of education have lost out. Less time is spent on cultural or musical activities. Right or wrong the allocation of classroom time has become a more open and debated rationing mechanism.

Not all rationing decisions have become more centralised. The devolution of budgets to schools and the inclusion of parents, teachers and the community representatives in budget making is an example. Not everyone agrees that a move to the left in **Figure 9.2** is such a good idea. It has been much debated in healthcare (Hunter, 1993, 1995; Klein et al, 1996; Klein, 1997; New and Le Grand, 1996; Lenaghan, 1997).

Regardless of the debate about explicit service rationing, there is little conflict about the case that financial rationing should be more accountable. In significant ways the public expenditure process has become a little more open than when Heclo and Wildavsky (1974) described it as *The private government of public money*. Much mystery still remains, but more recently it has been explored by Deakin and Parry (2000). To understand this most centralised of all rationing procedures we must, in the UK, begin with HM Treasury. Since Scottish,

Welsh and Northern Irish devolution, we must also be aware of some challenges to its 'supremacy'.

Containing public expenditure

All countries have their ministries of finance but the UK Treasury is almost uniquely powerful. We have already seen that nearly all revenue-raising powers in the UK lie with central government. Even local authorities, tiny though their local revenue is, are subject to restraint if they raise what central government deems to be excessive revenue. The Scottish Parliament can only add or subtract 3p in the pound from the national income tax.

With the Prime Minister, the Chancellor of the Exchequer is the only real arbiter of what tax levels shall be. In constitutional theory this power lies with Parliament – more precisely since 1911, with the House of Commons. A government department can only spend money with the approval of the House of Commons. Taxes can only be levied with the House of Commons' approval. The House of Commons' Public Accounts Committee and its officials, now in the National Audit Office, have a duty to ensure that money is only spent on purposes approved by Parliament. Moreover, this money has to be spent with due 'economy, efficiency and effectiveness' (1982 Local Government Finance Act, Section 26). The Audit Commission performs the same function for local authorities in England and Wales. The function in Scotland is performed by the Accounts Commission for Scotland and the Auditor General.

Long before proposals ever reach Parliament for usual rubber-stamping, the Treasury comes into action. It is a role that has developed and is still developing. Its 'supremacy' dates from Gladstone's period as Chancellor in the middle of the 19th century. As the role of government grew, so did the containing role of the Treasury. On a **Marxist** analysis it can be seen as the representative of capitalists' interests within government. It is driven by a traditional economistic view of the world, dedicated to a minimal state and seeking to frustrate social programmes and social progress at every turn. It tries to resolve the fundamental dilemma of modern capitalism – the economic need for growing social expenditure and the need to leave room for capital and the market to operate. It lies at the crux of this clash of irreconcilable forces (O'Connor, 1973; Gough, 1979).

For the **pluralist** political scientist, the Treasury represents some of the interests that have to find expression in any modern economy – the taxable limits of the average voter, the viability of a market economy that also needs public services. The Treasury's role is to manage these tensions. The classic statement of this view is to be found in Heclo and Wildavsky (1974) and Wildavsky (1974), who discuss the very different pattern in the US where Congress plays a much more important role.

In what follows we adopt what can be called a *neo-pluralist approach* (Dunleavy and O'Leary, 1987). The game fought out between the spending departments and the interests they represent is strongly affected by the state of the wider economy. In periods of economic crisis the Treasury becomes dominant and the rules of the game, which it sets, change accordingly. As the tensions have become central to modern politics so the Treasury's role in social policy formation has grown.

Treasury control

The Treasury's power derives from a series of constitutional conventions and gradually accumulating rules:

- No individual MP can rise in the House of Commons and put down a motion to spend public money as a congressman can in the US. No proposal to spend money can be tabled without the signature of a Treasury minister. Similar rules apply in the Scottish Parliament (Heald and McLeod, 2003).
- No proposal involving additional spending can be discussed by cabinet or a cabinet sub-committee unless it is accompanied by a Treasury paper on the economic and cost consequences. Major spending decisions of the cabinet are now only taken *once every two years* in the Comprehensive Spending Review.
- No spending proposals may be developed within a department unless the Treasury is informed and asked to comment.
- No department can spend money without regular Treasury approval. This used to be given so long as it had been voted by Parliament. Now the department is expected to be meeting performance targets agreed with the Treasury – *public service agreements*. An example is given in **Box 9.1**.

A section of the Treasury is devoted to keeping a continuing oversight of each spending department.

Despite these apparently draconian powers, the Treasury has not always won its battles to contain public spending. Political imperatives can ultimately overrule even the Treasury for a time. We have excellent documentary evidence of this from Lowe's (1989) account of the Treasury's attempt to cut back the scale of social spending in the 1950s. The Treasury fought back after the resignation of the Chancellor and his ministerial team when they argued that the Treasury had become unable to control public spending. An internal committee of enquiry was set up, chaired by Lord Plowden. Its report (HM Treasury, 1961) has set the basic ground rules for public spending control ever since. It argued:

- The pre-war consensus in favour of a small state and minimal spending had given way to a presumption of government spending to solve social problems. Natural restraint was not enough.

Box 9.1: Department of Health objectives and performance targets

Objective I: improve service standards

1 Reduce the maximum wait for an outpatient appointment to three months and the maximum wait for inpatient treatment to six months by the end of 2005, and achieve progressive further cuts with the aim of reducing the maximum inpatient and day case waiting time to three months by 2008.

2 Reduce to four hours the maximum wait in A&E from arrival to admission, transfer or discharge, by the end of 2004; and reduce the proportion waiting over one hour.

3 Guarantee access to a primary care professional within 24 hours and to a primary care doctor within 48 hours from 2004.

4 Ensure that by the end of 2005 every hospital appointment will be booked for the convenience of the patient, making it easier for patients and their GPs to choose the hospital and the consultant that best meets their needs.

5 Enhance accountability to patients and the public and secure sustained national improvements as measured by independently validated national surveys.

Objective II: improve health and social care outcomes for everyone

6 Reduce substantially the mortality rates from the major killer diseases by 2010: from heart disease by at least 40% in people under 75; from cancer by at least 20% in people under 75.

7 Improve life outcomes of adults and children with mental health problems; reduce the mortality rate from suicide and undetermined injury by at least 20% by 2010.

8 Improve the quality of life and independence of older people so that they can live at home wherever possible, by increasing by March 2006 the number of those supported intensively to live at home to 30% of the total being supported by social services.

...

11 By 2010 reduce inequalities in health outcomes by 10% as measured by infant mortality and life expectancy at birth.

Source: HM Treasury (2002d)

• Individual ministers could approach cabinet with one-off proposals to spend money which convinced their colleagues on their individual merits despite the Treasury's warnings. Such 'bubbling up' incremental growth led to unsustainable demands on taxation in the long run. Once politicians realised what the cumulative effect of their past decisions was going to mean for taxation or in the next economic crisis, public spending plans would be severely cut back. Such 'stop and go' measures were bad for the services and for the economy. What was needed was a long-term sustainable pattern of public spending growth. (Gordon Brown's speeches are continuous echoes of Plowden.)

- Policies were embarked upon without testing their long-run implications. A plan to build more teacher training places had consequences not just for the coming year when more students would attend college but in the future when the larger teacher stock would have to be paid.

Plowden's remedies followed:

- There should be regular comprehensive public spending plans encompassing the whole of the government's spending. No 'one-off' bright ideas could be considered at any other time. Every item would have to be considered in competition with every other new programme and long-standing claims. The spending time horizon should not be just for one year but five years ahead. (This time proved too long and was reduced to three before long.) Spending departments should then be held to those limits but also have the security of knowing that they were sure to get that sum of money for the medium term.
- Long-term spending plans should be considered alongside the economy's long-term capacity for growth. Unless ministers were prepared to see taxes rise, spending should be kept within the economy's ability to generate higher revenues from existing taxation rates. This would 'achieve greater stability in public spending decisions'.
- Those making long-term decisions should be better informed about the economic consequences of their choices. (For a review of the impact of Plowden's reforms on social policy departments, see Lowe, 1997a, 1997b.)

Achieving these goals has not been easy and the Treasury has manifestly failed on many occasions – most notably in the run-up to the economic crisis of 1976. Certain features have remained constant, however:

- the determination to consider all spending plans together on one occasion;
- to do so for an extended period;
- the attempt to link these planned levels of spending to economic growth.

The detailed implementation of these principles has changed.

Comprehensive plans

An expenditure division of the Treasury was created to oversee an annual cycle of bidding. Every spending department worked out early in the calendar year what it would need to meet existing policies for the next five years. Any hopes for additional programmes would be costed and considered, along with possible cuts required in time of economic crisis. In June-July each year the Treasury would produce a summation of all the spending bids and an assessment of what the economy could 'afford', given the expected growth rate. It would give options and a recommended path for the total growth rate in public spending. At this point, not knowing exactly what it would mean for their own departments, cabinet ministers would be forced to decide on an overall total. That agreed, it was then left to individual negotiations between spending departments and the Treasury to get plans trimmed to meet the predetermined target. However, it never really worked quite like that. Appeals to the Prime Minister might win the day. Hence a formal 'Star Chamber' of non-spending ministries was set up to hear appeals from aggrieved ministers chaired by a respected senior minister – Willie Whitelaw in Mrs Thatcher's time. In the 1990s, under Kenneth Clarke, a cabinet sub-committee called EDX did the job chaired by the Chancellor himself.

The annual routine would end in November with the announcement of public spending plans for the next year and the two beyond. This would be followed in March by the Budget – setting out the taxes needed to pay for these plans.

For a while in the mid-1990s these two processes were combined. The aim was to bring home to ministers the close link between taxes and new plans for spending. This was called the *unified budget*. Both the income and expenditure side of the National Accounts were presented as a single entity. It looked tidy but it nearly killed Treasury officials. Two of their major yearly activities had to be conducted at the same time. Annual bidding was enormously time-consuming and it encouraged departments to think of new plans each year. Not to do so would mean losing out against a more active ministry. Ministerial reputations would suffer if *extra* were not gained in the new round.

When Gordon Brown became Chancellor in 1997 he froze the spending levels set by the previous Conservative government for the next two years. The annual bidding round was abolished. Instead there was an in-depth look at everything each department did, and an opportunity to make a fundamental shift in priorities. The results of this first Comprehensive Spending Review were announced in July 1998 (HM Treasury, 1998). This covered the period 1999-2002. A second Review was published (HM Treasury, 2000) covering the period 2001-04. In July 2002 the latest Review covered the period 2003-06. We have moved from a one-year to a two-year cycle of bids. The Treasury would probably like to extend the 'period of stability'. Politicians feel the need to respond to events, public moods and upcoming elections.

Technical elements in the planning cycle have changed too, with important results. In the 1960s and early 1970s the plans were set in volume prices. These were essentially service specific price indices for each service. If the price of drugs, doctors' and nurses' salaries rose by 5% in a year, the NHS spending target was raised accordingly. This gave NHS managers more certainty about the real worth of their budget, but it gave them no incentive to keep down drug prices or salaries. After 1976, cash limits were set for the next year's spending. Whatever happened to prices or salaries they would not change. From 1982 this principle was applied to the three-year plans. The methodology was further refined in the 1990s. A department was told what its budget would be with a fairly low assumption about salary and price levels built in. Then, if the services gave in to higher salaries or if prices rose faster than expected, managers would have to reduce the scale of the services that they were able to provide. This was called *cash planning*. In essence it still applies. Thus, how much Gordon Brown's extra money will result in extra services will depend on what happens to public service pay and prices.

Not all spending can be controlled on a three-year horizon called the *departmental expenditure limits* (DELs). These limits comprise two categories: capital spending that is separately controlled, and resource budgets. These are calculated on an accruals basis, as used in private sector accounts. They take account of known debts incurred in the period and expected income. They also, and crucially, take account of the costs of the capital used by a service, land and buildings, and the depreciation of buildings over their life. Managers are forced to think about their use of buildings.

As we saw in Chapter Eight pensions and Income Support spending levels depend on benefit rates and the number of people who happen to qualify in any year. These are 'demand led' and come in a separate category called *annually managed expenditure* (AME). *Totally managed expenditure* is the total of DELs and AME.

Self-imposed prudence

Brown set himself two fiscal rules in 1997, which he has sustained:

• The *golden rule*: over the economic cycle the government will borrow only to cover the cost of capital expenditure and not to cover current expenditure – on health, pensions or Income Support. He could do so to cover current expenditure in a recession but only if the government ran a surplus in the good years, as it did in the late 1990s. Brown made use of this past prudence/ good fortune to sustain his spending plans despite the economic slowdown in 2002 and uncertainty about 2003. In fact, his claims in the November 2002 Pre-Budget Report (HM Treasury, 2002h) relied on an optimistic 'assumption' about UK growth in 2003 in the face of world, and especially European, growth prospects. It is an illustration of the temptation that faces all Chancellors, to be too optimistic about the country's growth potential so as to justify the spending plans they have had to agree to for political purposes.

- *Public debt* would be kept below 40% of GDP. Here Brown was well within this target if the economy did not deteriorate sharply.

Three years is a very short time horizon for economic trends, even if it is a long time in politics. The Treasury therefore subject current policies to a review of their implications over a *50-year* period. What are the implications of demographic trends and trends in the working population on future health and pensions spending and their finance? The results of such an analysis can be found in a document that accompanied the Pre-Budget Report in 2002 (HM Treasury, 2002g). It uses a very cautious prediction of productivity growth, yet even so, suggests that current levels of public spending included in the 2002 Comprehensive Spending Review and projected to continue are economically sustainable. Indeed, because of the UK's relatively low spending on public pensions and its relatively higher birth rate it will be in a much stronger relative position to cover its social spending than any other advanced economy. The study uses a computerised generation model to test how far present spending plans applied to future populations would imply raising future taxes. In the UK these are minimal, although in many other countries they are substantial. We discuss this more in Chapter Ten. Of course, a world economic slump could change that and many other predictions. Key areas of public policy such as health and public transport also have medium-term 10-year plans for service development. They set out various targets and ambitions, but the Treasury refuses to tie themselves to these aspirations.

Tax expenditure (see pages 9–10) is reported in the budget statement (HM Treasury, 2002a, Appendix A.3), but does not count as public expenditure, nor is it integrated into departmental accounts. The new Working and Child Tax Credits do not appear as public expenditure if they result in reduced levels of tax for a household rather than a cash payment. The old Working Families' Tax Credit figures will continue to count as public expenditure in the UK National Accounts but not in OECD international comparisons! Whatever the virtues of integrating the tax and benefits system it has caused considerable confusion in the statistics of public expenditure.

A more proactive role for the Treasury

Deakin and Parry (2000) sum up the traditional role of the Treasury's approach to social policy:

> ... we can detect the basic contours of the Treasury approach to social policy – politically aware, alive to economic analysis in a rudimentary way, not afraid to be opinionated, slightly defeatist,

seeking a more precise targeting on need so that people do not gain from misfortune, and wary of the spending departments. (p 24)

In the past the Treasury was a largely negative force. This changed in the 1990s. A series of circumstances led to its more proactive role – a series of Fundamental Expenditure Reviews were undertaken. The most significant was that of the Treasury itself. Like Plowden it was chaired by an outsider from industry – Sir Colin Southgate – but written by insiders (see Deakin and Parry, 2000, Chapter 4). The report was critical of the detailed Treasury oversight of spending decisions in departments. It was also critical of the negative view of public spending interest inherent in the old Gladstonian approach. The revolution in macroeconomic thinking in the 1980s had been to recognise that the government's role was not to try to fine-tune macroeconomic demand, but to improve the 'supply-side' of the economy – the efficiency with which economic institutions worked. In many instances this might mean *increasing* spending, for example, on training and education, or reorganising the benefits system in order to improve work incentives. Instead of blocking new spending plans, the Treasury should be involved in ensuring that policy improved the nation's efficiency, even if that meant some departments spending more. Many of these potential areas of active intervention would affect social policy.

The new spending directorate took on this enlarged more proactive role, not just overseeing spending departments, but conducting cross-departmental reviews. The notion of proactive teams separated from those doing the ordinary spending reviews did not last, but the proactive focus of their approach to the work was certainly sustained. Above all, the work on social security benefits policy moved centre-stage. The Treasury saw this in a different category – an area it had to get a grip on in order to achieve a major improvement in macroeconomic performance. Here it was fortunate in its new Chancellor, who was convinced of the same thing. It combined his belief in 'making work pay' and in redistribution. The Treasury became the lead social policy ministry as far as cash benefits were concerned. Benefits and tax policy became deliberately intertwined.

Territorial rationing

We have seen in preceding chapters how central funds are allocated down to local agencies: education, social and healthcare agencies *within* the nations of the UK. How are funds allocated *between* England, Scotland, Wales and Northern Ireland? Like so many financial allocations it is a rather hidden private arrangement which has only recently begun to attract some public attention. How much each country received could have been left to annual, or biannual, bargaining, just like departmental bargaining with the Treasury.

However, it would have been almost impossible to achieve 'closure'. A bargain settled about education spending would have still left a side argument about Scottish and Welsh bargaining, which could have reopened all the struck bargains between service departments. An agreed settlement, based on a formula, between the nations simplified the whole process. It reduced the transaction costs falling on the Treasury and the high political costs that would fall on politicians if the Scots, the English and the Welsh had a battle royal every year.

The first such formula was applied to Scotland in 1891 and is named after Lord Salisbury's Chancellor of the time, George Goshen. (For a history see Thain and Wright, 1995, from which this account is drawn.) It began as a way of allocating Scotland's share of education spending and was then applied to all public expenditure. The formula was simple enough. Scotland got 11/80ths of British spending service by service. That was Scotland's population share in 1891! As Scotland's population declined, so Scotland's share of resources relative to its population rose. Over time the formula practice was extended to Northern Ireland (1938), revised to take account of Northern Ireland's needs in 1950. The Welsh Office only came into existence in 1964 and was given a similarly crude formula based on population shares. In the late 1970s the Treasury was responsible for leading a review that tried to determine the 'relative needs' of the individual nations. An internal and cross-country battle, understandably, ensued (Heald, 1980). The consequence, in 1978, was a new formula based on the then population balance between England, Scotland and Wales in the ratio 85:10:5. This was called the 'Barnett formula' after the then Chief Secretary to the Treasury. The interdepartmental battles in England would determine how much each service would get, and the formula then determined how much Scotland and the rest would get assuming the same rate of growth in each service area. That would determine the overall size of the country block, but once allocated the individual Secretaries of State could decide what to do with the sum they received. A separate formula was applied to Northern Ireland. Social security as a UK-wide benefit system remains outside this process. The formula has been adjusted since 1978 to take account of population changes deriving from the 1991 Census. The rather shaky empirical foundations of the formula were exposed by the House of Commons Treasury Select Committee in 1997 (House of Commons Treasury Committee, 1997; Deakin and Parry, 2000, pp 162-78).

Essentially the same arrangements have survived devolution to the Scottish, Welsh and Northern Ireland Assemblies. They, rather than a Westminster-appointed Secretary of State, decide the internal allocations. Moreover, the Scottish Assembly has the power to raise an additional 3p income tax, not as yet used.

The 'blocks' of funds for each nation include more items, such as agriculture and forestry, and become the 'assigned budget'. It was agreed that the Barnett formula would be retained. It has been updated regularly in relation to the latest population estimates, and a mechanism has been established to resolve disputes.

Yet devolution has brought the funding mechanisms into the public domain and exposed their results. Table 9.1 shows the breakdown of spending by nation in 2000-01, the latest available figures. The shares of spending 80:10:6: 4 for England, Scotland, Wales and Northern Ireland were, to the nearest percentage point identical to those in 1997/98! A clear formulaic result. However, the result in terms of spending per head of population is strikingly different. Scots receive more than a quarter more education resources than the English and more than a fifth more health resources, an effect also largely unchanged. The English are now increasingly aware of this and are asking why.

The place of local authority spending

From the days of the Plowden Report the aim of the Treasury has been to control *Total Public Expenditure*. This includes not just the spending of central government but that of local government too. It included the nationalised industries, when there were any! Practically no other finance ministry in the world attempts to do this. The very idea that the government in Washington was trying to set limits to California's spending or to that of Little Rock Arkansas would be nearly enough to spark a second Civil War.

In the 19th century the Treasury was afraid that the new local government bodies would be profligate in their capital borrowing. Because they were public bodies they would land the Treasury with the task of bailing them out if they defaulted – a moral hazard problem. Hence the Treasury had a duty to restrict and approve all their borrowing, as it still does. Since the Keynesian era the Treasury have also maintained that, for reasons of macroeconomic planning, they have to be able to control the total level of public investment. In the more monetarist period the total level of public borrowing was seen to be critical in controlling the money supply. Thus, most economists are prepared to accept, for reasons that vary, that local authorities' capital spending should be subject to some central limits. Other countries' economies seem to survive with the normal mechanisms of interest rate policy. Be that as it may, there are still distinct capital spending limits set in the Comprehensive Spending Review. The amounts were controlled through 'credit approvals', or 'net capital allocations' in Scotland. These strict capital controls are being relaxed (see page 89).

Why the Treasury has sought to control current expenditure is less clear. In economic terms, a sum spent by a local authority must be taxed away from individuals. Councils must cover their expenditure each year. Thus, total

Table 9.1: Identifiable expenditure by country (2000/01)

	As a % of UK identifiable expenditure				Index (UK identifiable expenditure=100)			
	England	Scotland	Wales	N Ireland	England	Scotland	Wales	N Ireland
Education	81	11	5	4	96	124	98	138
Health and personal social services	81	10	6	3	97	116	112	110
Roads and transport	82	11	5	3	98	123	100	90
Housing	72	14	7	7	86	164	142	243
Other environmental services	79	11	8	3	94	124	160	103
Law, order and protective services	80	9	5	6	96	104	93	213
Trade, industry, energy and employment	73	13	5	9	87	154	108	315
Agriculture, fisheries, food and forestry	64	21	6	8	77	251	120	290
Culture, media and sport	82	8	8	3	98	91	162	91
Social security	81	9	6	3	97	110	116	120
Miscellaneous expenditure	80	7	6	8				
Total	**80**	**10**	**6**	**4**	**96**	**118**	**113**	**136**

Source: HM Treasury (2002e)

demand is not directly affected by councils' tax rates. The Treasury, however, worry that high local tax rates may reduce savings and the centre's capacity to tax. The 1984 Rates Act gave central government power to 'cap' the property tax income of local authorities. It then frequently did so or threatened to. The reserve powers remain, but the Labour government has not used them.

Local expenditure may therefore over- or undershoot central government's expectations. Hence *local authority self-financed expenditure* is not part of the Treasury's DELs in the Comprehensive Spending Review. This spending is that funded out of the Council Tax and local charges for services.

The Private Finance Initiative

The need to keep public spending and borrowing within tight limits sometimes produces some perverse consequences. One may be to try to redefine the spending so as to count it outside the limit government has set itself – bending the rules. Calling a social security benefit a tax credit has this effect, as we saw earlier. Shifting capital expenditure on schools and hospitals from the public accounts to the private sector is another example. Many claim that that is what the *Private Finance Initiative* (PFI) was all about. In fact, the case is more complex than that and it is worth trying to disentangle the good from the bad arguments.

Governments have always relied heavily on private construction companies to build schools, houses and other capital projects such as roads. They have borrowed money from the private sector to finance this building, just as a family does when it takes out a mortgage to buy a house or have one built. Beginning in 1992 the Conservative government took all this a stage further. Private companies could now not only undertake the building but also continue to own it and maintain it, indeed even staff it in some cases. The state would pay to lease the building for a period, or it might own it but contract with the private agency to run it. Many combinations were possible. In return the private company would raise the capital to fund the scheme itself. This took the whole capital expenditure and the borrowing out of the public accounts. After 1997 the Labour government pushed the scheme even more vigorously. The Chancellor could keep within his capital spending limits and have more schools and hospitals. Many projects were pushed ahead in ways that got them 'off budget'. Of course, this was, in part, a pure accounting trick. The real economic resources devoted to the projects were not any less and they had to be paid for. Future taxpayers would have to pay just as they had to for a more traditional scheme. Indeed, it was argued that many schemes had not been good value for money partly because local and health authorities were not used to making these kinds of contracts and were taken for a ride by companies who were. In a careful review of the evidence up to 2000 the

Commission on Public Private Partnerships (IPPR, 2001) concluded that there was evidence that in the case of roads and prisons some clear benefits had come from PFI projects. Elsewhere the evidence was thin. Yet there was an economic case for some PFI projects at least:

- putting large property and development deals together is not something the public sector does often or very well. A local health authority may want a walk-in facility as part of a shopping complex in a city centre. Contracting for space with a local developer may make a lot of sense. If it does not work the NHS can give up its lease;
- making the developer responsible and paying them a given sum at the outset puts the risk of overrunning costs on the developer;
- making the developer responsible for the building after it is completed may give the firm an incentive to design it in such a way that minimises maintenance costs.

In none of these cases is a PFI approach the only way to tackle the issues. Penalty clauses and better contracting might do as well, but at least PFI may be useful. As a mere accounting device it is probably counterproductive. For good and bad reasons it featured quite heavily in the Labour government's spending plans.

The 2002 Comprehensive Spending Review

The promises of spending contained in the 2002 Comprehensive Spending Review represent many months, if not years, of work by departments and the Treasury. They promise the fastest growth in health service, personal social services and education spending for many decades. Other service areas did not do so well. It is worth looking over the longer haul to get the promises into some perspective. Overall the plan is that public expenditure as a whole should amount to no more than 42% of GDP. This is only just above the figure for 1996/97, the year before the Labour government assumed office. So it is hardly an impossible burden (see **Table 9.2**). It does depend of course on how fast the GDP grows. The government is assuming a 2.5% per annum growth rate. If this is not achieved by 2006, the share will be more than 42%. Some newspapers have argued that if there is a recession the Chancellor will have to cut back his spending plans. This is not what a sensible Chancellor would do. Sustaining public spending in a recession is precisely what a government needs to do to prevent the recession getting worse. But if the long-term growth rate is not going to reach the hoped-for figure, then long-term rates of spending may have to be rethought.

As **Table 9.2** illustrates, there have been striking changes in the government's rationing priorities. The share of the GDP taken by the NHS will rise to its

Table 9.2: UK public spending^a: past and future (1984/85-2005/06)

Total managed expenditure as a share of GDP

	1984/ 85	1990/ 91	1996/ 97	1999/ 2000	2001/ 02	2005/ 06	% per annum growth 2002/03- 2005/06
Education	4.9	4.7	4.7	4.5	5.1	5.6	7.6
Health (net)	5.0	4.9	5.3	5.3	5.8	7.2	7.4
Personal social services	0.9	1.0	1.3	1.4	1.4	1.6	6.0
Housing	1.4	0.9	0.6	0.3	0.5	0.6	8.9
Social security	11.9	10.5	12.5	11.3	11.2	na	na
Law and order	1.9	2.0	2.1	2.1	2.3	2.5	5.0
Defence	5.2	3.8	2.8	2.5	2.4	2.3	1.2
Transport	2.0	1.7	1.3	0.9	1.0	1.3	12.1
Debt interest	5.3	3.6	3.7	2.8	2.2	na	na
Total^b	**48.0**	**39.9**	**41.0**	**37.7**	**39.2**	**41.9**	

Notes: ^a Estimates assuming 2.5% growth in GDP.
^b Includes other smaller programmes.
'na' refers to the fact that these items fall outside the departmental expenditure limits and depend on unforecastable changes in the economy.

Source: HM Treasury (2002a, 2002c, 2002e)

highest ever by a long way. Health has risen steadily in line with the public's expressed choices. Education was allowed to drop sharply but will recover, although not to the levels seen in the 1970s. Social housing has been a major casualty. (Notice the abolition of mortgage tax relief is not included in these figures.) Social security has taken a lower share as the level of unemployment fell. Defence has halved its share, a process that was underway before the fall of the Berlin Wall. Roads and public transport subsidies have been reduced. The biggest change in recent years has been the fall in the interest on government debt as a share of GDP. In the good years, particularly at the end of the 1990s, the debt was reduced. In addition interest rates have fallen. Consequently the Chancellor has saved a sum equivalent to the combined budgets of the personal social services, housing and public transport.

Although Chancellors may come and go, HM Treasury remains the key agency in social services rationing, now more than ever.

Overview

- Rationing has become more explicit and open as well as more centralised in many respects. There are some opposite tendencies – school budgets, for example. The invasion of professionals' previously guarded independence is one cause of their stated low morale.

- HM Treasury has developed a more proactive role in social policy as it came to be seen as critically important for the 'supply-side' of the economy.

- The Comprehensive Spending Reviews are more explicit and evidence-based than previous expenditure rounds. The Treasury's role looks likely to grow.

Questions for discussion

1. Who rations what kinds of social services resources?

2. Trace the development of Treasury control of public expenditure since 1961. What have been the most significant changes since 1997?

3. Why has the Treasury become more proactive in social policy? Give examples.

Further reading

Still the best, but dated, account of the Treasury's role is **Heclo and Wildavsky (1974)**. A recent account and one focused on its role in social policy formation is **Deakin and Parry (2000)**. For more detailed references in the period 1976-93, use **Thain and Wright (1995)**.

The latest Comprehensive Spending Review is a crucial reference **(HM Treasury, 2002e)**.

Lowe's (1989, 1997a, 1997b) descriptions of the Treasury's part in policy making from the official records in the Public Record Office give a real feel for the power-relations in Whitehall.

For a detailed account of public expenditure regulation in Scotland after devolution see **Heald and McLeod (2003)**. This is to be regularly updated by the authors (www.davidheald.com).

Do public services have a future?

Summary

- How much more do we need to pay for social services?

- What do the British public think about paying more in taxation to improve social services?

- Can the British electorate be encouraged to pay higher taxes for better public services?

- Are there other ways to raise the revenue?

> The fault, dear Brutus, is not in our stars, but in ourselves.
> (*Julius Caesar*, Act 1, p ii)

During the course of the book we have argued that there are strong reasons, grounded in economic theory, why public services are important for efficiency reasons, quite apart from any ethical considerations. Purely private markets fail badly in health, education and long-term care. Markets have greater advantages in pensions and housing, but even there they do not work well for those who have weak claims on the labour market for reasons of ill-health, disability or because of caring responsibilities.

We saw in the last chapter that, relative to other countries, the UK faces much less of a *public funding* dilemma. That is mainly because governments have been very cautious in their promises to future pensioners and because so much of the UK's pension provision is to be funded by private individuals, assuming that presumption holds. It is also a reflection of the fact that the UK's fertility rate has held up better than some other countries in Europe. Projecting present plans for the NHS and other social services into the future, and assuming modest productivity growth in line with post-war experience (2% per annum) the Treasury (2002g) show that future generations will have to pay negligibly more in taxes to support these improvements. Roughly speaking, over the next 50 years the growth in healthcare and education spending envisaged will be paid for by reductions in the social security budget. In most other advanced economies present commitments will result in a rising tax burden. To avoid future tax increases to finance its social policy budget the Italians would have to raise taxes today by two thirds, Japan by 15%, and the US and Germany by 10%. The comparable UK figure is about 2%. So the UK is in a relatively strong position.

These projections assume there will be no further pressure to improve social services, including uprating state pensions. But this must be in doubt. Public expectations, as we have seen, are rising all the time. The most recent survey of British public attitudes (Taylor-Gooby and Hastie, 2002) suggests that most people *do* want improved public services and say that they are prepared to pay more in taxation to achieve this (see **Table 10.1**). The crunch came when they were asked if they were prepared to pay *significantly* more – 3p in the pound in additional taxes to improve a particular service. Less than half said that they were prepared to do so. Asked if they were willing to spend this on the NHS, only 25% said they strongly agreed with such a proposition. This, remember, was the reply to a hypothetical question asked in the privacy of a person's living room without a real vote or the real prospect of losing such income. Support for higher unemployment benefits is minimal. A 3p increase would make a real difference to any *one* of the services discussed in this book. To improve all these services by spending a good deal more – say to Continental levels – would involve raising our level of taxation by about 10p in the pound.

It would involve increasing the take from 40% of all incomes to about 50%. There seems relatively little prospect of such a move. People want the ends but not the means. (Readers may recall the earlier quoted comment of the *Wall Street Journal* correspondent covering the 2001 General Election: "The trouble with the British is that they want European-level services with US levels of tax".)

Changing the tax structure

Perhaps the simplest remedy would be to raise the top level of tax – the 40% rate – on the incomes of the richest. Most on the Left of the Labour Party and many Liberal Democrats favour this. Surely the voters would agree. In fact, the results of the 1992 General Election suggest that the voters may not agree, especially those on middle incomes. They see themselves as one day moving into the top rate tax band. To raise the top rate tax eligibility much higher to avoid this political reaction seriously reduces the revenue gained quite rapidly. Moreover, we know that those on high incomes can employ accountants who manage to outwit the tax laws. The evidence we reviewed in Chapter Three suggests that this is not a particularly successful way to raise the kinds of revenue needed for a major improvement in public services. There may be redistributive or ethical grounds for doing so, but that is a different issue. We also reviewed proposals to rely more on 'hypothecated' taxes – health contributions or an education tax. We found some mileage in such ideas, as we did for taxing 'economic bads' – activities that cause pollution and economic waste, such as car travel in congested cities.

These taxes produce *economic efficiency gains* and should be considered on their own merits, regardless of revenue. As the fuel protests and the resistance of car owners to congestion charges show, this is not an easy route. However,

Table 10.1: **Depth of support for additional taxation**

% of British population saying they would agree to an increase in income tax on given services (pence in the pound)

	1p agree	1p strongly agree	3p agree	3p strongly agree
NHS	43	41	44	25
Schools	54	19	49	12
Public transport	34	8	26	5
Police	49	13	41	9
Retirement pensions	46	19	44	13
Unemployment benefits	14	2	9	2

Source: Data from Taylor-Gooby and Hastie (2002)

the more that we can awaken individuals to the widespread long-term costs of private actions the better.

The scale of public ignorance about how their taxes are spent is actually disturbing (Taylor-Gooby and Hastie, 2002). The belief that large sums are spent on unemployed people, refugees and asylum-seekers as well as lone parents is widespread. Too little is done to counter those prejudices. We saw that the UK is highly unusual in the low amounts of tax local government raises, and this does not help public awareness of the costs and benefits of public services. Taxes seem to go into a vast national black hole. In Sweden a local tax finances healthcare. Voters see local results for the taxes they pay. There is little point in local debate in the UK. Local tax changes and their impact are distorted by the high percentage of revenue coming from the centre. More local reliance on tax revenue could sharpen debate and improve local democracy.

Stealth taxes and beneficial taxes

In a review of tax and spending strategies in 19 rich democracies Wilensky (2002) concludes that those countries that have been most up-front about taxing their populations have been less successful at it. Those who have relied most on property taxes have been least successful of all. Property taxes – the old rates and the newer Council Tax – tend to come in large up-front annual claims. That is true in other countries as well as the UK. Everyone is faced with their total tax liability for the whole year. Few could tell you how much VAT they pay each year, although it is a much larger sum. Income taxes are almost as obvious. Countries that have relied most on this form of tax also attracted a taxpayer backlash. Those that hid their taxes in sales taxes or VAT or employer contributions to social security schemes did better, both in achieving high levels of tax and in sustaining them. It is not surprising that the UK Chancellor resorted to 'stealth' taxes. Yet, as we saw there are severe limits and costs to this approach. Employers' contributions raise the cost of employing labour and reduce wages or employment levels. People in sophisticated democracies soon rumble stealth taxes.

Another approach is to tax those who benefit disproportionately from a given service. The best example (see pages 118-20) is the graduate contribution. Another example would be road pricing. This has the added advantage of promoting economically efficient responses. Faced with the true price of imposing economic costs on others, people's behaviour may actually change.

A similar principle could be applied to long-term care. It could be made free at the point of use and the cost recovered from the estates of those who benefited when they die. This would also encourage families to think harder about supporting their parents.

Charging

This has already been taken a long way and, as we argued in Chapter Three, it is doubtful if there is much further mileage in the strategy. In the NHS, dental and optician care is now effectively charged at cost. Those on low incomes are exempt, along with a wide range of other groups, for example the elderly. Prescription charges are levied but reap little income as the exemptions are so broad. Extending charging to other areas of the healthcare system, such as attending a GP's surgery, is possible. As we saw, this is common in other countries but, as with prescription charges, revenue is likely to be small. The main effect may be to delay access and diagnosis, hence increasing the eventual costs. We saw that evidence from the US supports this view.

Social housing rents are already being raised. Charges exist for most social care services. Children are being charged considerable sums for out-of-school activities. All these charges are waived for the very poor but increase as household income rises. The result is that means testing now extends far up the income scale and it is doubtful whether it can be extended much without serious disincentives to work.

Selective universality

In the light of these difficulties of raising more in taxation, the strategy followed by Blair and Brown has been one of 'selective universality' (Hills and Lelkes, 1999; Glennerster, 2001a). During the last two decades of the 20th century the money spent on social policy has been increasingly targeted on the lower-income groups. This has been partly because social security has been subject to more means testing, but it is also because services in kind have been targeted. Subsidies to higher education have been reduced and the higher-income groups have lost most. Those in social housing are poorer. These are not all positive outcomes but the social wage is now much more pro-poor than it was in the 1970s when Le Grand (1982) characterised the welfare state as pro-middle class. Sefton (2002) shows that in-kind social spending (all the areas covered in this book excluding social security) was barely pro-poor in 1979. Now it is very definitely so. The poorest fifth now benefit twice as much as the richest fifth from these services. Social security already goes very largely to the poor. Large increases in spending have been awarded to the universal services – health and education – in the past five years, and much more is to come. Social care, which *most* older people will experience, is also to be expanded significantly, mainly because, as the Wanless Report pointed out, the NHS is dependent on good community-based social services. On the other hand, the social security budget, which used to form half of the social policy budget, has been held down to make way for the expansion. In Blair's first term in office most of the increase in health and education budgets came at the expense of social security and, as we saw, this is likely to continue to be the case. The outcome was partly achieved for reasons that everyone would applaud, an improved economic record and the reduction in long-term unemployment. A small part of the fall came about through the 'making work pay' and New Deal measures. A significant factor was the refusal to reverse previous Conservative government policy of linking insurance-based 'universal' benefits to prices, not earnings. The UK's low expenditure on future pensions will leave room for its health and education services to go on growing, and be provided at a standard that will keep the middle classes involved both as users and as voters. Such, at least, is the strategy.

It is one not without its problems. The growing number of older voters reliant on private and occupational pensions may become less and less willing to accept a fall in their standard of living. Private pensions did well in the 1980s and 1990s. If they do badly in the 21st century the retired will not remain politically passive. The US shows how powerful the older 'grey' vote could become. In Chapter Seven we reviewed the risks attached to funded private pension schemes. Inherent in a system of targeted state Income Support in old age is the disincentive to saving for those whose private pensions take them just above the Income Support level. We have already seen that the government has had to improve its pension promises. This may not be politically manageable. 'Selective universality' may not be robust in the long term.

Squeezing more out of each pound spent

Voters are increasingly reluctant to accept that their money is being well spent. Governments have certainly tried to squeeze more out of each tax pound. In the 1990s the Conservatives tried competition – the internal or quasi-market. Public and private suppliers competed to deliver public services paid for by public money. The current Labour government has kept some of this legacy, but instinctively has preferred using central targets and performance measures. The evidence we have reviewed on the success of these strategies suggests that both have some place but that competition, giving consumers 'exit power', is probably the most effective. Yet here too there have to be simple well understood performance measures in place so that consumers can both judge and choose. Schools have shown that this can work. It matters to the staff as, parents having made their choice, the state cash follows the pupil. National Curriculum Assessment tests have become well-appreciated measures of a child's performance. Judgements made about a school's performance in league tables may be unfair given a school's intake, but that is not impossible to remedy. Moreover, the fact that parents know how well their child is doing against some national benchmark has proved salutary.

The removal of what limited competitive pressure there was on hospital trusts in 1997 coincided with a sharp decline in their productivity, as we saw.

Social care has also shown the virtues of variety in the range of types of provider now operating.

Elaborate central guidelines and targets seem, on the other hand, counterproductive. Decentralised budgets, consumer choice and agency independence can produce good results for well-informed choosers. They can also lead some providers to cream-skim more able children or easy-to-treat clients, but old-style patterns of funding were equally at fault for ignoring frontline incentives. The details of funding mechanisms, at the institutional level, matter a lot. They matter not just in terms of getting efficiency incentives right, but in getting resources to where need is greatest.

Whatever we do, it costs

Protagonists on both sides of the argument tend to ignore reality. Reluctant taxpayers seem to forget that if the public sector collapses the private alternative would, for most, be exorbitant.

We have reviewed the evidence on private and public pension schemes. The harsh fact is that under both alternatives the pensions of more older people have to be paid for, one way or another, by those at work. This may mean people working longer or paying higher contributions, or a mixture of both.

In order to gauge the potential costs to a family, if they felt that they could no longer rely on the public services, we costed out the implications of 'going private'. We took as an example a family of two adults with children aged 14 and 18. In 2002 the Independent Schools Information Service advised us that day tuition fees varied from £1,800 to £3,500 per term for a child in secondary school. If parents had to pay the full cost of a university education it would depend on the choice of subject. A course in Social Science would require £10,000 a year, in Medicine nearly £21,000. Imperial College charges £13,500 for Computing. Maintenance costs, they advised, should be taken to be about £7,500; outside London it would be less.

Were the family to try to replicate NHS cover privately, assuming all of them were well and none had a poor health record, the annual premium would be between £1,600 and £1,900 a year.

If the parents wished to insure themselves against long-term care they would probably only be able to do so when they reached the age of 50. Again, for a healthy man the costs would amount to £2,904 and for a woman £4,056 per year.

In **Table 10.2** we include a quote for our family from the National Association of Pension Schemes. We asked what it would cost if the couple wished to have a pension equal to half the main earner's salary on retirement at the age of 65, assuming that the widow would get half this and that the pension was inflation proofed. We assumed that contributions would start at the age of 25. At August 2002 investment returns and annuity rates and assuming a 2.1% inflation and a 1.5% increase in salary above inflation, the advice was that such a couple would need to contribute about 11% of the husband's earnings. Were he to leave it to the age of 35 to start contributing, this would rise to over 17%.

Figures from the *Financial Times* (11/12 January 2003) suggest a 15% contribution from the age of 25. Some pension consultants suggest that a contributor wishing for a decent half-pay pension on retirement at the age of 65 should subtract five from his or her age and take that as the percentage of their income that they should pay in contributions. Thus a 25-year-old should consider paying a fifth of their income in pension contributions; beginning at the age of 30: a quarter. Of course, the employer might pay some of this.

Finally the family will have mortgage repayments. Outside London, for example, for a three-bedroomed house in Leeds, the repayments would amount to £6,300 per year. In London the costs would be much higher.

Taking all these costs together the burden of 'going private' might come to £40,000 per year (see **Table 10.2**).

This would still not cover long-term disability or mental health. These groups take much of the NHS budget so we must suppose taxes would still be levied to provide such services.

The impact on a family's decision to have children could be significant, but a lower birth rate would deepen the ageing crisis further. The ramifications of any failure to fund public services adequately are wider than is often appreciated.

Working longer

We saw that it is completely unrealistic to expect that individuals can work for shorter and shorter periods of their lives and expect their current contributions and taxes to support today's level of pensions, ungenerous as those are. The same holds true if we are talking about private pensions. Longer lives require longer working lives to finance an equivalent relative standard of living in retirement. From 1948-80, women who entered the labour force financed a substantial rise in social spending. They added to the available tax resources and real output. That gender dividend has been largely reaped. One of the important additional reasons for raising the work participation rate, in the fifth of families without an earner, is to increase government revenue as well as reduce the cost of social security. However, the really big shift will have to come in the age at which people leave the labour force. This may happen naturally as people find their pensions are too low to live on, and/or it can happen with financial inducements built into tax and benefit arrangements.

Table 10.2: **The costs of 'going private'**

Costs per annum for family: 2 adults, children 14 and 18

	£
School fees[a]	7,500
University tuition[b]:	
Social science	10,500
Computing	13,500
Medicine	20,700
Maintenance costs:	
London	7,500
Rest of country	5,000
Health – full family cover for a healthy family	
BUPA	1,920
Norwich Union	1,585
Long-term care[c]	
Healthy male aged 50	2,904
Female	4,056
Pension contributions[d]	10.8% of salary
Mortgage repayments (25-year loan):	
Outside London (Leeds)[e]	6,312
London	17,532-35,064

Notes and sources:
[a] The Independent Schools Information Service quoted a range of tuition fees of £1,800 per term to £3,500 per term. This figure is for a mid-range school.
[b] Overseas student fees represent the full cost of tuition. Figures from the London School of Economic and Political Science and Imperial College, London.
[c] Will bring a long-term care payment for a residential home or domiciliary services amounting to £3,000 a month if suffering from three kinds of disabling factors (Activities of Daily Living) quoted by BUPA.
[d] National Association of Pension Schemes estimated contribution as a percentage of salary to a personal pension plan that would secure a pension of 50% of final salary at 65 assuming contributions began at 24. (The contribution required starting at age 35 is 17.4%.) The scheme would be a joint life RPI linked pension, assuming 2.10% inflation, a 50% spouse's pension.
[e] Halifax Building Society (London prices £250,000-£500,000), three-bedroom house.

Vouchers and tax incentives

The standard economist's response to these dilemmas is the 'top-upable voucher' that we have discussed at various points in the book. Taxpayers implicitly decide how much they will spend on each child or patient. If that is less than a parent wishes to see spent it gives them a chance to pay more, adding to the tax-funded voucher whatever they deem fit in extra school fees at higher charging schools. We have seen that this could work best in education where it is feasible to allocate a single sum of money or voucher to each primary or secondary school child. Even here special needs children would require more. So too, arguably, would children from poorer homes. However, healthcare, long-term care or social care raise more difficult issues. Most of us use the NHS very little, but some use it a great deal. A uniform average cost voucher would be far too much for most of us. We could purchase a very generous health insurance package with monthly check-ups, sauna baths and massage while our sick neighbours failed to get the care they needed. To be at all equitable the vouchers would have to be 'risk-adjusted' – that is, related to our predicted level of need. This would require individualised assessment and be hopelessly impracticable or be so crude as to cause injustice. Much the same applies to long-term care.

This leaves education as the only feasible candidate. Yet, as we saw in Chapter Six, there are reasons unique to education that make that strategy problematic too. Voucher schemes are expressly designed to result in a variety of private schools, which attract children of parents with like incomes and, more importantly, like preferences. Children with parents who have a low priority for education will be collected together in the poor institutions. We know that the spin-off from lower achieving children mixing with and being taught with higher achievers is considerable. These effects are at least as important as moderate differences in education spending. Segregation reduces this 'spillover' benefit. If this is so, the overall 'investment' in children under such an arrangement may fall.

We saw that the whole theory of top-up vouchers depends on the assumption that the move to a largely privately provided and significantly privately funded system would not change voting preferences to pay taxes. It is at least possible that it would *erode* taxpayers' support. If education becomes largely a private act let the taxpayer forget it.

Tapping the willingness to pay

Are there other ways to tap a willingness to spend more, which nearly half the population has? Local taxation may be one possibility, but local councils seem even less popular than central government. It may be that smaller units with their own voluntary tax raising powers would be different. In our first flat as a young married couple we backed on to a communal garden in North Kensington. The houses around the garden – several hundred dwellings – had the power to vote to levy an add-on to the local rates. This dated back to a Victorian private act of Parliament. The sum raised could be used for the upkeep of the garden and other facilities. There were arguments about adding nursery facilities, I recall. Parish councils in rural areas had similar powers. The fact that local small communities decide how such money is spent on their very local facilities means they may be willing to levy extra taxes for local amenities. They may then be less prepared to pay national taxes! Evidence from the US suggests that this is not so. High tax-paying localities by choice also tend to vote for higher national taxes.

The idea could be extended to a national level. With modern computerisation, tax forms could include a section that enabled individuals to allocate part of their income – tax free – to any public purpose. Public agencies would be free to persuade taxpayers to support their cause just as charities do now. The money so designated on the tax return would come back to the school or hospital or local social services department. And why not?

Overview: Dear Brutus

Do public services have a future? Economic theory suggests that they should have. But there are no quick fixes. It will require higher taxes from a population that works for longer. But higher taxes require consent – the public must be convinced that public services are delivering high quality when they want them, where they want them and in the way that they want them. If public sector reforms can do this, governments may succeed in persuading them, particularly if taxpayers come to appreciate the price of private alternatives. That is the challenge the public services face.

Questions for discussion

1. What do public attitude surveys suggest about the British public's willingness to pay higher taxes to fund better social services?

2. What strategy would you adopt to pay for improved social services?

Further reading

The annual British Social Attitudes Surveys give the only time series describing changing views on the central questions posed in this chapter. The papers by **Hills and Lelkes (1999)** and **Taylor-Gooby and Hastie (2002)** should be read not only for the data but also for the discussion of the issues in the two rather different contributions.

References

Aaron, H. (1966) 'The social insurance paradox', *Canadian Journal of Economics,* vol 32, August, pp 371-4.

Aaron, H. (ed) (1999) *Behavioural dimensions of retirement economics,* Washington, DC: Brookings Institution.

Aaron, H. and Swartz, B. (1984) *The painful prescription*, Washington, DC: Brookings Institution.

Acheson Report (1998) *Independent Inquiry into Inequalities in Health: Report*, London: The Stationery Office.

Agulnik, P. (2000) 'Pension reform in the UK: evaluating retirement income policy', PhD thesis, London: London University.

Akerlof, G.A. (1970) 'The market for "lemons": qualitative uncertainty and the market mechanism', *Quarterly Journal of Economics*, vol 84, pp 488-500.

Alcock, P., Glennerster, H., Oakley, A. and Sinfield, A. (eds) (2001) *Welfare and wellbeing: Richard Titmuss's contribution to social policy*, Bristol: The Policy Press.

Allen, I. and Perkins, E. (eds) (1995) *The future of family care for older people*, London: HMSO.

Anderson, G.F. and Hussey, P.S. (2000) 'Population ageing: a comparison among industrial countries', *Health Affairs*, vol 19, no 3, pp 191-203.

Anheier, H.K. (2000) *Social services in Europe: An annotated bibliography*, London: Observatory for the Development of Social Services in Europe.

Arber, S. and Ginn, J. (1995) 'Gender differences in informal caring', *Health and Social Care in the Community*, vol 3, pp 19-31.

Arrow, K. (1951) *Social choice and individual values*, New York, NY: Wiley.

Atkinson, A.B. (1999) *The economic consequences of rolling back the welfare state*, Cambridge, MA: MIT Press.

Atkinson, A.B. and King, M.A. (1982) 'Housing policy taxation and reform', *Midland Bank Review*, Spring, pp 7-15.

Atkinson, A.B. and Micklewright, J. (1991) 'Unemployment compensation and labour market transitions: a critical review', *Journal of Economic Literature*, vol 29, no 4, pp 1679-727.

Audit Commission (1986) *Making a reality of community care*, London: HMSO.

Audit Commission (1996) *What the doctor ordered: A study of GP fundholders in England and Wales*, London: The Stationery Office.

Ball, S.J. (2002) *Class strategies and the education market: The middle classes and social advantage*, London: Routledge Farmer.

Barr, N. (1998) *The economics of the welfare state*, Oxford: Oxford University Press.

Barr, N. (ed) (2001a) *Economic theory and the welfare state*, vols 1-3, Cheltenham: Edward Elgar.

Barr, N. (2001b) *The welfare state as piggy bank: Information, risk, uncertainty and the role of the state*, Oxford: Oxford University Press.

Barr, N. (2003) *Financing higher education in the UK: The 2003 White paper*, Evidence given to the House of Commons Education and Skills Committee, March (http://econ.lse.ac.uk/staff/nb).

Becker, G.S. (1976) *The economic approach to human behaviour*, Chicago, IL: Chicago University Press.

Billis, D. and Glennerster, H. (1998) 'Human services and the voluntary sector: towards a theory of comparative advantage', *Journal of Social Policy*, vol 27, part 1, pp 79-98.

Blundell, R., Dearden, L., Meghir, C. and Sianesi, B. (1999) 'Human capital investment: the returns from education and training to the individual, the firm and the economy', *Fiscal Studies*, vol 20, no 1, pp 1-23.

Boadway, R. and Wildasin, D. (1996) 'Taxation and saving', in M.P. Devereux (ed) *The economics of tax policy*, Oxford: Oxford University Press, pp 55-106.

Borsch-Supan, A. (2000) 'A model under siege: a case study of the German retirement insurance system', *The Economic Journal*, vol 110, F24-F45.

Bosworth, B. and Burtless, G. (eds) (1998) *Ageing societies: The global dimension*, Washington, DC: Brookings Institution.

Bovaird, T. and Halachmi, A. (2001) 'Learning from international approaches to best value', *Policy & Politics*, vol 29, no 4, pp 451-63.

Bowley, M. (1945) *Housing and the state 1919-44*, London: Allen & Unwin.

Bradley, S. and Taylor, J. (2000) *The effect of the quasi-market on the efficiency–equity trade-off in the secondary school sector*, Centre for Research in the Economics of Education Discussion Paper EC9/00, Lancaster: Lancaster University.

Bradley, S., Johnes, G. and Millington, J. (1999) *School choice, competition and the efficiency of secondary schools in England*, Centre for Research in the Economics of Education Discussion Paper EC3/99, Lancaster: Lancaster University.

Bramley, G. (1998) *Where does public spending go? Pilot study to analyse the flows of public expenditure into local areas*, DETR Regeneration Research Report, London: DETR.

Brittain, J.A. (1972) *The pay roll for social security*, Washington, DC: Brookings Institution.

Bromley, N. and Stibbs, J. (2001) *Universal access, individual choice: International lessons for the NHS*, London: Centre for Reform.

Brooks, R., Regan, S. and Robinson, P. (2002) *A new contract for retirement*, London: IPPR.

Buchanan, J.M. (1975) *The limits of liberty: Between anarchy and Leviathan,* Chicago, IL: University of Chicago Press.

Bulmer, M. (1986) *Neighbours: The work of Philip Abrams*, Cambridge: Cambridge University Press.

Burchardt,T., Hills, J. and Propper, C. (1999) *Private welfare and public policy*, York: Joseph Rowntree Foundation.

Burgess, S. and Propper, C. (2002) 'The dynamics of poverty in Britain', in J. Hills, J. Le Grand, J. and D. Piachaud (eds) *Understanding social exclusion*, Oxford: Oxford University Press, pp 46-61.

Burtless, G. (1999) 'An economic view of retirement', in H. Aaron (ed) *Behavioral dimensions of retirement economics*, Washington, DC: Brookings Institution, pp 7-42.

Butler, D., Adonis, A. and Travers, T. (1994) *Failure in British government: The politics of the Poll Tax*, Oxford: Oxford University Press.

Calabresi, G. and Bobbitt, P. (1978) *Tragic choices*, New York, NY: Norton.

Callender, C. (2002) 'The costs of widening participation: contradictions in new Labour's student funding policies', *Social Policy and Society*, vol 1, no 2, pp 83-94.

Campbell, J.C. and Ikegami, I. (2000) 'Long-term care insurance comes to Japan', *Health Affairs*, vol 19, no 3, pp 26-39.

Cannan E. (1898) *The history of local rates in England* (2nd edn, 1912), London: King.

Care Development Group Report (2001) *Fair care for older people*, Edinburgh: Scottish Executive.

Chapman, B. (1997) 'Conceptual issues and the Australian experience with income contingent charges for higher education', *Economic Journal*, vol 107, May, pp 738-51.

Christie, I. and Leadbeater, C. (1998) *To our mutual advantage*, London: Demos.

Chubb, J.E. and Moe, T.E. (1990) *Politics, markets and America's schools*, Washington, DC: Brookings Institution.

Clarke, L. (1995) 'Family care and changing family structure: bad news for the elderly', in I. Allen and E. Perkins (eds) *The future of family care for older people*, London: HMSO.

Collard, D. (1978) *Altruism and economy: A study in non-selfish economics*, Oxford: Martin Robertson.

Commission on Taxation and Citizenship (2000) *Paying for progress: A new politics of tax for public spending*, London: Fabian Society.

Commonwealth of Australia (1997) *Learning for life: Review of higher education financing and policy: A policy discussion paper*, Canberra: AGPS.

Coons, J. and Sugarman, S. (1978) *Education by choice: The case for family control*, Berkeley, CA: University of California Press.

Corcoran, M. (2001) 'Mobility, persistence, and the consequences of poverty for children: child and adult outcomes', in S.H. Danziger and R.H. Haverman (eds) *Understanding Poverty*, Cambridge, MA: Harvard University Press, pp 127-61.

CPAG (Child Poverty Action Group) (2002) *Welfare benefits handbook*, London: CPAG.

Cuellar, A.E. and Weiner, J.M. (2000) 'Can social insurance for long-term care work? The experience of Germany', *Health Affairs*, vol 19, no 3, pp 8-25.

Deakin, N. (2001) *In search of civil society*, Basingstoke: Palgrave.

Deakin, N. and Parry, R. (2000) *The Treasury and social policy*, Basingstoke: Macmillan.

Dearing Committee (1997) *Higher education in the learning society*, NCIHE/97/856, London: The Stationery Office.

DETR (Department of the Environment, Transport and the Regions) (2000) *Quality and choice: A decent home for all – the way forward for housing*, London: DETR.

DETR (2001) *Guide to social rent reforms*, London: DETR.

Devereux, M.P. (1996) *The economics of tax policy*, Oxford: Oxford University Press.

DfES (Department for Education and Skills) (2003) *The future of higher education*, Cm 5735, London: The Stationery Office.

DfES and the Cabinet Office (2002) *Delivering for children and families*, London: The Cabinet Office Strategy Unit.

DHSS (Department of Health and Social Security) (1976) *Sharing resources for health in England*, Report of the Resource Allocation Working Party, London: HMSO.

Diamond, P. (1996) 'Social security reform in Chile: an economic perspective', in P. Diamond, D. Lindeman and H. Young (eds) *Social security: What role for the future?*, Washington, DC: National Academy of Social Insurance, pp 213-24.

Disney, R. (2000) 'Crises in public pension programmes in OECD: what are the reform options?', *The Economic Journal*, vol 110, pp F1-F23.

Disney, R., Emmerson, C. and Wakefield, M. (2001) 'Pension reform and saving in Britain', *Oxford Review of Economic Policy*, vol 17, no 1, pp 70-94.

Dixon, A. and Mossialos, E. (2002) *Health systems in eight countries: Trends and challenges*, London: London School of Economics and Political Science, European Observatory on Health Care Systems.

DoH (Department of Health) (1988) *Community care: Agenda for action*, London: HMSO.

DoH (1989) *Working for patients*, Cm 555, London: HMSO.

DoH (1998) *Modernising social services: Promoting independence, improving protection, raising standards*, Cm 4169, London: The Stationery Office.

DoH (1999) *A new approach to social service performance: Consultation document*, London: The Stationery Office.

DoH (2000) *The NHS plan: A plan for investment, a plan for reform*, Cm 4818-1, London: The Stationery Office.

DoH (2002a) *Delivering the NHS plan: Next steps on investment next steps on reform*, Cm 5503, London: The Stationery Office.

DoH (2002b) *Bulletin 2002/8 personal social services expenditure and unit costs: England 2000-2001*, London: DoH (www.doh.gov.uk).

DoH (2002c) 'Report', www.doh.gov.uk

Donnison, D. (1967) *The government of housing*, Harmondsworth: Penguin.

Donnison, D. and Ungerson, C. (1982) *Housing policy*, Harmondsworth: Penguin.

Dowling, B. (2000) *GPs and purchasing in the NHS*, Aldershot: Ashgate.

Doyal, L. and Gough, I. (1991) *A theory of human need*, London: Macmillan.

Dreze, J., Sen, A. and Hussain, A. (1995) *The political economy of hunger*, Oxford: Oxford University Press.

Dunleavy, P. (1991) *Democracy, bureaucracy and public choice*, Hemel Hempstead: Harvester Wheatsheaf.

Dunleavy, P. and O'Leary, B. (1987) *Theories of the state*, London: Macmillan.

DWP (Department for Work and Pensions) (2002a) *Social security statistics*, London: The Stationery Office.

DWP (2002b) *Simplicity, security and choice: Working and saving for retirement*, Cm 5677, London: The Stationery Office.

DWP (2002c) 'Building choice and responsibility: a radical agenda for housing benefit' (www.dwp.gov.uk/housingbenefit).

Endo, Y. and Katayama, E. (1998) 'Population ageing and Japanese economic performance', in B. Bosworth and G. Burtless (eds) *Ageing societies: The global dimension*, Washington, DC: Brookings Institution, pp 240-66.

Esteban, J.M. and Sakovics, J. (1993) 'Inter-temporal transfer institutions', *Journal of Economic Theory*, vol 61, pp 189-205.

EUEPC (European Union Economic Policy Committee) (2001) *Budgetary challenges posed by ageing populations*, Brussels: European Union (http://europa.eu.int/comm/economy_finance_en.htm).

European Observatory on Health Care Systems (1999) *Health care systems in transition: United Kingdom*, Copenhagen: WHO Regional Office for Europe (www.observatory.dk), p 75.

European Observatory on Health Care Systems (2001) *Health care systems in transition: Sweden*, Copenhagen: WHO Regional Office for Europe (www.observatory.dk).

Evandrou, M. (1998) 'Great expectations: social policy and the new millennium elders', in M. Bernard and J. Phillips (eds) *The social policy of old age*, London: Centre for Policy on Ageing.

Evandrou, M. and Falkingham, J. (1998) 'The personal social services', in H. Glennerster and J. Hills (eds) *The state of welfare: The economics of social spending*, Oxford: Oxford University Press, pp 189-256.

Evans, M. (1998) 'Social security: dismantling the pyramids?', in H. Glennerster and J. Hills (eds) *The state of welfare: The economics of social spending*, Oxford: Oxford University Press, pp 257-307.

Evans, M. (2001) *Welfare to work and the organisation of opportunity: Lessons from abroad*, CASE Report 15, London: Centre for Analysis of Social Exclusion, London School of Economics and Political Science.

Falkingham, J. and Hills, J. (1995) *The dynamic of welfare: The welfare state and the life cycle*, Hemel Hempstead: Prentice Hall.

Falkingham, J. and Rake, K. (1999) *Partnership in pensions: Delivering a secure retirement for women?*, CASE Paper 24, London: London School of Economics and Political Science.

Falkingham, S., Rake, K. and Paxton, W. (2002) 'Modelling pension choices for the 21st century', in R. Brooks, S. Regan and P. Robinson (eds) *A new contract for retirement: Modelling policy options for 2050*, London: IPPR.

Feder, J., Komisar, H.L. and Niefeld, M. (2000) 'Long-term care in the United States: an overview', *Health Affairs*, vol 19, no 3, pp 40-56.

Feldstein, M (1974) 'Social security, induced retirement and aggregate capital accumulation', *Journal of Political Economy*, vol 82, no 5, pp 905-26.

Feldstein, M. (1980) 'International differences in social security spending', *Journal of Public Economics*, vol 14, pp 225-44.

Field, F. and Piachaud, D. (1971) 'The poverty trap', *New Statesman*, 3 December.

Finch, J. (1995) 'Responsibilities, obligations and commitments', in I. Allen and E. Perkins (eds) *The future of family care for older people*, London: HMSO, pp 51-64.

Forder, J. (2000) *Regulating entrepreneurial behaviour in social care*, London: WHO Health Observatory, London School of Economics and Political Science.

Freeman, R., Topel, R. and Swedenborg, B. (eds) (1997) *The welfare state in transition: Reforming the Swedish model*, Chicago, IL: University of Chicago Press.

Friedman, M. (1962) *Capitalism and freedom*, Chicago, IL: University of Chicago Press.

Gerdtham, U.G. and Jonsson, B. (2000) 'Cross-country studies of health care expenditure', in J. Culyer and J. Newhouse (eds) *The handbook of health economics*, Amsterdam: North-Holland.

Gewirtz, S., Ball, S.J. and Bowe, R. (1995) *Markets, choice and equity in education*, Buckingham: Open University Press.

Glennerster, H. (1972) 'Education and inequality', in P. Townsend and N. Bosanquet (eds) *Labour and inequality*, London: Fabian Society, pp 83-107.

Glennerster, H. (1991) 'Quasi-markets for education?', *Economic Journal*, vol 101, no 408, pp 1268-86.

Glennerster, H. (1996) *Caring for the very old: Public and private solutions*, WSP/126, London: Sticerd, London School of Economics and Political Science.

Glennerster, H. (1998) 'Education: reaping the harvest?', in H. Glennerster and J. Hills (eds) *The state of welfare: The economics of social spending*, Oxford: Oxford University Press, pp 27-74.

Glennerster, H. (2000) *British social policy since 1945* (2nd edn), Oxford: Blackwell.

Glennerster, H. (2001a) 'Social Policy', in A. Seldon (ed) *The Blair effect*, London: Little, Brown and Co, pp 383-403.

Glennerster, H. (2001b) *United Kingdom education 1997-2001*, CASE Paper No 50, Centre for Analysis of Social Exclusion, London: London School of Economics and Political Science.

Glennerster, H. (2002) 'United Kingdom education, 1997-2001', *Oxford Review of Economic Policy*, vol 18, no 2, pp 120-36.

Glennerster, H., Cohen, A. and Bovell, V. (1998) 'Alternatives to fundholding', *International Journal of Health Services*, vol 28, no 1, pp 47-66.

Glennerster, H. with Korman, N. and Marslen-Wilson, F. (1983) *Planning for priority groups*, Oxford: Martin Robertson.

Glennerster, H. and Hills, J. (1998) *The state of welfare: The economics of social spending*, Oxford: Oxford University Press.

Glennerster, H. and Le Grand, J. (1995) 'The developments of quasi-markets in welfare provision in the United Kingdom', *International Journal of Health Services*, vol 25, no 2, pp 203-18.

Glennerster, H. and Wilson, G. (1970) *Paying for private schools*, London: Allen Lane, The Penguin Press.

Glennerster, H., Falkingham, J. and Barr, N. (1995) 'Education funding, equity and the life cycle', in J. Falkingham and J. Hills (eds) *The dynamic of welfare: The welfare state and the life cycle*, Hemel Hempstead: Harvester Wheatsheaf, p 119.

Glennerster, H., Hills, J. and Travers, T. (2000) *Paying for health, education and housing*, Oxford: Oxford University Press.

Glennerster, H., Matsaganis, M. and Owens, P. (1994) *Implementing GP fundholding: Wild card or winning hand*, Buckingham: Open University Press.

Glennerster, H., Wilson, G. and Merrett, S. (1968) 'A graduate tax', *Higher Education*, vol 1, no 1, pp 26-38 (reprinted with update 2003).

Goldstein, H. and Noden, P. (2003: forthcoming) 'Modelling social segregation', *Oxford Review of Education*, vol 29, no 2.

Goodin, R. and Le Grand, J. (1987) *Not only the poor: The middle classes and the welfare state*, London: Allen & Unwin.

Gorard, S. and Fitz, J. (1998) 'The more things change.... The missing impact of marketisation?', *International Studies in Sociology of Education*, vol 8, pp 299-314.

Gosden, P.H.J.H. (1976) *Education in the second world war*, London: Methuen.

Gough, I. (1979) *The political economy of the welfare state*, London: Macmillan.

Gough, I., Bradshaw, J., Ditch, J., Eardley, T. and Whiteford, P. (1997) 'Social assistance in OECD countries', *Journal of European Social Policy*, vol 7, no 1, pp 17-43.

Government Actuary's Department (2001) *Occupational pension schemes 1995 – tenth survey by the Government Actuary*, London: The Stationery Office.

Gravelle, H., Dusheiko, M. and Sutton, M. (2002) 'The demand for elective surgery in a public system: time and money prices in the UK National Health Service', *Journal of Health Economics*, vol 21, no 3, pp 423-49.

Grundy, E. (1995) 'Demographic influences on the future of family care', in I. Allen and E. Perkins (eds) *The future of family care for older people*, London: HMSO.

Gundlach, E., Woessman, L. and Gmelin, J. (2001) 'The decline of schooling productivity in OECD countries', *The Economic Journal*, vol 11, May, pp 135-47.

Guillebaud Committee (1956) *Committee of enquiry into the cost of the National Health Service*, Cmd 9663, London: HMSO.

Hall, A.S. (1974) *The point of entry*, London: Allen & Unwin.

Hansmann, H. (1980) 'The role of nonprofit enterprise', *Yale Law Journal*, vol 89, pp 835-901.

Hansmann, H. (1987) 'Economic theories of nonprofit organisation', in W.W. Powell (ed) *The nonprofit sector: A handbook*, New Haven, CT: Yale University Press.

Hansson, I. and Stuart, C. (1989) 'Social security as trade among living generations', *American Economic Review*, vol 17, December, pp 1182-95.

Harris, C. and Scrivener, G. (1996) 'Fundholders' prescribing costs: the first five years', *British Medical Journal*, vol 313, pp 1531-4.

Heady, C. (1996) 'Optimal taxation as a guide to tax policy', in M.P. Devereux (ed) *The economics of tax policy*, Oxford: Oxford University Press, pp 23-54.

Heald, D. (1980) *Territorial equity and public finance: Concepts and confusion*, Glasgow: Centre for the Study of Public Policy.

Heald, D. and McLeod, A. (2003) *The laws of Scotland, Stair Memorial Encyclopedia: Public expenditure*, London: Butterworths.

Heclo, H. and Wildavsky, A. (1974, 2nd edn 1981) *The private government of public money*, London: Macmillan.

Hill, M. (ed) (1993) *The policy process: A reader*, London: Harvester Wheatsheaf.

Hills, J. (1998) 'Housing: a decent home within the reach of every family?', in H. Glennerster and J. Hills (eds) *The state of welfare: The economics of social spending*, Oxford; Oxford University Press, pp 122-88.

Hills, J. (2000) *Reinventing social housing finance*, London: IPPR.

Hills, J. (2001a) 'Poverty and social security: what rights? Whose responsibilities?', in A. Park, J. Curtice, K. Thompson, L. Jarvis and C. Bromley (eds) *British Social Attitudes: The 18th Report: Public policy, social ties*, London: Sage Publications, pp 1-28.

Hills, J. (2001b) 'Inclusion or exclusion? The role of housing subsidies and benefits', *Urban Studies*, vol 38, no 11, pp 1887-902.

Hills, J. (2003) *Sixty years on from Beveridge: Is national insurance heading for retirement?*, CASE Paper, London: Centre for Analysis of Social Exclusion, London School of Economics and Political Science.

Hills, J. and Lelkes, O. (1999) 'Social security, selective universalism and patchwork redistribution', in R. Jowell, J. Curtice, A. Park and K. Thompson (eds) *British Social Attitudes: The 16th Report: Who shares New Labour values?*, London: Ashgate, pp 1-22.

Hills, J., Le Grand, J. and Piachaud, D. (2002) *Understanding social exclusion*, Oxford: Oxford University Press.

Hirsh, F. (1977) *Social limits to growth*, London: Routledge and Kegan Paul.

Hirschman, A.O. (1970) *Exit, voice and loyalty: Responses to decline in firms, organisations and states*, Cambridge, MA: Harvard University Press.

HM Treasury (1961) *Control of public expenditure*, The Plowden Report, Cm 1432, London: The Stationery Office.

HM Treasury (1998) *Modern public services for Britain: Investing in reform, Comprehensive Spending Review: 1999-2002*, Cm 4011, London: The Stationery Office (www.hm-treasury.gov.uk).

HM Treasury (2000) *Prudent for a purpose: Building opportunity and security for all. Spending Review: New public spending plans 2001-2004,* Cm 4807, London: The Stationery Office.

HM Treasury (2001) *Securing our future health: Taking a long-term view*, Interim Wanless Report, London: HM Treasury (www.hm-treasury.gov.uk).

HM Treasury (2002a) *Budget 2002*, HC 592, London: The Stationery Office (www.hm-treasury.gov.uk).

HM Treasury (2002b) *Securing our future health: Taking a long-term view*, Final Wanless Report (www.hm-treasury.gov.uk/wanless).

HM Treasury (2002c) *2002 Spending Review: New public spending plans 2003-2006*, Cm 5570, London: HM Treasury (www.hm-treasury.gov.uk).

HM Treasury (2002d) *2002 Spending Review, Public Service Agreements 2003-2006*, Cm 5571, London: The Stationery Office (www.hm.treasury.gov.uk).

HM Treasury (2002e) *Public expenditure 2002-03*, Cm 5401, London: The Stationery Office.

HM Treasury (2002f) *The role of the voluntary and community sector in service delivery: A cross cutting review*, London: HM Treasury.

HM Treasury (2002g) *Long-term public finance report: An analysis of fiscal sustainability*, London: HM Treasury.

HM Treasury (2002h) *Pre-budget report*, Cm 5664, London: HM Treasury (www.hm.treasury.gov.uk).

Hochman, H.M. and Rodgers, J.D. (1969) 'Pareto optimal redistribution', *American Economic Review*, vol 59, pp 542-7.

Holloway, S. and Tamplin, S. (2001) 'Valuing informal childcare in the UK', *Economic Trends*, September, London: The Stationery Office, pp 51-60.

Holmans, A.E. (1987) *Housing policy in Britain: A history*, London: Croom Helm.

House of Commons Treasury Committee (1997) *The Barnett formula*, HC 341, London: The Stationery Office.

House of Commons Education and Skills Committee (2002) *Post-16 support*, HC 445, London: The Stationery Office.

Hoxby, C.M. (2000) 'Does competition among public schools benefit students and taxpayers?', *The American Economic Review*, vol 90, pp 1209-38.

Hunter, D.J. (1993) 'Rationing and health care', *Critical Public Health*, vol 4, no 1, pp 27-33.

Hunter, D.J. (1995) 'Rationing health care: the political perspective', in R.J. Maxwell (ed) *British Medical Bulletin*, vol 51, no 4, Edinburgh: Churchill Livingstone.

IPPR (Institute of Public Policy Research) (2001) *Building better partnerships*, London: IPPR.

Jacobzone, S. (1999) *Ageing and care for frail elderly persons*, Paris: OECD.

Jones, A. and Posnett, S. (1993) 'The economics of charity', in N. Barr and D. Whynes (eds) *Current issues in the economics of welfare*, Basingstoke: Macmillan, pp 130-52.

Judge, K. (1978) *Rationing social services: A study of resource allocation in the personal social services*, London: Heinemann.

Judge, K. and Matthews, J. (1980) *Charging for care: A study of consumer charges and the personal social services*, London: Allen & Unwin.

Katz, B. (1999) 'Beyond city limits: a new metropolitan agenda', in H.J. Aaron and R.D. Reischauer (eds) *Setting national priorities*, Washington, DC: Brookings Institution, pp 303-31.

Kemp, P. (1998) *Housing Benefit: Time for reform*, York: Joseph Rowntree Foundation.

Kemp, P., Wilcox, S. and Rhodes, D. (2002) *Housing Benefit reform next steps*, York: Joseph Rowntree Foundation.

Kendall, J., Knapp, M. and Forder, J. (2003) 'Social care and the non profit sector in the western developed world', Mimeo, London: LSE Health and Social Care, *The non profit sector: A research handbook* (2nd edn), Harvard, MA: Yale University Press.

Kendall, J. with Almond, S. (1998) *The UK voluntary (third) sector in comparative perspective: Exceptional growth and transformation*, London: Personal Social Services Research Unit, London School of Economics and Political Science.

Kendall, J. and Knapp, M. (1996) *The voluntary sector in the UK*, Manchester: Manchester University Press.

King's Fund (2002) *The future of the NHS: A framework for debate*, London: King's Fund.

Klein, R. (1997) 'Defining a package of healthcare services the NHS is responsible for – the case against', *British Medical Journal*, vol 314, pp 506-9.

Klein, R., Day, P. and Redmayne, S. (1996) *Managing scarcity*, Buckingham: Open University Press.

Knapp, M. (1984) *The economics of social care*, London: Macmillan.

Knapp, M., Hardy, B. and Forder, J. (2001) 'Commissioning for quality: ten years of social care markets in England', *Journal of Social Policy*, vol 30, no 2, pp 283-306.

Ladd, H.F. (ed) (1996) *Holding schools accountable*, Washington, DC: Brookings Institution.

Layard, R. (1997) 'Preventing long-term unemployment: an economic analysis', in D.J. Snower and G. de la Dehesa (eds) *Unemployment policy*, Cambridge: Cambridge University Press, pp 333-49.

Leibenstein, H. (1966) 'Allocative efficiency versus X efficiency', *American Economic Review*, vol 56, pp 392-415.

Le Grand, J. (1982) *The strategy of equality*, London: Allen & Unwin.

Le Grand, J. (1991) 'The theory of government failure', *The British Journal of Political Science*, vol 21, pp 423-42.

Le Grand, J. (1997) 'Knights, knaves or pawns? Human behaviour and social policy', *Journal of Social Policy*, vol 26, part 2, pp 149-69.

Le Grand, J. (1999) 'Competition, cooperation, or control? Tales from the British National Health Service', *Health Affairs*, vol 18, no 3, pp 27-39.

Le Grand, J. (2002a) 'The Labour government and the National Health Service', *Oxford Review of Economic Policy*, vol 18, no 2, pp 137-53.

Le Grand, J. (2002b) 'Further tales from the British National Health Service', *Health Affairs*, vol 21, no 3, pp 116-28.

Le Grand, J. (2003) *From knave to knight, from pawn to queen, agency and public policy*, Oxford: Oxford University Press.

Le Grand, J. and Agulnik, P. (1998) *Tax relief and partnership pensions*, London: Centre for Analysis of Social Exclusion, London School of Economics and Political Science (http://sticerd.lse.ac.uk/case.htm).

Le Grand, J. and Vizard, P. (1998) 'The National Health Service: crisis, change, or continuity?', in H. Glennerster and J. Hills (eds) *The state of welfare: The economics of social spending*, Oxford: Oxford University Press, pp 75-121.

Le Grand, J., Mays, N. and Mulligan, J.A. (1998) *Learning from the NHS internal market*, London: King's Fund.

Lenaghan, J. (1997) 'Central government should have a greater role in rationing decisions – the case for', *British Medical Journal*, vol 314, pp 967-70.

Lévi-Strauss, C. (1969) *The elementary structures of kinship* (2nd edn), London: Eyre and Spottiswoode.

Lewis, J. and Glennerster, H. (1996) *Implementing the new community care*, Buckingham: Open University Press.

Lipsky, M. (1980) *Street-level bureaucracy: Dilemmas of the individual in public services*, New York, NY: Russell Sage Foundation.

Lødemel, I. and Trickey, H. (2001) *'An offer you can't refuse': Workfare in international perspective*, Bristol: The Policy Press.

Lowe, R. (1989) 'Resignation at the Treasury: the Social Services Committee and the failure to reform the welfare state 1955-57', *Journal of Social Policy*, vol 18, no 4, pp 505-26.

Lowe, R. (1997a) 'Milestone or millstone: the 1959-61 Plowden Committee and its impact on British welfare policy', *Historical Journal*, vol 40, no 2, pp 463-91.

Lowe, R. (1997b) 'The core executive, modernisation and the creation of PESC 1960-64', *Public Administration*, vol 75, Winter, pp 601-15.

Lusardi, A. (1999) 'Information, expectations, and savings for retirement', in H. Aaron (ed) *Behavioral dimensions of retirement economics*, Washington, DC: Brookings Institution, pp 81-115.

McKnight, A. (2002) 'Low-paid work: drip-feeding the poor. The dynamics of poverty in Britain', in J. Hills, J. Le Grand and D. Piachaud (eds) *Understanding social exclusion*, Oxford: Oxford University Press, pp 97-117.

Malthus, T.R. (1798) *Essay on the principle of population as it affects the future improvement of population*, London: J. Johnson (reprinted 1970, Penguin Books: Harmondsworth).

Malpass, P. (1990) *Reshaping housing policy: Subsidies, rents and residualisation*, London: Routledge.

Marsh, A. and Mullins, D (eds) (1998) *Housing and public policy*, Buckingham: Open University Press.

Marsh, A. and Riseborough, M. (1998) 'Expanding private renting: flexibility at a price', in A. Marsh and D. Mullins (eds) *Housing and public policy*, Buckingham: Open University Press, pp 99-123.

Marshall, T.H. (1950) *Citizenship and social class*, Cambridge: Cambridge University Press.

Marshall, J. and Peters, M. (eds) (1999) *Education policy*, Cheltenham: Edward Elgar.

Maslow, A. (1954) *Motivation and personality*, New York, NY: Harper.

Maynard, A. (1975) *Experiment with choice in education*, London: Institute of Economic Affairs.

Mayo, E. and Moore, H. (2001) *The mutual state: How local communities can run public services*, London: New Economics Foundation.

Merrett, S. (1979) *State housing in Britain*, London: Routledge and Kegan Paul.

Modigliani, F. and Brumberg, R (1954) 'Utility analysis and the consumption function: an interpretation of cross-section data', in K.K. Kurihara (ed) *Post Keynesian economics*, Rutgers: Rutgers University Press, pp 388-436.

Mossialos, E. and Thomson, S.M.S. (2001) *Voluntary health insurance in the European Union*, London: London School of Economics and Political Science, Health and Social Care.

Mueller, D.C. (ed) (1997) *Perspectives on public choice: A handbook*, Cambridge: Cambridge University Press.

National Assembly for Wales, Health and Social Services Committee (2001) *Targeting poor health: Professor Townsend's report of the Welsh Assembly's National Steering Group on the allocation of NHS resources*, Cardiff: National Assembly for Wales.

Naylor, R., Smith, J. and McKnight, A. (2002) *Sheer class: The extent and sources of variation in UK graduate earnings premium*, CASE Paper 54, London: Sticerd, London School of Economics and Political Science.

Netten, A. (1991) *Coming of age: The cost of social care support*, Personal Social Services Research Unit Discussion Paper 742, Canterbury: University of Kent.

Netten, A., Williams, W. and Darton, R. (2002) 'Care home closures: a market in crisis?', Paper presented at the Social Policy Association Annual Conference, Middlesbrough (www.uku.ac.uk).

Nevitt, A.A. (1966) *Housing, taxation and subsidies*, London: Nelson.

New, B. and Le Grand, J. (1996) *Rationing in the NHS: Principles and pragmatism*, London: King's Fund.

Nickell, S. and Quintini, G. (2002) 'The recent performance of the UK labour market', *Oxford Review of Economic Policy*, vol 18, no 2, pp 202-20.

Niskanen, W. (1971) *Bureaucracy and representative government*, Chicago, IL: Aldine Atherton.

Noden, P. (2002) 'Education markets and social polarisation: back to square one?', *Research Papers in Education*, vol 17, no 3, pp 409-12.

Nosick, R. (1974) *Anarchy, state and Utopia*, Oxford: Blackwell.

O'Connor, J. (1973) *The fiscal crisis of the state*, New York, NY: St Martin's Press.

ODPM (Office of the Deputy Prime Minister) (2002a) *A guide to the local government finance settlement*, London: ODPM.

ODPM (2002b) *Housing revenue account manual 2001*, London: The Stationery Office (www.housing.odpm.gov.uk).

OECD (Organisation for Economic Co-operation and Development) (2001a) *Education at a glance: OECD indicators 2001*, Paris: OECD.

OECD (2001b) *Knowledge and skills for life. First results from PISA 2000*, Paris: OECD.

OECD (2001c) *Ageing and income, financial resources and retirement in 9 OECD countries*, Paris: OECD.

OECD (2002a) *Revenue statistics*, Paris: OECD.

OECD (2002b) *Education at a glance: OECD indicators 2002*, Paris: OECD.

Offe, C. (1984) *Contradictions of the welfare state*, London: Hutchinson.

Okun, A.M. (1975) *Equality and efficiency: The big trade off*, Washington, DC: Brookings Institution.

ONS (Office for National Statistics) (annual) *General Household Survey*, London: The Stationery Office.

ONS (1999) *Economic Trends*, no 544, London: The Stationery Office, pp 49-63.

ONS (2001) *United Kingdom national accounts*, London: The Stationery Office.

ONS (2002a) 'The effects of taxes and benefits on household income, 2000-01', *Economic Trends*, no 582, pp 33-80.

ONS (2002b) *Annual abstract of statistics*, London: The Stationery Office (www.statistics.gov.uk).

Paine, T. (1791/92, 1969) *Rights of man*, Harmondsworth: Penguin.

Park, A. and Roberts, C. (2002) 'The ties that bind', in A. Parl, J. Curtis, K. Thompson, L. Jarvis and C. Bromley (eds) *British Social Attitudes Survey 19th report*, London: Sage Publications, pp 183-207.

Parker, G. and Lawton, D. (1994) *Different types of carer: Evidence from the General Household Survey*, London: HMSO.

Parker, G. (1990) *With due care and attention* (2nd edn), London: Family Policy Studies Centre.

Parker, R.A. (1967) 'Social administration and scarcity: the problem of rationing', *Social Work*, April, pp 9-14.

Parker, R.A. (1976) 'Charging for the social services', *Journal of Social Policy*, vol 5, no 4, pp 359-73.

Pauly, M.V. (1974) 'Overinsurance and the public provision of insurance: the roles of moral hazard and adverse selection', *Quarterly Journal of Economics*, vol 88, pp 44-62.

Pickard, L., Wittenberg, R., Cosmas-Herrera, A., Davies, B. and Darton, R. (2000) 'Relying on informal care in the new century? Informal care for elderly people in England to 2031', *Ageing and Society*, vol 20, pp 745-72.

Power, A. (1987) *Property before people: The management of twentieth-century council housing*, London: Allen & Unwin.

Power, A. (1993) *Hovels to high rise: State housing in Europe since 1850*, London: Routledge.

President's Commission (2002) *Strengthening social security and creating personal wealth for all Americans*, Washington, DC: Government Printing Office.

Propper, C. (2001) 'Expenditure on healthcare in the UK: a review of the issues', *Fiscal Studies*, vol 22, no 2, pp 151-83.

Propper, C. and Green, K. (2001) 'A larger role for the private sector in financing UK health care: the arguments and the evidence', *Journal of Social Policy*, vol 30, no 4, pp 685-704.

Propper, C., Burgess, S. and Abraham, D. (2003) *Competition and quality: Evidence from the NHS internal market 1991-1999*, Bristol: Centre for Market and Public Organisation, Department of Economics, University of Bristol.

Propper, C., Croxson, B. and Shearer, A. (2002) 'Waiting times for hospital admissions: the impact of GP fundholding', *Journal of Health Economics*, vol 21, no 2, pp 227-52.

Rafferty, T., Wilson-Davis, K. and McGavoek, H. (1997) 'How has fundholding in Northern Ireland affected prescribing patterns? A longitudinal study', *British Medical Journal*, vol 315, pp 166-70.

Raftery, J. and McLeod, H. (1998) *Hospital activity changes and total purchasing: National evaluation of total purchasing pilot projects*, Working Paper, London: Kings' Fund.

Ranade, W. (1998) 'Reforming the British National Health Service: all change, no change?', in W. Ranade (ed) *Markets and healthcare: A comparative analysis*, London: Longman, pp 101-21.

Rawls, J. (1972) *A theory of justice*, Oxford: Oxford University Press.

Richards, E. with Wilsdon, T. and Lyons, S. (1996) *Paying for long term care*, London: IPPR.

Robinson, R. and Dixon, A. (2002) *Completing the course: Health to 2010*, London: Fabian Society.

Rogers, R. and Power, A. (2000) *Cities for a small country*, London: Faber and Faber.

Rowntree, B.S. (1902) *Poverty: A study of town life*, London: Nelson, reissued (2000) by The Policy Press for the Joseph Rowntree Foundation, Bristol.

Royal Commission on Long-Term Care (1999) *With respect to old age*, Cm 4192, London: The Stationery Office.

Ruhm, C.J. (2000) *Parental employment and child cognitive development*, Working Paper 7666, Cambridge, MA: National Bureau of Economic Research (www.nber.org/papers/w766).

Salamon, L. (1987) 'Partners in public service: voluntary failure and third party government: toward a theory of government-nonprofit relations', in W.W. Powell (ed) *The nonprofit sector: A research handbook*, New Haven, CT: Yale University Press.

Samuelson, P.A. (1958) 'An exact consumption-loan model of interest with or without the social contrivance of money', *Journal of Political Economy*, vol 66, December, pp 467-82.

Savas, E.S. (1977) 'Policy analysis for local government: public versus private refuse collection', *Policy Analysis*, vol 3, pp 44-74.

Savas, E.S. (1982) *Privatising the public sector: How to shrink government*, Chatham, NJ: Chatham House.

Scott, A.J., Lewis, A. and Lea, S.E.G. (2001) *Student debt: The causes and consequences of undergraduate borrowing in the UK*, Bristol: The Policy Press.

Scottish Executive (1999) *Fair shares for all: Report of the national review of resource allocation for the NHS in Scotland*, Edinburgh: Scottish Executive Health Department.

Sefton, T. (2002) *Recent changes in the distribution of the social wage*, CASE Paper 62, London: Centre for Analysis of Social Exclusion, London School of Economics and Political Science.

Sen, A. (1981) *Poverty and famines*, Oxford: Oxford University Press.

Smith, A. (1776) *The wealth of nations* (Penguin edn, 1974), Harmondsworth: Penguin.

Sparkes, J. and Glennerster, H. (2002) 'Preventing social exclusion: education's contribution', in J. Hills, J. Le Grand and D. Piachaud (eds) *Understanding social exclusion*, Oxford: Oxford University Press, pp 178-201.

Takayama, N. (1992) *The greying of Japan: An economic perspective on public pensions*, Oxford: Oxford University Press.

Taylor-Gooby, P. (1995) 'Comfortable, marginal and excluded', in R. Jowell, J. Curtice, A. Park, L. Brook and D. Ahrendt (eds) *British Social Attitudes: 12th Report*, Aldershot: Dartmouth.

Taylor-Gooby, P. and Hastie, C. (2002) 'Support for state spending: has New Labour got it right?', in A. Park, J. Curtis, K. Thompson, L. Jarvis and C. Bromley (eds) *British Social Attitudes: 19th Report*, London: Sage Publications, pp 75-96.

Thain, C. and Wright, M. (1995) *The Treasury and Whitehall: The planning and control of public expenditure, 1976-1993*, Oxford: Oxford University Press.

Tiebout, C. (1956) 'A pure theory of public expenditure', *Journal of Political Economy*, vol 64, no 5, pp 416-24.

Timmins, N. (2002) 'A time for change in the British NHS: an interview with Alan Milburn', *Health Affairs*, vol 21, no 3, pp 129-35.

Titmuss, R.M. (1958) *Essays on the 'welfare state'*, London: Allen & Unwin.

Titmuss, R.M. (1970) *The gift relationship*, London: Allen & Unwin.

Tullock, G. (1976) *The vote motive*, London: Institute of Economic Affairs.

US Senate Committee on Ageing (2002) *Hearing finding summary, June 2002*, Washington, DC: US Government Printing Office.

Uthwatt Committee (1942) *Compensation and betterment*, Cmd 6386, London: HMSO.

Vandenberghe, V. (1996) *Functioning and regulation of educational quasi-markets*, Louvain-la-Neuve: Catholic University.

Vandenberghe, V. (1998) 'Education quasi-markets: the Belgian experience', in W. Bartlett, J. Roberts and J. Le Grand (eds) *A revolution in social policy: Quasi-market reforms in the 1990s*, Bristol: The Policy Press, pp 79-94.

Walker, B. (1998) 'Incentives, choice and control in the finance of council housing', in A. Marsh and D. Mullins (eds) *Housing and public policy*, Buckingham: Open University Press, pp 153-74.

Weisbrod, B.A. (1986) 'Toward a theory of the voluntary nonprofit sector in a three-sector economy' (original version, 1972), in S. Rose-Ackerman (ed) *The economics of nonprofit institutions*, Oxford: Oxford University Press.

West, A., Pennell, H. and West, R. (2000) 'New Labour and school-based education in England: changing the system of funding?, *British Educational Research Journal*, vol 26, no 4, pp 523-36.

Whitty, G., Power, S. and Halpin, D. (1998) 'Self-managing schools in the market place: the experience of England, the USA and New Zealand', in W. Bartlett, J. Roberts and J. Le Grand (eds) *A revolution in social policy: Quasi-market reforms in the 1990s*, Bristol: The Policy Press.

Wildavsky, A. (1974) *The politics of the budgetary process*, Boston, MA: Little Brown.

Wilensky, H.L. (2002) *Rich democracies: political economy, public policy, and performance*, Berkeley, CA: University of California Press

Wilson, R. and Walley T. (1995) 'Prescribing costs in general practice fundholding', *Lancet*, vol 346, pp 1710-11.

Wistow, G., Knapp, M., Hardy, B., Forder, J., Kendall, J. and Manning, R. (1996) *Social care markets: Progress and prospects*, Buckingham: Open University Press.

Wittenberg, R., Pickard, L., Comtas-Herrera, A., Davies, B. and Darton, R. (2001) 'Demand for long-term care for older people in England to 2031', *Health Statistics Quarterly*, vol 12, pp 5-17.

Wittenberg, R., Hancock, R., Lomas-Herrera, A. and Pickard, L. (2002) 'Demand for long-term care in the UK', in R. Brooks, S. Regan and P. Robinson (eds) *A new contract for retirement: Modelling policy options to 2050*, London: IPPR, pp 65-120.

World Bank (1994) *Averting the old age crisis*, Oxford: Oxford University Press.

Index

A

Aaron, Henry 17, 142, 154
Abrams, Philip 16-17
Access Regulator 119
additional educational needs funding 110
additional state pension 141, 143
Additional Voluntary Contributions
    141-2
'administrative rationing' 179
advanced corporation tax 40
adverse selection 23, 56, 80
Advisory Committee on Resource
    Allocation 64-5
ageing population
    healthcare costs 59
    and income security 129
    informal care costs 81-2
    longer working lives 204
    pensions saving 142, 153
agency of user 11-14
    see also consumer choice
Akerlof, George 23
allocative efficiency 17
Almond, S. 83-4
annually managed expenditure (AME)
    187
approved personal pensions 141
Arbuthnott Review 66
assisted places scheme 112-13
Atkinson, Tony 48, 49, 150
Audit Commission 8, 76, 89, 91, 182
Australia
    graduate tax 125-6
    pension scheme 143, 148, 155
autonomy
    agency of user 11-14
    'critical autonomy' 5
    pensions savings 130
    see also consumer choice
average tax rate 44

B

Barnett formula 190-1
Barr, N. 153
basic credit approvals 191
basic human needs 1-6
    economic theory 16, 25
    financing provision 6-9, 10tab
    hierarchy of needs 2-3
    housing as 160
    and life cycle 6
    measuring need for healthcare funding
        63-6, 67
    theory of human need 3-5
bed blocking 76, 90
Belgium: education funding 31, 124
Best Value regime 31-2, 92
Bevan, Aneurin 91
Beveridge, W.H. 61, 130
Billis, D. 32-3
Blair, Tony 9, 59
Bobbett, P. 180
Bradley, S. 122
Bramley, G. 64
Brown, Gordon 38, 185, 186
    NHS spending 60-1
    prudent aims 187-8
building societies 163
Burchardt, T. 11-13
bureaucrats' self-interest 27-9
Butler, D. 43
buyer/seller information imbalances 23-4

C

Calabresi, G. 180
Canada: pension policy 146
capital gains tax 164
capitation payments 58, 63
Care trusts 90
caring see informal caring; social care
cash planning 187
cash support 9-10
Centre for Analysis of Social Exclusion
    (CASE) 121, 137
Centre for Health Economics, University
    of York 64, 87
Chancellor of the Exchequer 182
    see also Brown, Gordon
charging for services 50
    healthcare 12-13, 57-8, 68, 71, 201
    higher education 115-20, 125, 200
    social care 91, 201
charitable giving 14, 21, 32, 50-1
    see also voluntary sector
Charles I, king of England 36
Chartered Institute of Public Finance 89
Child Tax Credit 7, 52, 137, 188
childcare provision

by schools 113
informal costs 81
tax credits for 136-7
women's role 5
Chile: pensions policy 130*fig*, 131, 148, 155
Church
church schools 112, 123-4
as social care provider 83-4
tithes 36
civil servants *see* bureaucrats
civil society: mutuality principle 33
classical economic theory 16-18
collective activity 3-4
and public goods 19, 36-7
colleges of further education 113
Commission for Health Improvement 74
Commission for Healthcare Audit and
Inspection (CHAI) 75-6
Commission on Public Private
Partnerships 193-4
Commission for Social Care Inspection
101
community care tendering 30
companionship as human need 2, 3
competition
in education 120-1, 122-3
'tax competition' 37
see also market efficiency; private sector
provision
comprehensive spending plans 185-7
Comprehensive Spending Reviews 38,
180, 183, 186, 191
2002 review 194-5
Compulsory Competitive Tendering
(CCT) 30
Conservative governments (1979-97)
202
compulsory competitive tendering 30
education funding 111-12, 114, 116
mortgage relief 164
pensions policy 131
poll tax 43
privatisation 193
taxation 37-8
consumer choice 11-14, 31
and cash benefits 7
in education 105, 120-1, 122, 123
and government failure 26
of healthcare provider 75, 77
information failure 22, 56, 80, 133
information for 22
in insurance-based healthcare systems
69
limited in social care 80
rising expectations 59, 67, 178, 180

sanctions 29-30, 122
consumer sovereignty 17
corporate taxation 46
cost-of-living assistance in Germany 144
Council Tax 46, 84, 85, 86, 89-90, 109,
193, 200
cream-skimming 23, 69, 121, 124, 203
credit approvals 89, 191
'critical autonomy' 5
Cubie Committee 117

D

Deakin, N. 181, 188-9
Dearing Committee and Report 116,
117, 124
defined benefit pension schemes 152
defined contribution pension schemes
152
'demand-led' financing
healthcare 57-8
social security 138
Denmark
healthcare funding 57, 69
pensions policy 146
social care provision 95
taxation 37, 38*tab*, 70-1
Department of Health: public service
agreement 184
departmental expenditure limits (DELs)
187
devolution
and central funding mechanisms 190-1,
192*tab*
and taxation 43
Diagnostic Related Groups (DRGs) 75
direct-grant schools 112
direct taxation 44, 47*tab*
district health authorities 73
domiciliary care 92-3
Donnison, David 172
Doyal, L. 3-5
drug rationing 59, 72
Dunleavy, P. 28
dynamic efficiency 17

E

earning power
and life cycle 6
limitations on women 5
economic efficiency 25, 199
of education 121-3
of social security 149-56
economic theory of markets 16-18
education 103-27

allocation of funds 108–20
  additional educational needs funding
    110
  central government funding 109,
    110–11, 112
  Formula Spending Share 110
  LEA funding of schools 111–113
  for private school places 112–13
  for special initiatives 112
charging for services 201
choice of school 11, 12, 24, 31
costs of 105–8, 201–2
  international comparison 106–8,
    109*tab*
  and life cycle 6
  in family 5
financial benefits to consumer 105, 115,
  118–19
higher education costs and funding
  113–20
  student loan system 115–20, 125
international comparisons 31, 123–6
market failure 105, 115
market provision 7, 120–1
monopolies in provision 105
non-educational services 113
performance measures 121–3, 202
private sector costs 203, 205*tab*
public–private financing 8, 9
quasi-markets 31, 120–1, 122–3, 124
rationing of scarce resources 181, 195
service providers 8
taxation for 41
voucher systems 31, 120, 121, 206
Education Action Zones 112
Education Reform Act (1988) 111, 120
Education (Student Loans) Act (1990)
  115
efficiency *see* economic efficiency;
  market efficiency
employers' contributions 10, 40, 68–9
Estate Tax 49
European Union Economic Policy
  Committee (EUEPC) 97
Excellence in Cities programme 112
exit sanctions 29–30
externalities 19–21
  income externalities 20–1

F

Fabian Society Commission on Taxation
  39, 40–1
Falkingham, J. 6
family support and social care 81–2
fees for services *see* charging for services

Feldstein, Martin 150
Field, Frank 27
fiscal welfare 10, 51–2, 136–7
Fitz, J. 121
food
  ability to purchase 2
  and autonomy 5
  finance for 6–7
Formula Grant/formula spending share
  (FSS)
  for education 110
  for social care 85–8
foundation hospitals 9, 75
France
  education funding 123, 124, 125
  housing policy 173–4
  pensions policy 130*fig*, 131, 148
  private insurance 69–70
  social care provision 94, 96
  social insurance 40, 68, 69, 144–5
  taxation 37, 38*tab*
free market economic theory 16, 17–18
  failure of 25
  see also private sector provision
free riding 19, 21, 36
Fundamental Expenditure Reviews 189

G

'gatekeeper' principle 56, 58
geographical monopolies 18
Germany
  cost-of-living assistance 144
  education funding 124–5
  healthcare provision 7, 31, 51, 69
  housing policy 173
  pensions policy 130*fig*, 131, 147–8
  service providers 7
  social care provision 95, 96, 99
  social security contributions 40
  taxation 37, 38*tab*, 42*tab*, 43
giving *see* charitable giving
Gladstone, W.M. 182
Glennerster, H. 32–3, 117–18
Gorard, S. 121
Goshen formula 190
Gough, I. 3–5
government failure theory 25–30
GP fundholding 31, 72–3
GP funding
  capitation payments 58, 63
  changes to system 63
graduate tax 117, 119, 125–6, 200
grant-maintained schools 112
grants for students 113–14, 125
Greater London Authority 43

Greece: pensions policy 148
Griffiths Report 91
group identity 4-5
group personal pensions 141
Guillebaud Committee 90
Gundlach, E. 122

H

habitations à loyer modéré (HLMs) 173-4
Hampden, John 36
Hansmann, H. 32
Hastie, C. 39
Heady, C. 48
Health Act (1999) 90
health inequalities adjustment 64-5, 66
Health Resource Groups (HRGs) 75
Health Service Corporation 76-7
healthcare 7, 10*tab*, 55-77
  ageing population 59
  capital building programme 66
  capitation payments 58, 63
  charging for services 12-13, 57-8, 68,
    71, 201
  consumer expectations 59, 67, 180
  costs of 56-67, 201-2
  'demand-led' finance 57-8
  funding alternatives 67-71
  health inequalities 66-7
  health inequalities adjustment 64-5, 66
  hypothecating taxation for 40-1, 67,
    199
  incentives 75, 76
  insurance-based systems 23, 56, 57-8,
    59, 67-9
  market failure 56
  market forces factor 64, 66
  market mechanisms 72-6
  measuring need 63-6, 67
  mixed financing 9, 11-13
  private cover costs 203, 205*tab*
  privatisation and quasi-markets 30-1,
    72-6, 202-3
  productivity measures 74-5
  public service agreements 184
  purchaser–provider split 30, 69, 72-3
  rationing of scarce resources 59, 72,
    180-1, 186-7, 194-5
  regulation 75-6
  service providers 7, 8
  social care overlap 89-91, 97, 98, 99,
    100-1
  tax-financed systems 56-7, 61, 67, 69,
    71
  voucher system 206
Heclo, H. 181, 182

higher education 9, 113-20
  consumer benefits 105, 115, 118-19
  costs of provision 113, 203, 205*tab*
  funding systems 115-20
    Access Regulator 119
    as deterrent to poorer students 116,
      118-19
    economists' case for 105, 115-16
    graduate tax 117, 119, 125-6, 200
    income contingent loans 116, 119
    international comparison 124-6
    Labour policy 116-20
    research funding 114-15, 120
    student grants 113-14, 125
    White Paper on Higher Education
      Funding 118-20
  market failure 115
  performance incentives 123
Higher Education Funding Council 114
Hills, J. 6, 39
Hirschman, A.O. 29-30
Hochman, H.M. 21
Holloway, S. 81
horizontal redistribution 6, 44
housing 7, 9, 159-74
  as alternative to long-term care 98
  as basic human need 160
  benefits *see* Housing Benefit
  costs to the individual 165, 204, 205*tab*
  costs to the state 162, 165-7, 168-70
  evolution of housing policy 160-2
  improving choice and efficiency 171-2
  international comparison 172-4
  market failure 161
  market forces 160
  rent control and regulation 162-3, 166,
    167-8, 169, 171
  rise of owner-occupation 163
  social housing 9, 161-3, 166-8
  state intervention 160, 161-2
  subsidies for 162, 168-9
  tax benefits of home ownership 51,
    163-5
Housing Acts 162, 166, 168
housing association grant (HAG) 167-8
housing associations 9, 161, 162, 170
  in Europe 173
  as social housing providers 166, 167-8
Housing Benefit 7, 9, 162, 165, 166, 169,
  170
  criticisms of system 171-2
  reform proposals 172
Housing Corporation 167, 170
Housing Finance Act (1972) 162
housing revenue accounts 168-9

Housing the Working Classes Act (1890) 160-1
Hoxby, C.M. 123
human needs *see* basic human needs
hypothecation: healthcare 40-1, 67, 199

I

'imperfect markets' 18
incidence of taxation 44
income contingent loans 116, 119, 126
'income effect' 48
income externalities 20-1
income replacement 130-1
Income Support 7, 91, 133-4, 138, 144, 150, 171
income support systems 2
  see also social security
income tax 45, 47*tab*, 51-2, 200
  see also fiscal welfare; taxation
Independent Schools Information Service 203, 205*tab*
indirect taxation 44, 46, 47*tab*
informal care 81-2
  costs of 81
  impact of ageing population 81-2
  pension implications 156
  support function 81
  women's role 5, 81
information failure 22-5, 56, 80, 133
inheritance tax 49
innovation 17
Institute for Public Policy Research 101, 143
insurance
  healthcare financing 23, 56, 57-8, 59, 67-9
  information failure 23, 24-5, 56, 133
  private provision 6, 23, 24-5, 56, 69-70, 80
  pensions 131-2
  social care financing 82-3, 94, 95
  see also National Insurance; social insurance
interest group politics 163
Ireland: pension policy 146
Italy
  education funding 124
  pensions policy 130*fig*, 131
  social care provision 95
  social security contributions 40

J

Japan
  pensions crisis 148

social care provision 95, 96
taxation 37, 38*tab*
'Jarman' index 63
joint finance initiative 90

K

Kemp, P. 171
Kendall, J. 14, 83-4
King's Fund 76-7
Knapp, M. 92-3

L

Labour government (1997–)
  budgetary prudence 187-8
  education funding 112, 114
  student loan system 116-20
  fiscal welfare 7, 10
  fuel protests 37
  healthcare
    increase in spending 59-61
    market mechanisms 72-6
  local authority controls 43
  mortgage relief 164
  pensions policy 145
  Private Finance Initiative 193-4
  public expenditure controls 186-95
  public–private healthcare finance 9
  selective universality 201-2
  taxation 40, 41-2
labour market
  competition in 40
  effects of taxation 46-8
  as free market 17-18
Le Grand, Julian 17, 29, 73, 201
Leibenstein, H. 28
Lelkes, O. 39
Lévi-Strauss, Claude 178
life cycle and needs 6
life expectancy measure 63-5, 66-7
loan sanctions 89, 191
local authorities
  Best Value regime 31-2, 92
  capital spending 89, 169, 191
  central control of spending 191, 193
  education funding 109-13
  history of house building 160-2
  housing expenditure 168-70
    capital spending 169
    housing associations 170
    Housing Benefit 170
    housing revenue accounts 168-9
    see also social housing
  housing regulation 160
  long-term care 82, 84

funding complexities 97-101
as purchasers 31-2, 72, 92-3
rent controls 162-3
revenue 84-5
  changes to 85-6
social services *see* social care
taxation at local level 42-3, 67, 70-1,
  84, 200, 206-7
Local Education Authorities (LEAs)
  109-13
Local Government Finance Act (1988)
  85
Local Management of Schools (LMS)
  111
Local Prudential Regimes 89
long-term care provision 7, 8
  asset tests 97-8, 99, 100
  bed blocking 76, 90
  choice of provider 13, 92-3
  costs of 82, 83*tab*, 205*tab*
  funding complexities 97-101
  healthcare overlap 89-91, 97, 99, 100-1
  information failure 24, 80
  not-for-profit providers 83-4, 94, 95, 96
  nursing care funding 82, 100, 101
  private insurance for 24-5, 80, 96-7,
    98-9
  private provision 82-3, 92-3
  social security payments for 90-1, 92,
    93
  taxation for 200
  voucher system 206
love as basic human need 3
Lowe, R. 182
loyalty of consumer 30

M

McKnight, A. 150
Malthus, Thomas 4
marginal taxes 44, 46, 171
market efficiency 7, 16-18
  allocative efficiency 17
  dynamic efficiency 17
  economic efficiency 25
  productive efficiency 17
  and taxation 46-52
  X-inefficiency 17, 28, 29, 30
market failure 18-25, 198
  education 105, 115
  externalities 19-21
  government failure theory 25-30
  healthcare 56
  housing 161
  income support 133-4
  information failure 22-5, 56, 80, 133

privatisation and quasi-markets 30-2,
  202
public goods 18-19
social care 80, 96-7
market provision *see* private sector
  provision
Marshall, T.H. 3
Maslow, A. 2-3
means testing
  as form of taxation 48
  for pensions 131, 140, 143
  for student loan system 116-17
Medicaid 96
Medicare 95
Minimum Income Guarantee 140, 143,
  155
Mirlees, James 48
mixed financing 9, 10*tab*, 11-13
  see also Private Finance Initiative;
    Private–Public Finance Partnerships
modernisation fund 67
monopolies 18
  in education 105
  geographical monopolies 18
  of healthcare providers 71-2
  public services as 27, 30, 71-2
moral hazard 24, 56, 80, 133, 191
mortality measure 63-5, 66-7
mutuality in civil society 33
'myopia' 80, 133

N

National Assistance Act (1948) 144
National Association of Pension Schemes
  203, 205*tab*
National Audit Office 8, 182
National Care Standards Commission 76,
  101
National General Household Survey 59
National Institute for Clinical Excellence
  (NICE) 59, 74, 180*fig*, 181
National Insurance 46, 61, 67, 132,
  134*tab*, 135*tab*
  2002 increase 39-40
National Minimum Wage 150
National Service Frameworks 61
needs *see* basic human needs
negative externalities 20
negative income tax 51, 137
neo-pluralist approach to public
  expenditure 182-3
Netherlands
  education funding 31, 124, 125
  private pension funding 145, 146
  sick clubs 31, 69

neutral taxation 44
New Labour *see* Labour government
New Zealand
  education funding 124, 126
  healthcare funding 57
  pensions policy 130*fig*, 131, 148
NHS
  allocation of funds 60*fig*, 61-6
  capital building programme 66
  compulsory competitive tendering 30
  finance for trust hospitals 9, 73, 76-7
  geriatric care 98
  increase in expenditure on 59-61
  market mechanisms 71-6
  nursing care funding 82, 100, 101
  perverse incentive problem 89-91
  productivity measures 74-5
  public service agreement 184
  rationing of scarce resources 59, 72,
    180-1, 186-7
  regional differences 61-2
  see also healthcare
NHS and Community Care Act (1990)
  30, 92
Niskanen, W. 27-8
non-excludability property 19
non-refundable tax credits 44
non-rivalry 19
Northern Ireland
  allocation of central funds 61-2, 189-
    91, 192*tab*
  higher education funding 117
  taxation 43
Norway: social security 145
Nosick, Robert 21
not-for-profit sector *see* voluntary sector
nursing care definition 101

O

occupational pensions 141, 143, 152
occupational welfare 10, 40, 68-9
Offe, Claus 178
Office for National Statistics 46, 137
oligopolies 18
'opportunity costs' 81
Organisation for Economic Co-operation
  and Development (OECD) 96, 107-8,
  137, 138

P

Parry, R. 181, 188-9
'pathfinder areas' 172
pauperisation 21
PAYG schemes 147, 150, 151, 153, 155

Pension Credit 140, 143, 155
Pension Policy Institute 143
pensions 129-56
  complexity of system 141-2, 156
  defined benefit schemes 152
  defined contribution schemes 152
  funding for 131-8, 139*tab*, 198
  government policy 26-7, 145
    consultative paper 142-3
    stealth taxes 40
    tax allowances 52, 137-8
  insurance markets 131-2
  international comparison 130-1, 145-9
  long-term care deductions 98, 99
  private provision 131-2, 133-4, 137-8,
    143, 150-5, 198, 202
    costs of 203-4, 205*tab*
    and uncertainty 24
  reform options 145-6
  state pensions 7, 140, 142
    as disincentive to saving 155, 202
    PAYG system 147, 150, 151, 153, 155
  targeted social security 155-6
  types of provision 140-2
Pensions Commission 142
personal care definition 99
personal pensions 141
personal social services 86-7
Personal Social Services Research Unit,
  Kent University 88
physiological needs 2-3
planning for public expenditure 186-7
Plowden Report 183-5
pluralist approach to public expenditure
  182
political activity 4-5
poll taxes 43, 85
Ponzi, Charles 154
poverty
  food provision 6-7
  housing provision 7
  incidence of 129
  methods of relief 21, 130-1
  state role 130-1
  and taxation levels 46, 47*tab*, 48
  see also basic human needs; social
    security
price-elasticity 44
primary care trusts (PCTs) 74-5
  long-term care funding 82
'primary goods' 3
prison service as public sector service 8-9
Private Finance Initiative (PFI) 193-4
private sector provision 6, 8, 10*tab*
  education 109, 112-13, 121, 203
  in US 123-4

housing 7, 160-2
insurance 6, 24-5
  health insurance 23, 56, 69-70
  for social care 24-5, 80, 94, 95, 97-8, 98-9
  pensions 131-2, 133-4, 137-8, 139*tab*, 141, 143
  market failure 23, 133-4
  move towards 145, 146, 147-8, 150-5, 202
  public–private welfare 9, 10*tab*, 11-13
  of social care 82-3, 92-3
  see also market efficiency; market failure
Private–Public Finance Partnerships (PPFPs) 89, 193-4
privatisation 13, 30-2
productive efficiency 17
profit motive 17
progressive taxation 44, 45
property taxes 200
  see also Council Tax
proportional taxation 44
Propper, C. 70, 76
public assistance schemes 143-5
public attitudes
  consent to taxation 36-43
  rising expectations 59, 67, 198
  management of 177-95
  towards raising taxation to pay for services 198-9, 206-7
  see also self-interest
public expenditure 7
  budget maximisers 27-8
  containment measures 181, 182-95
  Treasury role 182-3
  education 105-8, 201-2
  finance–provision distinction 7-8, 11-13
  funding private sector 11-12, 14
  funding voluntary sector 14
  healthcare 56-67, 201-2
  housing 162, 165-7, 168-70
  for public goods 18-19
  quasi-markets 31-2, 72-6, 202
  rationing scarce resources 177-95
  social security 41, 137, 138, 201-2
  tax credit accounting 137
  wholly public finance 8-9
public goods 18-19, 25-6, 32
  education as 105, 116
  taxation for 19, 36-7
public servants
  pension rights in France 148
  as self-interested parties 27-9
public service agreements 183, 184
public service provision 6-7, 197-207

and food 6-7
government failure theory 25-30
in monopolies 27, 30, 71-2
privatisation and quasi-markets 30-2, 72-6, 202
public–private welfare 9, 10*tab*, 11-13
rationing scarce resources 177-95
  economic concept of 179-80
  healthcare 59, 72
  political rationing 180-2
  public expenditure constraints 182-95
  territorial rationing 61-2, 189-91, 192*tab*
  rising expectations 59, 67, 178, 198
  shrinking base 13
  X-inefficiency 17, 28, 29, 30
  see also public goods
Public–Private Partnerships (PPPs) 89, 193-4
purchaser–provider split in healthcare 30, 69, 72-3
purchasing power 2
pure public goods 19

Q

quasi-markets 30-2, 202
  and educational performance 120-1, 122-3, 124, 202
  in healthcare 72-6
queuing gap 179

R

Rates Act (1984) 193
rationing gap 179-80
rationing scarce resources 177-95
  economic concept 179-80
  sociological concept 178
Rawls, John 3
redistribution 44
  to square life cycle 6
  see also fiscal welfare
refundable tax credits 44
regressive taxation 44
regulation
  free markets 18
  health service 74, 75-6
  housing 160
  long-term care 101
  pension schemes 134
  public services 30
religion *see* Church
rent control and regulation 162-3, 166, 167-8, 169, 171
Resource Allocation Working Party 63-4

Revenue Minimum d'Insertion (RMI) 145
Revenue Support Grant 85
Richards, E. 81
right-to-buy scheme 166
'rights of citizenship' 3
rising expectations 59, 67, 177-95, 198
risk
  and insurance savings 131-2
  and market failure 23, 24, 56
Rogers, A.D. 21
rough sleepers: healthcare needs 66
Rowntree, B.S. 6
Royal Commission on Long-Term Care 82, 90, 98-100

S

safety as basic human need 2-3
Salamon, L. 32
Samuelson, P.A. 154
savings
  disincentives 155
  effect of taxation 48
  incentives 150-1
  see also pensions; social security
Scandinavia
  education funding 124, 125
  healthcare funding 57
  housing policy 174
  social care provision 94, 95
  social security provision 144, 145
  taxation 37, 38*tab*
Scotland
  allocation of central funds 61-2, 189-91, 192*tab*
  financing healthcare 66
  healthcare cooperatives 76
  higher education funding 117
  long-term care funding 82, 101
  public expenditure control 182
  taxation 43
second state pension 141, 143
Sefton, T. 201
selective universality 201-2
self-esteem as basic human need 3, 5
self-interest
  of bureaucrats 27-9
  in economic theory 16-18
  and government failure 26-7
seller/buyer information imbalances 23-4
Sen, Amartya 2
SERPS 141
service charges *see* charging for services
service providers 7-9

see also private sector provision; public service provision
ship money 36
sick pay 133
Smith, Adam 16-17, 18, 43, 45
Social Attitudes Survey 39
social care 79-102
  allocation of funds 84-91
    formula spending share 85-8
    perverse incentive problem 89-91, 99
    specific grants 88
  bed blocking 76, 90
  charges for services 91, 201
  expansion of 201
  healthcare overlap 89-91, 97, 98, 99, 100-1
  informal care 81-2
  international overview 94-7
  long-term care funding complexities 97-101
  market failure 80, 96-7
  mixed market provision 92-3
  personal social services 86-7
  privately funded care 82-3, 97-8
  rationing of scarce resources 195
  revenue sources 84-5
social class
  and choice in education 121
  and entry into higher education 115, 116
  self-interested voters 26-7
social division of welfare 9-11
social exclusion 144-5
social housing 9, 161-3, 166-8, 195, 201
  housing associations as providers 166, 167-8
  international models 173-4
  right-to-buy scheme 166
  shortcomings of system 171-2
  see also Housing Benefit
social insurance systems 7, 31, 67-9, 94, 95, 130, 143-5
  employers' contributions 40, 68-9
social security 2, 129-56
  allocation of funds 138-49
  costs of 41, 132-8
  decrease in spending 201-2
  drawbacks to targeting 155-6
  economic efficiency 149-56
    work incentives 149-50
  employer contributions 40
  market failure 133-4
  merging benefits and income tax systems 51-2, 188, 189
  payments for residential care 90-1, 92, 93

pensions forecast 142-3
pro-poor policies 201
public assistance schemes abroad 143-5
tax credits 136-7
tax-funded benefits 135, 136
unfunded social security 154-5
see also Housing Benefit; Income
   Support; pensions; tax credits
Southgate, Sir Colin 189
Spain: social care provision 95
stakeholder pensions 141
state provision
   poverty relief 130-1
   see also public expenditure; public
   service provision
statutory agencies 8
stealth taxes 40, 200
Stern, Nic 48
student grants 113-14, 125
student loan system 115-20, 125
subsidiarity 83
'substitution effect' 47
supplementary credit approvals 191
Sweden
   education funding 125
   pensions policy 130*fig*, 131, 147
   taxation 37, 38, 42*tab*, 43, 70-1, 200

'income effect' 48
localisation of 42-3, 67, 70-1, 84, 200,
   206-7
merging benefits and income tax
   systems 51-2, 188, 189
public attitudes towards 40-3, 198-200
of 'public bads' 20, 41-2, 199
for public goods 19, 36-7, 198-200
rates of taxation 37-8
social security financing 135, 136
subsidies for private health insurance 70
'substitution effect' 47
tax terms 44
Treasury control 182
voluntary donations 206-7
Taylor, J. 122
Taylor-Gooby, P. 39
Teaching Quality Review 114
Tiebout, Charles 26
tithes 36
Titmuss, R.M. 2, 10, 51
top-up voucher systems 205-6
total public expenditure 191
totally managed expenditure (TME) 187
Treasury 28, 182-95
treatment rationing 59, 72
Tullock, G. 27

T

Tamplin, S. 81
tax allowances 9-10, 44, 51, 137-8
'tax competition' 37
tax credits 7, 9-10, 44, 52, 136-7, 188,
   193
   for housing 171-2
tax expenditures 10, 44, 51, 137, 188
tax relief 44
tax restraint 37
tax thresholds 44
taxable capacity 38
taxable income 44
taxation 35-52
   alternatives to 50-2
   avoidance/evasion 37
   capital gains tax 164
   consent for 36-40
   effects of state intervention 48-9
   efficiency of 46-52
   equity of system 43-6, 47*tab*
   for externalities 20, 21
   graduate tax 117, 119, 125-6, 200
   healthcare financing 56-7, 61, 67, 68,
   71
   and home ownership 163-5
   hypothecation 40-1, 67, 199

U

uncertainty 24-5, 56, 134
unemployment
   social security 133, 149-50
   and uncertainty 24
unified budgets 186
unintended consequences 163
United States
   choice of school 11
   education funding 123-4
   higher education 115, 126
   housing policy 174
   pensions policy 130*fig*, 131, 147, 151
   social care provision 95, 96-7
   social security 144
   taxation 37, 38*tab*, 49
universality: selective universality 201-2
universities
   changes in funding system 113-20
   student loan system 115-20
   White Paper on fees 118-20
   income sources 9
   research funding 114-15, 120

V

Value Added Tax (VAT) 46, 200
vertical redistribution 6, 44
voice of consumer 30
voluntary sector 7, 8, 14, 32-3
  healthcare proposal 76-7
  housing in Europe 173-4
  international overview 94-6
  social care provision 83-4, 92, 94, 95
  supply side argument for 33
  'voluntary failure' 32
  see also charitable giving
voters: self-interested voters 26-7
voucher systems 205-6
  education 31, 120, 121, 206
  for refugees 5
vulnerable people 80

W

Wales
  allocation of central funds 61-2,
    189-91, 192*tab*
  financing healthcare 66
  financing social care 101
  higher education funding 117
  taxation 43
Wall Street Journal 39
Wanless Report 60-1, 71, 201
wealth tax 45, 49
Weisbrod, B.A. 32
welfare: social division of 9-11
welfare dependency 21
White Paper on Higher Education
    Funding 118-20
Wildavsky, A. 181, 182
Wilensky, H.L. 200
women
  pension prospects 156
  unpaid labour 5
  see also informal care
work incentives 149-50
workhouse test 149
working life span 204
Working Tax Credit 7, 52, 137, 188
World Bank 148

X

X-inefficiency 17, 28, 29, 30

Benefits

A Journal of Social Security Research, Policy and Practice

(3 issues) February, June and October
ISSN 0962 7898

"Benefits *provides an authoritative, up-to-date and lively insight into an important and fast-moving policy area. It is essential reading for anyone with an interest in social security policy, practice and research.*" **Jane Millar, Department of Social and Policy Sciences, University of Bath**

FREE sample issue online at
www.policypress.org.uk/benefits.htm

FREE online access to subscribers

"*... essential reading for all service providers. We ensure that it is available to all our team as it covers both policy and practice issues in a stimulating way.*"
John Hannam, Head of Welfare Rights, Nottinghamshire County Council

Benefits is the only journal focusing specifically on social security, social inclusion and anti-poverty policies in the UK. Established over ten years ago, the journal has a well-earned reputation for up-to-date information and analysis of development in policy and practice. Edited and written by both academics and practitioners, the journal is essential reading for anyone studying, researching or practising in the social security and welfare rights fields. It is highly accessible and each issue provides a wide range of articles around a theme alongside popular regular features, such as Research Round-up and Policy Review.

Who should read *Benefits*?

- Welfare rights workers in both the statutory and voluntary sectors
- Frontline and managerial staff working in the Pensions Service, Department for Work and Pensions and Jobcentre Plus
- Policy makers
- Academics, researchers and teachers in the field of social policy and related disciplines
- Students of social policy and related disciplines

To subscribe, please contact:

The Policy Press
c/o Portland Press Ltd
Commerce Way
Whitehall Industrial Estate
Colchester CO2 8HP
UK
Tel: +44 (0)1206 796351
Fax: +44 (0)1206 799331
E-mail: sales@portlandpress.co.uk